TEXT/REFERENCE BOOKS ON DATA COMMUNICATIONS AND COMPUTER ARCHITECTURE
(Available from Macmillian Publishing Co.)

DATA AND COMPUTER COMMUNICATIONS, SECOND EDITION

A broad but detailed survey, covering four main areas: (1) data communications, including transmission, media, signal encoding, link control, and multiplexing; (2) communication networks, including circuit- and packet-switched, local, packet radio, and satellite; (3) communications architecture, including the OSI model and related protocols; and (4) ISDN.

LOCAL NETWORKS: AN INTRODUCTION, THIRD EDITION

An in-depth presentation of the technology and architecture of local networks. Covers topology, transmission media, medium access control, standards, internetworking, and interface issues.

COMPUTER ORGANIZATION AND ARCHITECTURE, SECOND EDITION

A unified view of this broad field. Covers fundamentals such as CPU, control unit, microprogramming, instruction set, I/O, and memory. Also covers advanced topics such as RISC and parallel organization.

ISDN: AN INTRODUCTION

An in-depth presentation of the technology and architecture of integrated services digital network (ISDN). Covers the integrated digital network (IDN), ISDN services, architecture, signaling system no. 7 (SS7), and detailed coverage of the 1988 CCITT standards.

BUSINESS DATA COMMUNICATIONS

A comprehensive presentation of data communications and telecommunications from a business perspective. Covers voice, data, image, and video communications and applications technology, and includes a number of case studies.

> All of these books include a glossary, a list of acronyms, homework problems, and recommendations for further reading. These books are suitable as references, for self-study, and as textbooks.

Handbook of
COMPUTER-
COMMUNICATIONS
Standards

Handbook of
COMPUTER-
COMMUNICATIONS
Standards

Volume 2, Second Edition

Local Area Network Standards

William Stallings, Ph.D.

HOWARD W. SAMS & COMPANY

A Division of Macmillan, Inc.
11711 North College, Suite 141, Carmel, IN 46032 USA

SECOND EDITION
FIRST PRINTING—1990

International Standard Book Number: 0-672-22698-7
Library of Congress Catalog Card Number: 87-14062

Acquisitions Editor: Scott Arant
Development Editor: C. Herbert Feltner
Manuscript Editor: Phil Kennedy
Compositor: Compset, Inc.

Printed in the United States of America

Again, for Tricia

Contents

Preface

The key to the development of the local area network (LAN) market is the availability of a low-cost interface. The cost to connect equipment to a LAN must be much less than the cost of the equipment alone. This requirement, plus the complexity of the LAN protocols, dictate a VLSI solution. However, chip manufacturers will be reluctant to commit the necessary resources unless there is a high-volume market. A LAN standard would assure that volume. A second benefit of a LAN standard is that it supports a multiple-vendor environment, giving the customer greater flexibility and control.

This line of reasoning has inspired two important and successful LAN standard efforts. The IEEE 802 LAN standards address the needs of the office and the factor for a spectrum of low- and medium-speed LANs, covering twisted pair and coaxial cable media, and bus and ring topologies. The fiber distributed data interface standard addresses the need for a high-speed LAN for computer room and backbone applications, using an optical fiber ring.

Objectives

This book is one of a series of books that provides a comprehensive treatment of computer communications standards. The series systematically covers the major standards topics, providing the introductory and tutorial text material missing from the actual standards. The books function as a primary reference for those who need an understanding of the technology, implementation, design, and application issues that relate to the standards. The books also function as companions to the standards documents for those who need to understand the standards for implementation or product assessment purposes.

In terms of content, the objectives for this and the other volumes are:

- Clear tutorial exposition
- Discussion of relevance and value of each standard
- Analysis of options within each standard
- Explanation of underlying technology
- Manageable and consistent treatment of a variety of standards
- Comparative assessment of alternative standards and options

This volume, Volume II, covers standards that have been developed for local networks. These standards were developed by two separate groups. The IEEE 802 committee, set up by the IEEE Computer Society, has prepared a set of standards covering low- to medium-speed local networks. These standards were initially approved in 1985 and were revised in 1987. One chapter is devoted to each of the major components of this standard. The Accredited Standards Committee X3T95, accredited by the American National Standards Institute, has prepared a standard for a high-speed local network, known as the fiber distributed data interface. This standard was approved in 1987. A chapter is devoted to this standard. All of these standards are in the process of becoming international standards, published by the International Organization for Standardization.

Intended Audience

This book is intended for a broad range of readers interested in local network standards:

- *Students and professionals in data processing and data communications:* This book is intended as a basic tutorial and reference source for this exciting area within the broader fields of computer science and data communications.
- *Local network customers and system managers:* The book provides the reader with an understanding of what features and architecture are needed in a local network facility, as well as a knowledge of current and evolving standards. This information provides a means of assessing specific implementations and vendor offerings.
- *Local network designers and implementers:* The book discusses critical design issues and explores approaches to meeting user requirements.

Related Materials

The author has prepared a number of related materials that may be of interest to the reader. A videotape course that covers the material of this text is available from the Instructional Television Department, College of Engineering, University of Maryland, College Park, MD 20742; telephone (301) 454–7451.

Local Networks, Second Edition (1987, Macmillan) covers the fundamental topics in local network technology, as well as related topics, such as performance, internetworking, network management, and security. This is one of a number of books the author has written for Macmillan; these are described on the inside front cover of this book.

Local Network Technology, Second Edition (1985, IEEE Computer Society Press) contains reprints of many of the key references cited herein. The IEEE Computer Society is at P.O. Box 80452, Worldway Postal Center, Los Angeles, CA 90080; telephone (800) 272-6657.

Acknowledgments

David Carlson (802.2), Don Loughry (802.3), Bob Douglas (802.4), and Jackie Winkler (802.5) of the IEEE 802 committee, and Floyd Ross of the FDDI committee reviewed the descriptions of the respective standards; of course, any remaining errors in the text are my responsibility.

The Second Edition

This second edition provides an update that reflects changes and additions to the set of local area network standards since the publication of the first edition. These include

- Addresses (Chapter 2): Standard address formats and codes have been developed for both MAC and SAP addresses.
- IEEE 802.3 (Chapter 4): A new option, 10BASET, which is a 10-Mbps system running on unshielded twisted pair, has been added. In addition, a fiber-optic interrepeater link has been defined.
- IEEE 802.4 (Chapter 5): A new option has been added. This is an optical fiber specification for an active or passive star topology, operating at 5, 10, and 20 Mbps.
- MAC bridges (Chapter 8): Both the 802.1 and 802.5 committees have been working on specifications for bridge devices that are used to interconnect LANs. This work is nearing final standardization, and a new chapter has been added to describe these specifications.

In addition, some of the original discussion has been reworked and expanded to improve clarity.

1

Local Network Technology

The principal technology ingredients that determine the nature of a local network are:

- Topology
- Transmission medium
- Medium access control technique

Together, they determine the type of data that may be transmitted, the speed and the efficiency of communications, and even the kinds of applications that a network may support.

This chapter surveys the topologies and the transmission media that, within the state of the art, are appropriate for local networks. For more detail, see [STAL90c]. The issue of access control is also briefly raised, to be pursued in greater depth in the remainder of the book. We begin by defining the term local network.

1.1 A DEFINITION

To formulate a definition of the term *local network,* and to characterize the purposes of such networks, it is important to understand the trends that have brought about local networks.

Of most importance is the dramatic and continuing decrease in computer hardware costs, accompanied by an increase in computer hardware capability. Today's microprocessors have speeds, instruction sets, and memory capacities comparable to the most powerful minicomputers of a few years ago. This trend has spawned a number of changes in the way information is collected, processed, and used in organizations. There is increasing use of small, single-function systems, such as word processors and small business computers, and of general-purpose microcomputers, such as personal computers and UNIX-based multiuser workstations. These small, dispersed systems are more accessible to the user, more responsive, and easier to use than large central time-sharing systems.

All of these factors lead to an increased number of systems at a single site: office building, factory, operations center, and so on. At the same time there is likely to be a desire to interconnect these systems for a variety of reasons, including:

- To share and exchange data between systems
- To share expensive resources

The ability to exchange data is a compelling reason for interconnection. Individual users of computer systems do not work in isolation, and will want to retain some of the benefits provided by a central system. These include the ability to exchange messages with other users, the ability to access data from several sources in the preparation of a document or for an analysis, and the opportunity for multiple users to share information in a common file.

To appreciate the second reason, consider that although the cost of data processing hardware has dropped, the cost of essential electromechanical equipment, such as bulk storage and line printers, remains high. In the past, with a centralized data processing facility, these devices could be attached directly to the central host computer. With the dispersal of computer power, these devices must somehow be shared.

All of these requirements can be met by a local network, which is defined as follows:

A local network is a communications network that provides interconnection of a variety of data communicating devices within a small area.

There are three elements of significance in this definition. First, a local network is a communications network. That is, it is a facility for moving bits of data from one attached device to another. The application-level software and protocols that are required for attached devices to function cooperatively are beyond the scope of this book. As a corollary to this definition, note that a collection of devices interconnected by individual point-to-point links is not included in the definition or in this book.

Second, we interpret the phrase *data communicating devices* broadly, to include any device that communicates over a transmission medium. Examples:

- Computers
- Terminals
- Peripheral devices
- Sensors (temperature, humidity, security alarm sensors)
- Telephones
- Television transmitter and receivers
- Facsimile

Of course, not all types of local networks are capable of handling all of these devices.

Third, the geographic scope of a local network is small. The most common occurrence is a network that is confined to a single building. Networks that span several buildings, such as on a college campus or military base, are also common. A borderline case is a network with a radius of a few tens of kilometers. With appropriate technology, such a system will behave like a local network.

1.2   TOPOLOGIES

In the context of a communications network, the term *topology* refers to the way in which the end points, or stations, attached to the network are interconnected. The common topologies for local networks (Figure 1.1) are star, ring, and bus or tree. The bus is a special case of the tree, with only one trunk and no branches; we shall use the term bus/tree when the distinction is unimportant.

The Star Topology

In the *star topology,* each station is connected by a point-to-point link to a common central switch. Communication between any two stations is via circuit switching. For a station to transmit data, it must first send a request to the central switch, asking for a connection to some destination station. Once the circuit is set up, data may be exchanged between the two stations as if they were connected by a dedicated point-to-point link.

This topology exhibits a centralized communications control strategy. All communications are controlled by the central switch, which must set up and maintain a number of concurrent data paths. Consequently, the central switch node is rather complex. On the other hand, the com-

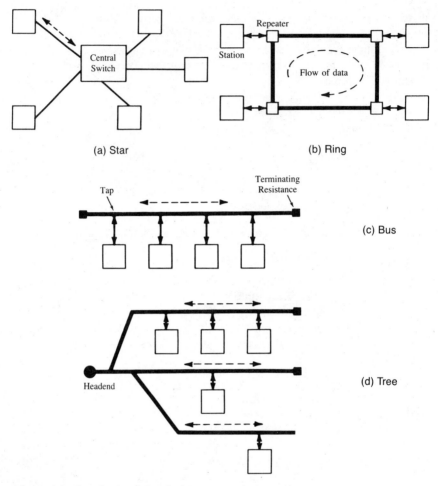

Figure 1.1.   Local network topologies

munications processing burden on the stations is minimal. Other than some rudimentary logic for requesting and accepting connections, the stations need only be concerned with the simple communications requirements of a point-to-point link.

The star topology is used for digital data switch and digital PBX products. Although such products can function as local networks, their operation has not been standardized, and they are not further explored in this book.

The Ring Topology

In the *ring topology,* the local network consists of a set of *repeaters* joined by point-to-point links in a closed loop. Hence each repeater participates in two links. The repeater is a comparatively simple device, capable of receiving data on one link and transmitting it, bit by bit, on the other link as fast as it is received, with no buffering at the repeater. The links are unidirectional; that is, data are transmitted in one direction only, and all oriented in the same way. Thus data circulate around the ring in one direction (clockwise or counterclockwise).

Each station attaches to the network at a repeater. Data are transmitted in blocks, called frames or protocol data units (PDUs). Each frame contains data to be transmitted plus some control information, including the address of the intended destination station. For large blocks of data, the sending station breaks the data up into smaller blocks and sends each block out in a frame. For each frame that a station wishes to transmit, it waits for its next turn and then transmits the frame. As the frame circulates past all the other stations, the destination station recognizes its address and copies the frame into a local buffer as it goes by. The frame continues to circulate until it returns to the source station, where it is removed.

Because multiple devices share the ring, control is needed to determine at what time each station may insert frames. This is almost always done with some form of distributed control. Each station contains access logic that controls transmission and reception.

Note the contrast between the ring and the star topologies. The star topology involves rather complex network processing functions with minimal burden on the stations. In the ring topology, the network devices are the relatively simple repeaters. However, the stations must provide the framing and access control logic.

The Bus and the Tree Topologies

With the *bus topology,* the communications network is simply the transmission medium—no switches and no repeaters. All stations attach, through appropriate hardware interfacing, directly to a linear transmission medium, or *bus*. A transmission from any station propagates the length of the medium and can be received by all other stations.

The tree topology is a generalization of the bus topology. The transmission medium is a branching cable with no closed loops. The tree layout begins at a point known as the *headend*. One or more cables start at the headend, and each of these may have branches. The branches in turn may have additional branches to allow quite complex layouts. Again, a transmission from any station propagates throughout the medium and can be received by all other stations. For both bus and tree topologies, the medium is referred to as *multipoint*.

Because all nodes on a bus or tree share a common transmission link, only one station can transmit at a time. Some form of access control is required to determine which station may transmit next.

As with the ring, packet transmission is typically used for communication. A station wishing to transmit breaks its message into packets and sends these one at a time. For each packet that a station wishes to transmit, it waits for its next turn and then transmits the packet. The intended destination station will recognize its address as the packets go by, and copy them. There are no intermediate nodes and no switching or repeating is involved.

As with the ring, the stations attached to a bus- or tree-topology LAN must supply the framing and access control logic; the processing burden is of roughly the same order of magnitude. The network is relieved of the entire communications processing burden; it is simply a passive (from the point of view of communications) transmission medium.

1.3   TRANSMISSION MEDIA

The transmission medium is the physical signal path between transmitter and receiver. The media that have commonly been used for local networks are twisted pair, coaxial cable, and optical fiber. Tables 1.1 and 1.2 summarize representative, commercially available parameters for these media in point-to-point (ring) and multipoint (bus/tree) local networks. The reader will note that performance for a given medium is considerably better for the ring topology compared with the bus/tree topology. In the bus/tree topology, each station is attached to the medium by a tap, and each tap introduces some attenuation and distortion to the signal as it passes by. In the ring, each station is attached to the medium by a repeater, and each repeater generates a new signal to compensate for effects of attenuation and distortion.

In this section, we describe these media using a set of characteristics based on that proposed in [ROSE82]. The characteristics are:

- *Physical description:* The nature of the transmission medium
- *Transmission characteristics:* Include whether analog or digital signaling is used, modulation technique, capacity, and the frequency range over which transmission occurs
- *Connectivity:* Point-to-point or multipoint
- *Geographic scope:* The maximum distance between points on the network; whether suitable for intrabuilding, interbuilding, and/or intracity use
- *Noise immunity:* Resistance of medium to contamination of the transmitted data
- *Relative cost:* Based on cost of components, installation, and maintenance

Table 1.1.   TRANSMISSION MEDIA FOR LOCAL NETWORKS: RING

Transmission Medium	Data Rate (Mbps)	Distance Between Repeaters (km)	Number of Repeaters
Unshielded twisted pair	4	0.1	72
Shielded twisted pair	16	0.3	250
Baseband coaxial cable	16	1.0	250
Optical fiber	100	2.0	240

Table 1.2.   TRANSMISSION MEDIA FOR LOCAL NETWORKS: BUS/TREE

Transmission Medium	Data Rate (Mbps)	Range (km)	Number of Taps
Twisted pair	1–2	< 2	10s
Baseband coaxial cable	10; 50 with limitations	< 3	100s
Broadband coaxial cable	500; 20 per channel	< 30	1000s
Optical fiber	10	< 1	10s

Twisted Pair

By far the most common transmission medium, for both analog and digital data, is *twisted pair.* The wiring within a building to connect the telephones is twisted pair, as are the "local loops" that connect all of the phones in a limited geographic area to a central exchange.

Physical Description.   A twisted pair consists of two insulated wires arranged in a regular spiral pattern. The wires are copper- or steel-coated with copper. The copper provides conductivity; steel may be used for strength. A wire pair acts as a single communication link. Typically, a number of these pairs are bundled together into a cable by wrapping them in a tough protective sheath. Over longer distances, cables may contain hundreds of pairs. The twisting of the individual pairs minimizes electromagnetic interference between the pairs. The wires in a pair have thicknesses of from 0.016 to 0.036 inch.

Transmission Characteristics.   Wire pairs may be used to transmit both analog and digital signals. For analog signals, amplifiers are required about every 5 to 6 km. For digital signals, repeaters are used every 2 or 3 km.

The most common use of wire pair is for analog transmission of voice. Although frequency components of speech may be found between 20 Hz and 20 kHz, a much narrower bandwidth is required for intelligible speech reproduction [FREE81]. The standard bandwidth of a full-duplex voice channel is 300 to 3400 Hz. Multiple voice channels can be multiplexed, using frequency-division multiplexing (FDM), on a single wire pair. A bandwidth of 4 kHz per channel provides adequate separation between channels. Twisted pair has a capacity of up to 24 voice channels using a bandwidth of up to 268 kHz.

Digital data may be transmitted over an analog voice channel using a modem. With a current modem design, speeds of up to 9600 bps using phase-shift keying (PSK) are practical. On a 24-channel wire pair, the aggregate data rate is 230 kbps.

It is also possible to use digital or baseband signaling on a wire pair. Bell offers a T1 circuit using twisted pair that handles 24 PCM voice channels, for an aggregate data rate of 1.544 Mbps. Higher data rates, depending on distance, are possible. A data rate of four megabits per second represents a reasonable upper limit.

Connectivity.   Twisted pair can be used for point-to-point and multipoint applications. As a multipoint medium, twisted pair is a less-expensive, lower-performance alternative to coax cable but supports fewer stations. Point-to-point usage is far more common.

Geographic Scope.   Twisted pair can easily provide point-to-point data transmission to a range of 15 km or more. Twisted pair for local networks is typically used within a single building or just a few buildings.

Noise Immunity.   Compared to other guided media, twisted pair is limited in distance, bandwidth, and data rate. The medium is quite susceptible to interference and noise because of its easy coupling with electromagnetic fields. For example, a wire run parallel to an ac power line will pick up 60-Hz energy. Signals on adjacent pairs of cables may interfere with each other, a phenomenon known as crosstalk.

Several measures can be taken to reduce impairments. Shielding the wire with metallic braid or sheathing reduces interference. The twisting of the wire reduces low frequency interference, and the use of different twist lengths in adjacent pairs reduces crosstalk. These measures are effective for wavelengths much greater than the twist length of the cable. Noise immunity can be as high or higher than for coaxial cable for low frequency transmission. However, above 10 to 100 kHz, coaxial cable is typically superior.

Cost. Twisted pair is less expensive than either coaxial cable or fiber in terms of cost per foot. However, installation costs may approach that of other media due to labor costs.

Coaxial Cable

The most versatile transmission for local networks is *coaxial cable*. Indeed, many people think of coaxial cable as the *only* local network transmission medium, despite the widespread use of twisted pair.

In this section we discuss two types of coaxial cable currently in use for local network applications: 75-ohm cable, which is the standard used in *community antenna television* (CATV) systems, and 50-ohm cable. Typically, 50-ohm cable is only used for digital signaling, called *baseband;* 75-ohm cable is used for analog signaling with FDM called *broadband,* and for high-speed digital signaling and analog signaling in which no FDM is possible. The latter is sometimes referred to as *single-channel broadband.*

Physical Description. Coaxial cable, like twisted pair, consists of two conductors, but it is constructed differently to permit it to operate over a wider range of frequencies. It consists of a hollow outer cylindrical conductor that surrounds a single inner wire conductor. The inner conductor can be either solid or stranded; the outer conductor can be either solid or braided. The inner conductor is held in place by either regularly spaced insulating rings or a solid dialectric material. The outer conductor is covered with a jacket or a shield. A single coaxial cable has a diameter of from 0.4 to about 1 inch.

Transmission Characteristics. The 50-ohm cable is used exclusively for digital transmission. Manchester encoding (see Appendix B) is typically used. Data rates of up to 10 Mbps can be achieved.

CATV cable is used for both analog and digital signaling. For analog signaling, frequencies up to 300 to 400 MHz are possible. Analog data, such as video and audio, can be handled on CATV cable in much the same way as free-space radio and TV broadcasting. TV channels are each allocated 6 MHz of bandwidth; each radio channel requires much less. Hence a large number of channels can be carried on the cable using FDM.

When FDM is used, the CATV cable is referred to as *broadband.* The frequency spectrum of the cable is divided into channels, each of which carries analog signals. In addition to the analog data referred to above, digital data may also be carried in a channel. Various modulation schemes have been used for digital data, including ASK, FSK, and PSK (see Appendix B). The efficiency of the modem will determine the bandwidth needed to support a given data rate. A good rule of thumb

[STAH82] is to assume 1 Hz per bps for rates of 5 Mbps and above and 2 Hz per bps for lower rates. For example, a 5-Mbps data rate can be achieved in a 6-MHz TV channel, whereas a 4.8-kbps modem might use about 10 kHz. With current technology, a data rate of about 20 Mbps is achievable; at this rate, the bandwidth efficiency may exceed 1 bps/Hz.

To achieve data rates above 20 Mbps, two approaches have been taken. Both require that the entire bandwidth of the 75-ohm cable be dedicated to this data transfer; no FDM is employed. One approach is to use digital signaling on the cable, as is done for the 50-ohm cable. A data rate of 50 Mbps has been achieved with this scheme. An alternative is to use a simple PSK system; using a 150-MHz carrier, a data rate of 50 Mbps has also been achieved. Much lower data rates are achieved using FSK.

Connectivity.   Coaxial cable is applicable to point-to-point and to multipoint configurations. Baseband 50-ohm cable can support on the order of 100 devices per segment, with larger systems possible by linking segments with repeaters. Broadband 75-ohm cable can support thousands of devices. The use of 75-ohm cable at high data rates (50 Mbps) introduces technical problems that limit the number of devices to 20 to 30.

Geographic Scope.   Maximum distances in a typical baseband cable are limited to a few kilometers. Broadband networks can span ranges of tens of kilometers. The difference has to do with the relative signal integrity of analog and digital signals. The types of electromagnetic noise usually encountered in industrial and urban areas are of relatively low frequencies, where most of the energy in digital signals resides. Analog signals may be placed on a carrier of sufficiently high frequency to avoid the main components of noise.

High-speed transmission (50 Mbps), digital or analog, is limited to about 1 km. Because of the high data rate, the physical distance between signals on the bus is very small. Hence very little attenuation or noise can be tolerated before the data are lost.

Noise Immunity.   Noise immunity for coaxial cable depends on the application and implementation. In general, it is superior to that of twisted pair for higher frequencies.

Cost.   The cost of installed coaxial cable falls between that of twisted pair and optical fiber.

Optical Fiber Cable

The most exciting developments in the realm of local network transmission media are in the area of *fiber optics*. Because the technology is changing rapidly, this section can provide only a current snapshot of fiber optic capability.

Physical Description.   An optical fiber is a thin (2 to 125 μm), flexible medium capable of conducting an optical ray. Various glasses and plastics can be used to make optical fibers [JORD85]. The lowest losses have been obtained using fibers of ultrapure fused silica. Ultrapure fiber is difficult to manufacture; higher-loss multicomponent glass fibers are more economical and still provide good performance. Plastic fiber is even less costly and can be used for short-haul links, for which moderately high losses are acceptable.

An optical fiber cable has a cylindrical shape and consists of three concentric sections: the core, the cladding, and the jacket. The *core* is the innermost section, and consists of one or more very thin strands, or fibers, made of glass or plastic. Each fiber is surrounded by its own *cladding,* a glass or plastic coating that has optical properties different from those of the core. The outermost layer, surrounding one or a bundle of cladded fibers, is the *jacket.* The jacket is composed of plastic and other materials layered to protect against moisture, abrasion, crushing, and other environmental hazards.

Transmission Characteristics.   Optical fiber transmits a signal-encoded beam of light by means of total internal reflection. Total internal reflection can occur in any transparent medium that has a higher index of refraction than the surrounding medium. In effect, the optical fiber acts as a waveguide for frequencies in the range 10^{14} to 10^{15} Hz, which covers the visible spectrum and part of the infrared spectrum.

Figure 1.2 shows the principle of optical fiber transmission. Light from a source enters the cylindrical glass or plastic core. Rays at shallow angles are reflected and propagated along the fiber; other rays are absorbed by the surrounding material. This form of propagation is called multimode, referring to the variety of angles that will reflect. When the fiber core radius is reduced, fewer angles will reflect. By reducing the radius of the core to the order of a wavelength, only a single angle or mode can pass: the axial ray. This provides superior performance to multimode for the following reason. With multimode transmission, multiple propagation paths exist, each with a different path length and hence time to traverse the fiber. This causes signal elements to spread out in time and limits the rate at which data can be accurately received. Since there is a single transmission path with single-mode transmission, such distortion cannot occur. Finally, by varying the index of refraction of the core, a third type of transmission, known as multimode graded index, is possible. This type is intermediate between the other two in characteristics. The variable refraction has the effect of focusing the rays more efficiently

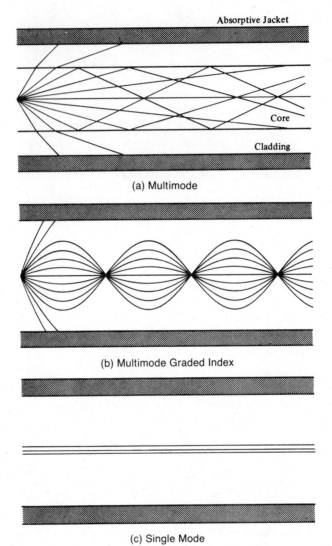

(a) Multimode

(b) Multimode Graded Index

(c) Single Mode

Figure 1.2.   Optical fiber transmission modes

than ordinary multimode, also known as multimode step-index. Table 1.3 compares the three fiber transmission modes. As can be seen, tremendous capacities can be achieved, far exceeding those of coaxial cable or twisted pair.

Two different types of light source are used in fiber optic systems [WERN86]; the *light-emitting diode* (LED) and the *injection laser diode* (ILD). The LED is a solid-state device that emits light when a current is applied. The ILD is a solid-state device that works on the laser principle in which quantum electronic effects are stimulated to produce a superradiant beam of narrow bandwidth. The LED is less costly, operates over

Table 1.3.   COMPARISON OF THREE TYPES OF OPTICAL FIBERS

	Step-index Multimode	Graded-Index Multimode	Single-mode
Light source	LED or laser	LED or laser	Laser
Bandwidth	Wide (up to 200 MHz/km)	Very wide (200 MHz-3 GHz/km)	Extremely wide (3 GHz-50 GHz/km)
Splicing	Difficult	Difficult	Difficult
Typical application	Computer data links	Moderate-length telephone lines	Telecommunication long lines
Cost	Least expensive	More expensive	Most expensive
Core diameter (μm)	50–125	50–125	2–8
Cladding diameter (μm)	125–440	125–440	15–60

a greater temperature range, and has a longer operational life. The ILD is more efficient and can sustain greater data rates.

The detector used at the receiving end to convert the light into electrical energy is a *photodiode*. Two solid-state devices have been used [FORR86]: the PIN detector and the APD detector. The PIN photodiode has a segment of intrinsic (I) silicon between the P and N layers of a diode. The APD, avalanche photodiode, is similar in appearance but uses a stronger electric field. Both devices are basically photon counters. The PIN is less expensive and less sensitive than the APD.

Modulation of the light carrier is a form of ASK called *intensity modulation*. Typically, the two binary digits are represented by the presence or absence of light at a given frequency. Both LED and ILD devices can be modulated in this fashion; the PIN and APD detectors respond directly to intensity modulation.

Data rates as high as a few gigabits per second have been demonstrated in the laboratory. Current practical applications are in the range of a few hundreds of megabits per second over a few kilometers.

There is a relationship among the wavelength employed, the types of transmission, and the achievable data rate [MIER86]. Both single mode and multimode can support several different wavelengths of light and can employ laser or LED light sources. In glass-composition fiber, light propagates best in three distinct wavelength "windows," centered on 850, 1300, and 1500 nanometers (nm). The loss is lower at higher wavelengths, allowing greater data rates over longer distances (Table 1.4). Most local applications today use 850-nm LED light sources. Although this is relatively inexpensive, this combination is generally limited to data rates under 100 Mbps and distances of a few kilometers. To achieve higher data

Table 1.4.   TRANSMISSION LOSSES OF VARIOUS TYPES OF OPTICAL FIBER [FREE85]

		Transmission Loss (dB/km)		
Mode	Material Core/Cladding	850 nm	1300 nm	1500 nm
Single mode	Silica glass/silica glass	2	0.5	0.2
Step-index multimode	Silica glass/silica glass	2	0.5	0.2
	Silica glass/plastic	2.5	High	High
	Multicomponent glass/ multicomponent glass	3.4	High	High
Graded-index multimode	Silica glass/silica glass	2	0.5	0.2
	Multicomponent glass/ multicomponent glass	3.5	High	High

rates and longer distances, a 1300-nm LED or laser source is needed. Thus although the 850-nm source is attractive for most local area networks, the 1300-nm source is more appropriate for high-speed local area networks. The highest transmission capacities and longest distances achievable today require 1500-nm light sources. These require lasers and are used in some long-distance applications, but are currently too expensive for local networks.

Currently, a single carrier frequency is used for optical fiber transmission. Future advance will permit practical FDM systems, also referred to as wavelength division multiplexing or color division multiplexing.

Connectivity.   The most common use of optical fiber is for point-to-point links. Experimental multipoint systems using a bus topology have been built, but are too expensive to be practical today. In principle, however, a single segment of optical fiber could support many more drops than either twisted pair of coaxial cable, because of fiber's lower power loss, lower attenuation characteristics, and greater bandwidth potential.

Geographic Scope.   Present technology supports transmission over distances of 6 to 8 km without repeaters. Hence, optical fiber is suitable for linking local networks in several buildings via point-to-point links.

Noise Immunity.   Optical fiber is not affected by electromagnetic interference or noise. This characteristic permits high data rates over long distance and provides excellent security.

Cost.   Fiber optic systems are more expensive than twisted pair and coaxial cable in terms of cost per foot and required components (transmitters, receivers, connectors). While costs of twisted pair and coaxial cable are unlikely to drop, engineering advances should reduce the cost of fiber optics to be competitive with these other media.

1.4   THE BUS/TREE TOPOLOGY

So far, the bus and the tree topologies have been the most common ones used to implement local networks. Ethernet [METC76] was one of the earliest local networks and is still the best known; it uses a baseband bus architecture. MITREnet [HOPK79] is an early bus/tree broadband system that has been the basis of much government-sponsored research and development and of a number of commercial products. Many of the popular, low-cost twisted-pair local networks for personal computers use a bus topology. Finally, the oldest and most popular high-speed local network, HYPERchannel [CHRI79], uses a baseband bus architecture.

In this section, we first describe key characteristics common to all bus and tree configurations, and then look in more detail at baseband and broadband local networks.

Characteristics of Bus/Tree Local Networks

The operation of the bus/tree local network can be summarized briefly. Because multiple devices share a single data path, only one may transmit at a time. A station usually transmits data in the form of a frame containing the address of the destination. The frame propagates throughout the medium and is received by all other stations. The addressed station copies the frame as it goes by.

Two transmission techniques are in use: baseband and broadband. Baseband, using digital signaling, can be employed on twisted-pair or coaxial cable. Broadband, using analog signaling in the radio-frequency (RF) range, employs coaxial cable. Some of the differences are highlighted in Table 1.5, and this section explores the two methods in some detail. There is also a variant, known as *single-channel broadband,* that has the signaling characteristics of broadband but some of the restrictions of baseband. This is also covered later.

Table 1.5.   BUS/TREE TRANSMISSION TECHNIQUES

Baseband	Broadband
Digital signaling	Analog signaling (requires RF modem)
Entire bandwidth consumed by signal—no FDM	FDM possible—multiple data channels, video, audio
Bidirectional	Unidirectional
Bus topology	Bus or tree topology
Distance: up to a few kilometers	Distance: up to tens of kilometers

The multipoint nature of the bus/tree topology gives rise to several problems. First is determining which station may transmit at any point in time. With point-to-point links this is a fairly simple task. If the line is full-duplex, both stations may transmit at the same time; if the line is half-duplex, a rather simple mechanism is needed to ensure that the two stations take turns. Historically, the most common shared access scheme has been the multidrop line, in which access is determined by polling from a controlling station. The controlling station may send data to any other station, or it may issue a poll to a specific station, asking for an immediate response. This method, however, negates some of the advantages of a distributed system and is awkward for communication between two non-controller stations. A variety of distributed strategies, referred to as medium access control protocols, have now been developed for bus and tree topologies.

A second problem has to do with signal balancing. When two devices exchange data over a link, the signal strength of the transmitter must be adjusted to be within certain limits. The signal must be strong enough so that, after attenuation across the medium, it meets the receiver's minimum signal strength requirements. It must also be strong enough to maintain an adequate signal to noise ratio. On the other hand, the signal must not be so strong that it overloads the circuitry of the transmitter, which creates harmonics and other spurious signals. Although easily done for a point-to-point link, signal balancing is no easy task for a multipoint line. If any device can transmit to any other device, then the signal balancing must be performed for all permutations of stations taken two at a time. For n stations that works out to $n \times (n - 1)$ permutations. Therefore, for a 200-station network (not a particularly large system), 39,800 signal strength constraints must be satisfied simultaneously. With interdevice distances ranging from tens of thousands of meters, this is an impossible task for any but small networks. In systems that use RF signals, the problem is compounded because of the possibility of RF signal interference across frequencies. The solution is to divide the medium into segments within which pairwise balancing is possible, using amplifiers or repeaters between segments.

Baseband Systems

The principal characteristics of a baseband system are listed in Table 1.5. As mentioned earlier, a baseband local network is defined as one that uses digital signaling. (This is a restricted use of the word *baseband*, which has become accepted in local network circles. More generally, baseband refers to the transmission of an analog or digital signal in its original form, without modulation.) Digital signals are inserted on the line as voltage pulses, usually using either Manchester or Differential Manchester encoding. The entire frequency spectrum of the medium is used to form the signal; hence, frequency-division multiplexing (FDM) cannot be used. Transmission is bidirectional. That is, a signal inserted at any point on the medium propagates in both directions to the ends, where it is absorbed (Figure 1.3a). The digital signaling requires a bus topology. Unlike analog signals, digital signals cannot easily be propagated through the splitters and joiners required for a tree topology. Baseband systems can extend only a limited distance, about 1 km at most. This is because the attenuation of the signal, which is most pronounced at higher frequencies, causes a blurring of the pulses and a weakening of the signal to the extent that communication over larger distances is impractical.

Baseband Coax.   Most baseband coaxial cable systems use a special 50-ohm cable rather than the standard CATV 75-ohm cable. These values refer to the impedance of the cable. Roughly speaking, impedance is a measure of how much voltage must be applied to the cable to achieve a given signal strength. For digital signals, the 50-ohm cable suffers less intense reflections from the insertion capacitance of the taps, and provides better immunity against low-frequency electromagnetic noise. The simplest baseband coaxial bus local network consists of an unbranched

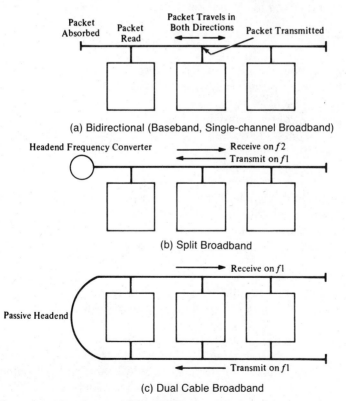

(a) Bidirectional (Baseband, Single-channel Broadband)

(b) Split Broadband

(c) Dual Cable Broadband

Figure 1.3.   Baseband and broadband transmission techniques

length of coaxial cable with a terminating resistance at each end. The value of the resistance is set equal to the impedance of the cable; this prevents reflection by absorbing any signal on the cable.

As with any transmission system, there are engineering trade-offs involving data rate, cable length, number of taps, and electrical characteristics of the transmit and receive components for a baseband coaxial system. For example, the lower the data range, the longer the cable can be. That latter statement is true for the following reason: when a signal is propagated along a transmission medium, the integrity of the signal suffers due to attenuation, noise, and other impairments. The longer the length of propagation, the greater the effect, increasing the probability of error. At a lower data rate, however, the individual pulses of a digital signal last longer and can be recovered in the presence of impairments more easily than higher-rate, shorter pulses.

An example from the IEEE 802.3 standard illustrates some of the tradeoffs. The original 802.3 standard specified 0.4-inch diameter cable and a data rate of 10 Mbps. With these parameters, a maximum length of 500 m is recommended to guarantee signal quality. Stations attach to the cable by means of a tap, with the distance between any two taps being a multiple of 2.5 m; this is to ensure that reflections from adjacent taps do not add in phase. Studies have shown that if this spacing is not enforced, signal quality does suffer [YEN83]. A maximum of 100 taps is recommended. A later edition of the 802.3 standard uses 0.25-inch cable, which causes greater attenuation. Accordingly, the cable length is limited to 200m, and the number of taps is limited to 30.

To extend the length of the network, a repeater may be used. It consists, in essence, of two transceivers joined together and connected to two different segments of coax cable. The repeater passes digital signals in both directions between the two segments, amplifying and regenerating the signals as they pass through. A repeater is transparent to the rest of the system; as it does no buffering, it in no sense isolates one segment from another. So, for example, if two stations on different segments attempt to transmit at the same time, their packets will interfere with each other (collide). To avoid multipath interference, only one path of segments and repeaters is allowed between any two stations.

Twisted-Pair Baseband.   A twisted-pair baseband LAN is intended for low-cost, low-performance requirements. This type of system supports fewer stations at lower speeds than a coax baseband local network, but at far lower cost.

Twisted pair is a good medium for several reasons. First, it has lower cost than coaxial cable while providing almost equal noise immunity. Second, virtually anyone can install the network, which consists of laying the cable and connecting the controllers. The task requires only a screwdriver and a pair of pliers, and is similar to hooking up hi-fi speakers.

Broadband Systems

Like the term baseband, *broadband* is a word co-opted into the local network vocabulary from the telecommunications world, with a change in meaning. In general, broadband refers to any channel having a bandwidth greater than a voice-grade channel (4 kHz). To local network aficionados, the term is reserved for coaxial cable on which analog signaling is used. A further restriction to transmission techniques that allow FDM on the cable is usually applied. We will generally mean systems capable of FDM when using the term broadband. Systems intended to carry only a single analog signal will be referred to as single channel broadband.

FDM Broadband.   Table 1.5 summarizes the key characteristics of broadband systems. As mentioned, broadband implies the use of analog signaling. FDM is possible: the frequency spectrum of the cable can be divided into channels or sections of bandwidth. Separate channels can support data traffic, TV, or radio signals. Broadband components allow splitting and joining operations; hence both bus and tree topologies are possible. Much greater distances—tens of kilometers—are possible with broadband compared to baseband. This is because the analog signals that carry the digital data can propagate greater distances before the noise and attenuation damage the data.

As with baseband, stations attach to the cable by means of a tap. Unlike baseband, however, broadband is inherently a unidirectional medium; signals inserted onto the medium can propagate in only one direction. The primary reason for this is that it is infeasible to build amplifiers that will pass signals of one frequency in both directions. This unidirectional property means that only those stations downstream from a transmitting station can receive its signals. How, then, to achieve full connectivity?

Clearly, two data paths are needed. These paths are joined at a point on the network known as the *headend*. For bus topology, the headend is simply one end of the bus. For tree topology, the headend is the root of the branching tree. All stations transmit on one path toward the headend (inbound). Signals received at the headend are then propagated along a second data path away from the headend (outbound). All stations receive on the outbound path.

Physically, two different configurations are used to implement the inbound and outbound paths (Figure 1.3b and c). On a *dual-cable* configuration, the inbound and outbound paths are separate cables, with the headend simply a passive connector between the two. Stations send and receive on the same frequency.

By contrast, on the *split* configuration, the inbound and outbound paths are different frequency bands on the same cable. *Bidirectional amplifiers* pass lower frequencies inbound, and higher frequencies outbound.

(Note that this is a different sense of the word bidirectional.) Between the inbound and the outbound frequency bands is a guardband. The guardband carries no signals and separates signals in the other two bands. The headend contains a device, known as a *frequency translator,* for translating inbound frequencies to outbound frequencies.

The frequency translator at the headend can be either an analog or a digital device. An analog device simply translates signals to a new frequency and retransmits them. A digital device recovers the digital data from the analog signal and then retransmits the cleaned-up data on the new frequency.

Split systems are categorized by frequency allocation to the two paths, as shown in Table 1.6. Subsplit, commonly used by the CATV industry, was designed for metropolitan area television distribution, with limited subscriber-to-central office communication. It provides the easiest way to upgrade existing one-way cable systems to two-way operation. Subsplit has limited usefulness for local area networking because a bandwidth of only 25 MHz is available for two-way communication. Midsplit is more suitable for LANs, as it provides a more equitable distribution of bandwidth. However, midsplit was developed at a time when the practical spectrum of a CATV cable was 300 MHz, whereas spectrums surpassing 400 MHz are now available. Accordingly, a highsplit specification has been developed to provide the maximum two-way bandwidth for a split cable system.

The differences between split and dual are minor. The split system is useful when a single cable plant is already installed in a building. Also, the installed system is about 10 to 15 percent cheaper than a dual-cable system [HOPK79]. On the other hand, a dual cable has over twice the capacity of midsplit. It does not require the frequency translator at the headend, which on the split system may need to be redundant for reliability.

Broadband systems use standard, off-the-shelf CATV components, including 75-ohm coaxial cable. All end points are terminated with a 75-ohm terminator to absorb signals. Broadband is suitable for tens of kilo-

Table 1.6. COMMON CABLE FREQUENCY SPLITS

Format	Inbound Frequency Band (MHz)	Outbound Frequency Band (MHz)	Maximum Two-way Bandwidth (MHz)
Subsplit	5–30	54–400	25
Midsplit	5–116	168–400	111
Highsplit	5–174	232–400	168
Dual Cable	40–400	40–400	360

meters radius from the headend and hundreds or even thousands of devices.

Cables used in broadband networks are of three types. *Trunk cable,* typically 0.5 to 1.0 inch in diameter with attenuation of 0.7 to 1.2 dB per 100 ft of cable at 300 MHz, might form the spine of a large LAN system. Typically, trunk cables are sheathed in a rigid aluminum shield and range in length from a few kilometers to tens of kilometers. *Distribution cables,* typically 0.4 to 0.5 inch in diameter with attenuation of 1.2 to 2.0 dB per 100 ft, are used for shorter distances and for branch cables. They may be semirigid or rigid. *Drop cables,* typically 0.25 inch in diameter with attenuation of 4 to 6 db per 100 ft, are flexible, short, and used to connect stations to the local network.

Amplifiers may be used on trunk and distribution cables to compensate for cable attenuation. Amplifiers must have a *slope* to account for the variability of attenuation as a function of frequency; less amplification is needed at lower frequencies. For split systems, amplifiers must be bidirectional, passing and amplifying lower frequencies in one direction and higher frequencies in the other.

Single-Channel Broadband.   An abridged form of broadband, known as single-channel broadband or carrierband, is one in which the entire spectrum of the cable is devoted to a single transmission path for analog signals.

In general, a single-channel broadband local network has the following characteristics. Bidirectional transmission, using a bus topology, is employed. Hence there can be no amplifiers, and there is no need for a headend. Some form of FSK is used, generally at a low frequency (a few MHz). This is an advantage because attenuation is less at lower frequencies.

Because the cable is dedicated to a single task, it is not necessary to take care that the modem output be confined to a narrow bandwidth. Energy can spread over the cable's spectrum. As a result, the electronics are simple and inexpensive. This scheme would appear to give comparable performance, at a comparable price, to baseband.

1.5 THE RING TOPOLOGY

The major alternative to the bus/tree topology for local networks is the ring. The ring has enjoyed considerable popularity in Europe but has only recently gained acceptance in the United States, where Ethernet and MITREnet were largely responsible for shaping the early direction of activity. The current U.S. popularity of the ring local network dates from the introduction of IBM's product in 1985 [DERF86], which was quickly followed by compatible products from other vendors.

Characteristics of Ring Local Networks

The ring consists of a number of repeaters, each connected to two others by unidirectional transmission links to form a single closed path. Data are transferred sequentially, bit by bit, around the ring from one repeater to the next. Each repeater regenerates and retransmits each bit.

For a ring to operate as a communications network, three functions are required: data insertion, data reception, and data removal. These functions are provided by the repeaters. Each repeater, in addition to serving as an active element on the ring, serves as a device attachment point for data insertion. Data are transmitted in frames, each of which contains a destination address field. As a frame circulates past a repeater, the address field is copied to the attached station. If the station recognizes the address, then the remainder of the frame is copied.

A variety of strategies can be used for determining how and when frames are added to and removed from the ring. The strategy can be viewed, at least conceptually, as residing in a medium access control layer, discussed in Chapter 2.

Repeaters perform the data insertion and reception functions in a manner not unlike that of taps, which serve as device attachment points on a bus or a tree. Data removal, however, is more difficult on a ring. For a bus or a tree, signals inserted onto the line propagate to the end points and are absorbed by terminators. Hence, shortly after transmission ceases, the bus or the tree is clear of data. Because the ring is a closed loop, however, data will circulate indefinitely unless removed. A frame may be removed by the addressed repeater. Alternatively, each frame could be removed by the transmitting repeater after it has made one trip around the loop. The latter approach is more desirable because (1) it permits automatic acknowledgment and (2) it permits multicast addressing: one frame sent simultaneously to multiple stations.

The repeater, then, can be seen to have two main purposes: (1) to contribute to the proper functioning of the ring by passing on all the data that comes its way and (2) to provide an access point for attached stations to send and receive data. Corresponding to these two purposes are two states (Figure 1.4): the listen state and the transmit state.

In the *listen state,* each bit that is received is retransmitted with a small delay, required to allow the repeater to perform necessary functions. Ideally, the delay should be on the order of one bit time (the time it takes for a repeater to transmit one complete bit onto the outgoing line). These functions are:

- Scan passing bit stream for pertinent patterns. Chief among these is the address or addresses of attached devices. Another pattern, used in the token control strategy explained later, indicates permission to transmit. Note that to perform the scanning function, the repeater must have some knowledge of frame format.

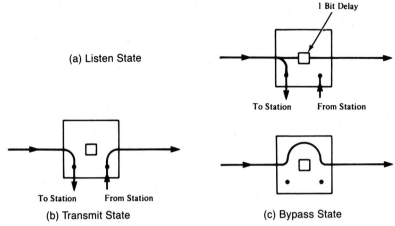

(a) Listen State

(b) Transmit State

(c) Bypass State

Figure 1.4. Ring repeater states

- Copy each incoming bit and send it to the attached station, while continuing to retransmit each bit. This will be done for each bit of each frame addressed to this station.
- Modify a bit as it passes by. In certain control strategies, bits may be modified to, for example, indicate that the frame has been copied. This would serve as an acknowledgment.

When a repeater's station has data to send and when the repeater, based on the control strategy, has permission to send, the repeater enters the *transmit state*. In this state, the repeater receives bits from the station and retransmits them on its outgoing link. During the period of transmission, bits may appear on the incoming ring link. There are two possibilities, and they are treated differently:

- The bits could be from the same packet that the repeater is still sending. This will occur if the *bit length* of the ring is shorter than the frame. In this case, the repeater passes the bits back to the station, which can check them as a form of acknowledgment.
- For some control strategies, more than one frame could be on the ring at the same time. If the repeater, while transmitting, receives bits from a frame it did not originate, it must buffer them to be transmitted later.

These two states, listen and transmit, are sufficient for proper ring operation. A third state, the *bypass state,* is also useful. In this state, a bypass relay is activated, so that signals propagate past the repeater with no delay other than medium propagation. The bypass relay affords two benefits: (1) it provides a partial solution to the reliability problem, discussed later, and (2) it improves performance by eliminating repeater delay for those stations that are not active on the network.

Ring Benefits

Until recently the ring topology LAN was little known in the United States. While much work has been done in Europe, the emphasis in the United States was on the bus/tree topologies. The strengths of the bus/tree approach, discussed in the preceding section, are well known. The benefits of the ring have been less well known, but interest is beginning to build. A good deal of research into overcoming some of the weaknesses of the ring has been done at M.I.T. [SALT79, SALT83] and at IBM [BUX83, STRO83, DIXO83]. The result has been a proliferation of ring-based LAN products, most notably the appearance of the IBM product in 1985, followed by a number of compatible products from other vendors [DERF86, STRO86].

Like the bus and the tree, the ring is also a shared-access or multiaccess network. Hence, the benefits of this type of medium include the ability to broadcast and incremental cost growth. There are other benefits provided by the ring that are not shared by the bus/tree topology.

The most important benefit or strength of the ring is that it uses point-to-point communication links. There are a number of implications of this fact. First, because the transmitted signal is regenerated at each node, greater distances can be covered than with baseband bus. Broadband bus/tree can cover a similar range, but cascaded amplifiers can result in loss of data integrity at high data rates. Second, the ring can accommodate optical fiber links, which provide very high data rates and excellent electromagnetic interference (EMI) characteristics. Finally, the electronics and maintenance of point-to-point lines are simpler than for multipoint lines.

Another benefit of the ring is that fault isolation and recovery are simpler than for bus/tree. This is discussed in more detail later in this section and in Chapter 7.

With the ring, the *duplicate address* problem is easily solved. If, on a bus or tree, two stations are by accident assigned the same address, there is no easy way to sort this out. A relatively complex algorithm must be incorporated into the LAN protocol. On a ring, the first station with an address match that is encountered by a frame can modify a bit in the packet to acknowledge reception. Subsequent stations with the same address will easily recognize the problem.

Potential Ring Problems

The potential problems of a ring are, at first blush, more obvious than the benefits:

1. *Cable vulnerability:* A break on any of the links between repeaters disables the entire network until the problem can be isolated and a

new cable installed. The ring may range widely throughout a building and is vulnerable at every point to accidents.

2. *Repeater failure:* As with the links, a failure of a single repeater disables the entire network. In many networks, it will be common for many of the stations not to be in operation at any time; yet all repeaters must always operate properly.

3. *Perambulation:* When either a repeater or a link fails, locating the failure requires perambulation of the ring, and thus access to all rooms containing repeaters and cable. This is known as the *pocket full of keys* problem.

4. *Installation headaches:* Installation of a new repeater to support new devices requires the identification of two nearby, topologically adjacent repeaters. It must be verified that they are in fact adjacent (documentation could be faulty or out of date), and cable must be run from the new repeater to both of the old repeaters. These are several unfortunate consequences. The length of cable driven by the source repeater may change, possibly requiring retuning. Old cable, if not removed, accumulates. In addition, the geometry of the ring may become highly irregular, exacerbating the perambulation problem.

5. *Size Limitations:* There is a practical limit to the number of repeaters on a ring. This limit is suggested by the reliability and maintenance problems cited earlier, the timing jitter discussed later, and the accumulating delay of large numbers of repeaters. A limit of a few hundred repeaters seems reasonable.

6. *Initialization and recovery:* To avoid designating one ring node as a controller (negating the benefit of distributed control), a strategy is required to assure that all stations can cooperate smoothly when initialization and recovery is required. This need arises, for example, when a frame is garbled by a transient line error; in that case, no repeater may wish to assume the responsibility of removing the circulating frame.

7. *Timing Jitter:* This is a subtle problem having to do with the clocking or the timing of a signal in a distributed network.

Problems 1 and 2 are reliability problems. These two problems, together with problems 3, 4, and 5, can be ameliorated by a refinement in the ring architecture, explained in the next section. Problem 6 is a software problem, to be dealt with by the various LAN protocols discussed in later chapters. A discussion of problem 7 is deferred until Chapter 6.

The Star-Ring Architecture

Two observations can be made about the basic ring architecture described above. First, there is a practical limit to the number of repeaters on a ring. As mentioned in problem 5 above, a number of factors combine to limit the practical size of a ring local network to a few hundred repeaters. Sec-

ond, the cited benefits of the ring do not depend on the actual routing of
the cables that link the repeaters.

These observations have led to the development of a refined ring
architecture, the star-ring, which overcomes some of the problems of the
ring and allows the construction of large local networks [SALW83].

As a first step, consider the rearrangement of a ring into a star. This
is achieved by having the interrepeater links all thread through a single
site (Figure 1.5). This ring wiring concentrator has a number of advantages. Because there is access to the signal on every link, it is a simple
matter to isolate a fault. A message can be launched into the ring and
tracked to see how far it gets without mishap. A faulty segment can be
disconnected—no pocket full of keys needed—and repaired at a later
time. New repeaters can easily be added to the ring: simply run two cables from the new repeater to the site of ring wiring concentration and
splice into the ring.

The bypass relay associated with each repeater can be moved into
the ring wiring concentrator. The relay can automatically bypass its repeater and two links for any malfunction. A nice effect of this feature is
that the transmission path from one working repeater to the next is ap-

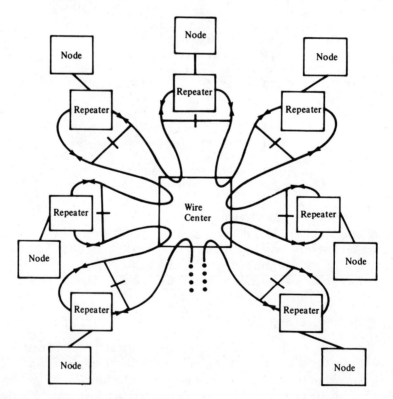

Figure 1.5.   Ring wiring concentrator

proximately constant; thus the range of signal levels to which the transmission system must automatically adapt is much smaller.

The ring wiring concentrator greatly alleviates the perambulation and installation problems mentioned earlier. It also permits rapid recovery from a cable or repeater failure. Nevertheless, a single failure could, at least temporarily, disable the entire network. Furthermore, throughput and jitter considerations still place a practical upper limit on the number of repeaters in a ring. Finally, in a spread out network, a single wire concentration site dictates a lot of cable.

To attack these remaining problems, consider a local network consisting of multiple rings. Each ring consists of a connected sequence of

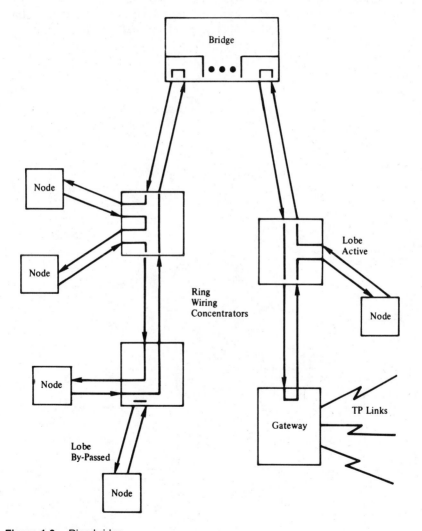

Figure 1.6. Ring bridge

wiring concentrators, and the set of rings is connected by a bridge (Figure 1.6). The bridge routes data frames from one ring subnetwork to another, based on addressing information in the frame so routed. From a physical point of view, each ring operates independently of the other rings attached to the bridge. From a logical point of view, the bridge provides transparent routing among the rings.

The bridge must perform five functions:

- *Input filtering:* For each ring, the bridge monitors the traffic on the ring and copies all frames addressed to other rings on the bridge. This function can be performed by a repeater programmed to recognize a family of addresses rather than a single address.
- *Input buffering:* Received frames may need to be buffered, either because the interring traffic is peaking, or because the target output buffer is temporarily full.

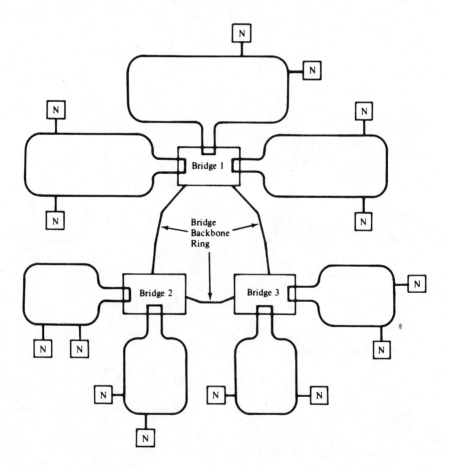

Figure 1.7. Multiple bridges

- *Switching:* Each frame must be routed through the bridge to its appropriate destination ring.
- *Output buffering:* A frame may need to be buffered at the threshold of the destination ring, waiting for an opportunity to be inserted.
- *Output transmission:* This function can be performed by an ordinary repeater.

For a small number of rings, a bridge can be a reasonably simple device. As the number of rings on a bridge grows, the switching complexity and load on the bridge also grow. For very large installations, multiple bridges, interconnected by high-speed trunks, may be needed (Figure 1.7).

Three principal advantages accrue from the use of a bridge. First, the timing jitter problem, which becomes more difficult as the number of repeaters on a ring grows, is bounded by restricting the size of the ring. Second, the failure of a ring, for whatever reason, will disable only a portion of the network; failure of the bridge does not prevent intraring traffic. Finally, multiple rings may be employed to obtain a satisfactory level of performance when the throughput capability of a single ring is exceeded.

There are several pitfalls to be noted. First, the automatic acknowledgment feature of the ring is lost; higher level protocols must provide acknowledgment. Second, performance may not significantly improve if there is a high percentage of interring traffic. If it is possible to do so, network devices should be judiciously allocated to rings to minimize interring traffic.

2

Local Network Standards

The remainder of this book is devoted to an examination of standards for local networks. Before proceeding to specific standards, beginning in Chapter 3, this chapter provides an overview. First, we examine the importance of standards, and then look at the key organizations involved in the development of standards. Following this, various concepts and issues related to local network protocols are discussed. This is followed by an overview of the two sets of standards that are presented in the remainder of the book: IEEE 802 and FDDI.

2.1 STANDARDS

The Importance of Standards

It has long been accepted in the communications industry that standards are required to govern the physical, electrical, and procedural characteristics of communication equipment. In the past, this view has not been embraced by the computer industry. Whereas communication equipment vendors recognize that their equipment will generally interface to and communicate with other vendors' equipment, computer vendors have traditionally attempted to monopolize their customers. The proliferation of computers and distributed processing has made that an untenable position. Computers from different vendors must communicate with each other and, with the ongoing evolution of protocol standards, customers will no longer accept special-purpose protocol conversion software development. The day is quickly coming when the standards discussed in this book and in the other books in this series will dominate the marketplace.

The key advantages of standardization are:

- A standard assures that there will be a large market for a particular piece of equipment or software. This encourages mass production and, in some cases, the use of large-scale integration (LSI) or very-large-scale integration (VLSI) techniques, resulting in lower costs.
- A standard allows products from multiple vendors to communicate, giving the purchaser more flexibility in equipment selection and use.

The principal disadvantage of standards is that they tend to freeze technology. By the time a standard is developed, subjected to review and compromise, and promulgated, more efficient techniques are possible. Nevertheless, the advantages of standards are so great that customers are willing to pay this price.

So far, we have not given a definition of the term *standard*. Although there is no widely accepted and quoted definition, the following definition from the 1979 National Policy on Standards for the United States encompasses the essential concept [NSPA79]:

A prescribed set of rules, conditions, or requirements concerning definition of terms; classification of components; specification of materials, performance, or operations; delineation of procedures; or measurement of quantity and quality in describing materials, products, systems, services, or practices.

In this book, we are concerned with standards that have been developed to specify services and protocols used for local networks.

Standards and Regulation

It is helpful for the reader to distinguish three concepts [CERN84]:

- Voluntary standards
- Regulatory standards
- Regulatory use of voluntary standards

Voluntary standards are developed by standards-making organizations such as the International Organization for Standardization (ISO) and the American National Standards Institute (ANSI). They are voluntary in that the existence of the standard does not compel its use. That is, manufacturers voluntarily implement a standard if they perceive a benefit to themselves, and in a legal sense the practical consequences of departing from a standard are minimal. Voluntary standards are also voluntary in the sense that they are developed by volunteers who are not paid for their efforts by the standards-making organization. These volunteers are generally employees of interested organizations, such as governments and industry groups. Voluntary standards work because they are generally developed on the basis of broad consensus and because the customer demand for standard products encourages the implementation of these standards by the producers.

In contrast, a regulatory standard is developed by a government regulatory agency to meet some public objective such as economic, health, and safety. These standards have the force of regulation behind them and must be met by providers in the context in which the regulations apply.

A relatively new, or at least newly prevalent, phenomenon is the regulatory use of voluntary standards. A typical example of this is a regulation that requires that a government purchase of a product be limited to products that conform to some referenced set of voluntary standards. This approach has a number of salutory effects:

- It reduces the rule-making burden on government agencies.
- It encourages cooperation between government and standards organizations to produce standards of broad applicability.
- It reduces the variety of standards that providers must meet.

2.2 STANDARDS ORGANIZATIONS

In this book, we look at the major standards developed for local networks. The two groups involved in developing these standards are the IEEE 802 committee, sponsored by the IEEE Computer Society, and the X3 committee, accredited by ANSI. The goal of both efforts is the development of standards to be adopted by the ISO. This section provides a brief description of the relevant organizations.

International Organization for Standardization

ISO is an international agency for the development of standards on a wide range of subjects. It is a voluntary, nontreaty organization whose members are designated standards bodies of participating nations and nonvoting observer organizations. Although ISO is a nongovernmental organization, more than 70 percent of ISO member bodies are governmental standards institutions or organizations incorporated by public law. Most of the remainder have close links with the public administrations in their own countries. The United States member body is ANSI.

ISO was founded in 1946 and has issued more than 5000 standards on a broad range of areas. Its purpose is to promote the development of standardization and related activities to facilitate international exchange of goods and services, and to develop cooperation in the sphere of intellectual, scientific, technological, and economic activity. Standards have been issued to cover everything from screw threads to solar energy. ISO is organized as a group of technical committees chartered to produce standards in various areas. The area of work of relevance to this book is handled by Technical Committee 97 (TC97), Information Processing Systems. As with all ISO technical committees, TC97 is organized into subcommittees and working groups that actually do the work of producing the standards. The work related to OSI (see Appendix A) is carried on by subcommittees SC6 and SC21 (Table 2.1).

The development of an ISO standard from first proposal to actual publication of the standard follows a seven-step process. The objective is to ensure that the final result is acceptable to as many countries as possible. The steps can be briefly described as follows (time limits are the minimum time in which voting could be accomplished, and amendments require extended times) [LOHS85].

1. A new work item is assigned to the appropriate technical committee (TC), and within that TC, to the appropriate working group (WG). The WG prepares the technical specifications for the proposed standard and publishes these as a draft proposal (DP). This DP is circulated among interested members for balloting and technical comment. At least 3 months is allowed, and there may be iterations. When there is "substantial support," the DP is sent to the administrative arm of ISO, known as the Central Secretariat.
2. The DP is registered at the Central Secretariat within 2 months of final approval by the TC.

Table 2.1. SUBCOMMITTEES OF ISO TC97 CONCERNED WITH OSI

SC6   Telecommunications and Information Exchange Between Systems
  WG 1   Data link layer
  WG 2   Network layer
  WG 3   Physical interface characteristics
  WG 4   Transport layer
  WG 5   Architecture and coordination of layers 1–4

SG21   Information Retrieval, Transfer, and Management for OSI
  WG 1   OSI architecture
  WG 2   Computer graphics
  WG 3   Database
  WG 4   OSI management
  WG 5   Specific application services and protocols
  WG 6   Session, presentation, common application service elements, and
         upper layer architecture

3. The Central Secretariat edits the document to ensure conformity with ISO practices; no technical changes are made. The edited document is then issued as a Draft International Standard (DIS).
4. The DIS is circulated for a 6-month balloting period. For approval, the DIS must receive a majority approval by the TC members and 75 percent approval of all voting members. Revisions may occur to resolve any negative vote. If more than two negative votes remain, it is unlikely that the DIS will be published as an International Standard.
5. The approved DIS and revisions are returned within 3 months to the Central Secretariat for submission to the ISO Council, which acts as the board of directors of ISO.
6. The DIS is accepted by the Council as an International Standard (IS).
7. The IS is published by ISO.

As can be seen, the process of issuing a standard is a slow one. Certainly, it would be desirable to issue standards as quickly as the technical details can be worked out, but ISO must assure that the standard will receive widespread support.

American National Standards Institute and Accredited Standards Committee X3

ANSI is a nonprofit, nongovernment federation of standards-making and standards-using organizations [SHER86b]. Its members include professional societies, trade associations, governmental and regulatory bodies, industrial companies, and consumer groups. ANSI is the national clearinghouse for voluntary standards in the United States and is also the U.S.-designated voting member of the ISO.

ANSI publishes national standards but does not develop them. Rather, standards are developed by other groups that are accredited to develop standards for ANSI consideration. Much of this work is done directly by ANSI member organizations, such as IEEE. Additionally, an important group of standards is developed by quasi-independent committees, known as Accredited Standards Committees (ASCs), which are administered by ANSI member organizations.

One such organization is the Accredited Standards Committee for Information Processing Systems, ASC X3 [ROBI86]. ASC X3 is sponsored and administered by the Computer and Business Equipment Manufacturers Association (CBEMA). CBEMA is a trade association that represents the information processing, communications, and business products sector of industry. ASC X3 has a broad charter to develop standards relating to information processing. It also acts as the ANSI-appointed Technical Advisory Group (TAG) for ISO TC97.

X3 itself is composed of 41 members from the producer, consumer, and general organizations in the information processing industry. The work is organized into TCs, which actually develop draft standards. Once a consensus is reached on the content of a standard within a committee, it is published for open public review. If and when ANSI determines that there is consensus, the proposal is adopted as an American National Standard.

IEEE and the IEEE Computer Society

The Institute of Electrical and Electronics Engineers (IEEE) is the world's largest professional society, with some 275,000 members. Its activities are organized under a number of boards, one of which is the IEEE Standards Board. The Standards Board directs the development of IEEE standards. The IEEE is accredited by ANSI for the development of standards, and IEEE standards are submitted to ANSI for consideration as national standards. Standards work in the areas of communications and information systems is performed primarily by committees set up under the IEEE Communications Society [COHE85] and the IEEE Computer Society [BUCK86, WILK87].

The development of standards within the IEEE is performed by participating members and the results are balloted among interested professional members. The result is that IEEE standards have reached a consensus acceptable to ANSI and are quickly adopted as national standards. The time period between the start of a project and the adoption as a national standard is generally shorter under the IEEE process than under the X3 process [SHER86a].

2.3 LOCAL NETWORK PROTOCOLS

A Local Network Reference Model

The following discussion assumes a basic understanding of the OSI reference model. For the reader unfamiliar with this model, an overview is provided in Appendix A. The local network model developed here is based on an IEEE 802 working document [IEEE86], but the same concepts apply to the fiber distributed data interface (FDDI) standard.

In making use of the services of a communications network, the open systems interconnection (OSI) model dictates that layers 1 through 3 are required. Briefly, these layers can be described as follows:

1. *Physical layer:* Concerned with transmission of unstructured bit stream over physical link. Involves such parameters as signal voltage swing and bit duration. Deals with the mechanical, electrical, and procedural characteristics to establish, maintain, and deactivate the physical link.

2. *Data link layer:* Provides for the reliable transfer of data across the physical link; sends blocks of data (frames) with the necessary synchronization, error control, and flow control.
3. *Network layer:* Provides upper layers with independence from the data transmission and switching technologies used to connect systems; responsible for establishing, maintaining, and terminating connections.

We now turn to the question of what layers are required for the proper operation of the LAN. For the sake of clarity, we examine the question in the context of the OSI reference model. Two characteristics of LANs are important in this context. First, data are transmitted in addressed frames. Second, there is no intermediate switching, hence no routing required (repeaters are used in rings and may be used in baseband bus LANs, but do not involve switching or routing).

These two characteristics essentially determine the answer to the question: What OSI layers are needed? Layer 1, certainly. Physical connection is required. Layer 2 is also needed. Data transmitted across the LAN must be organized into frames and control must be exercised. But what about layer 3? The answer is yes and no. If we look at the functions performed by layer 3, the answer would seem to be no. First, there is routing. With a direct link available between any two points, this is not needed. The other functions—addressing, sequencing, flow control, error control, and so on—are also performed by layer 2. The difference is that layer 2 performs these functions across a single link, whereas layer 3 may perform them across the sequence of links required to traverse the network. But as only one link is required to traverse the LAN, these layer 3 functions are redundant and superfluous!

From the point of view of an attached device, the answer would seem to be yes, the LAN must provide layer 3. The device sees itself attached to an access point into a network supporting communication with multiple devices. The layer for assuring that a message sent across that access point is delivered to one of a number of end points would seem to be a layer 3 function. So we can say that although the network provides services up through layer 3, the characteristics of the network allow these services to be implemented on two OSI layers. Thus, the minimum essential communications functions that must be performed by the LAN correspond to layers 1 and 2 of the OSI model.

With the points above in mind, let us now think about the functional requirements for controlling a local network and examine these from the top down. We follow the reasoning, illustrated in Figure 2.1, used by the IEEE 802 committee [IEEE86].

At the highest level are the functions associated with accepting transmissions from and delivering receptions to attached stations. These functions include:

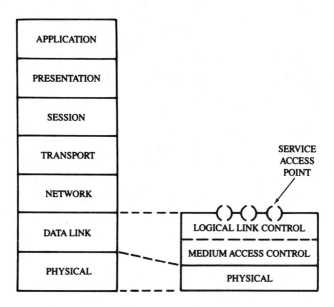

Figure 2.1. Local network communication architecture compared to OSI

- Provide one or more service access points (SAP). A SAP is a logical interface between two adjacent layers.
- On transmission, assemble data into a frame with address and error-detection fields.
- On reception, disassemble frame, perform address recognition and error detection.
- Manage communication over the link.

These are the functions typically associated with layer 2, the data link layer. The first function, and related functions, are grouped into a logical link control (LLC) layer by IEEE 802. The last three functions are treated as a separate layer, called *medium access control* (MAC). This is done for the following reasons:

- The logic required to manage access to a multiple-source, multiple-destination link is not found in traditional layer 2 link control.
- For the same LLC, several MAC options may be provided, as we shall see.

Finally, at the lowest layer, are the functions generally associated with the physical layer. These include:

- Encoding/decoding of signals
- Preamble generation/removal (for synchronization)
- Bit transmission/reception

As with the OSI model, these functions are assigned to a physical layer in the IEEE 802 standard.

The functions performed by the physical layer are straightforward. However, the functional split between MAC and LLC warrants further elaboration. In the remainder of this section, we examine these two layers, and also address the important issue of addressing.

Medium Access Control for Local Networks

All local networks consist of collections of devices that must share the network's transmission capacity. Some means of controlling access to the transmission medium is needed so that, when required, two particular devices can exchange data.

The key parameters in any medium access control technique are where and how. *Where* refers to whether control is exercised in a centralized or distributed fashion. In a centralized scheme, a controller is designated that has the authority to grant access to the network. A station wishing to transmit must wait until it receives permission from the controller. In a decentralized network, the stations collectively perform a medium access control function to dynamically determine the order in which stations transmit. A centralized scheme has certain advantages, such as:

- It may afford greater control over access for providing such things as priorities, overrides, and guaranteed bandwidth.
- It allows the logic at each station to be as simple as possible.
- It avoids problems of coordination.

Its principal disadvantages include:

- It results in a single point of failure.
- It may act as a bottleneck, reducing efficiency.

The pros and cons for distributed control are mirror images of the points made above.

The second parameter, *how*, is constrained by the topology and is a trade-off among competing factors: cost, performance, and complexity. In general, we can categorize access control techniques as being either synchronous or asynchronous. With synchronous techniques, a specific capacity is dedicated to a connection. Such techniques are not optimal in LANs because the needs of the stations are generally unpredictable. It is preferable to be able to allocate capacity in an asynchronous (dynamic) fashion, more or less in response to immediate needs. The asynchronous approach can be further subdivided into three categories: round robin, reservation, and contention.

Round Robin. Round robin techniques are conceptually simple, based on the philosophy of "give everybody a turn." Each station in turn is given an opportunity to transmit. During that opportunity, the station may decline to transmit or may transmit subject to a certain upper bound, usually expressed as a maximum amount of data or time for this opportunity. In any case, the station, when it is finished, must relinquish its turn, and the right to transmit passes to the next station in logical sequence. Control of turns may be centralized or distributed. Polling on a multidrop line is an example of a centralized technique.

When many stations have data to transmit over an extended period of time, round robin techniques can be very efficient. If only a few stations have data to transmit at any given time, other techniques may be preferable, largely depending on whether the data traffic is *stream* or *bursty*. Stream traffic is characterized by lengthy and fairly continuous transmissions. Examples are voice communication, telemetry, and bulk file transfer. Bursty traffic is characterized by short, sporadic transmissions. Interactive terminal-host traffic fits this description.

Reservation. For stream traffic, reservation techniques are well suited. Typically, time on the medium is divided into slots, much as with synchronous time-division multiplexing (TDM). To transmit, a station reserves future slots for an extended or indefinite period. Again, reservations may be made in either a centralized or a distributed fashion.

Contention. For bursty traffic, contention techniques are usually appropriate. With these techniques, no control is exercised to determine whose turn it is; all stations contend for time in a way that can be, as we shall see, rather rough and tumble. These techniques are of necessity distributed in nature. Their principal advantage is that they are simple to implement and, under light to moderate load, efficient. For some of these techniques, however, performance tends to collapse under heavy load.

Although both centralized and distributed reservation techniques have been implemented in some LAN products, round robin and contention techniques are the most common. We will see in the following chapters that the local network standards employ round robin and contention techniques.

Data Link Control for Local Networks

As with all data link control standards, LLC is concerned with the transmission of a frame of data between two stations, with no intermediate switching nodes.

It differs from traditional link layers in three ways:

- It must support the multiaccess nature of the link.
- It is relieved of some details of link access by the MAC layer.
- It must provide some layer 3 functions.

Figure 2.2 helps clarify the requirements for the link layer. We consider two stations or systems that communicate via a LAN (bus or ring). Higher layers (the equivalent of transport and above) provide end-to-end services between the stations. Below the link layer, a MAC layer provides the necessary logic for gaining access to the network for frame transmission and reception.

At a minimum, the link layer should perform those functions normally associated with that layer:

- *Error control:* End-to-end error control and acknowledgment. The link layer should guarantee error-free transmission across the LAN.
- *Flow control:* End-to-end flow control.

These functions are provided in much the same way as for high-level data link control (HDLC) and other point-to-point link protocols—by the use of sequence numbers.

It has already been mentioned that because of the lack of intermediate switching nodes, a LAN does not require a separate layer 3; rather, the essential layer 3 functions can be incorporated into layer 2:

- *Connectionless:* Some form of connectionless service is needed for efficient support of highly interactive traffic.
- *Connection-oriented:* A connection-oriented service is also usually needed.
- *Multiplexing:* Generally, a single physical link attaches a station to a LAN; it should be possible to provide data transfer with multiple end points over that link.

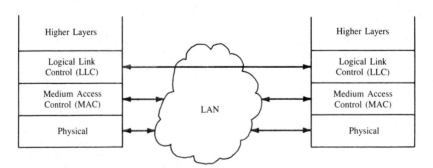

Figure 2.2. LAN communication architecture

Because there is no need for routing, the above functions are easily provided. The connectionless service simply requires the use of source and destination address fields. The station sending the frame must designate the destination address, so that the frame is delivered properly. The source address must also be indicated so that the recipient knows where the frame came from.

Both the connection-oriented and multiplexing capabilities can be supported with the concept of the service access point (SAP). As an example, Figure 2.3 shows three stations attached to a LAN. Each station has an address. Furthermore, the link layer supports multiple SAPs, each with its own address. The link layer provides communication between SAPs. Assume that a process or application X in station A wishes to send a message to a process in station C. X may be a report generator program in microcomputer A. C may be a printer and a simple printer driver. X attaches itself to SAP 1 and requests a connection to station C, SAP 1

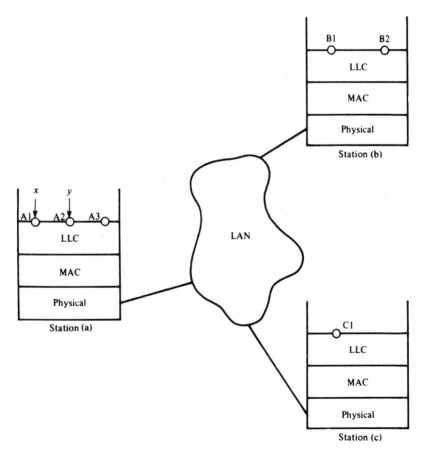

Figure 2.3. LAN link control scenario

(station C may have only one SAP if it is a single printer). Station A's link layer then sends to the LAN a *connection-request* frame that includes the source address (A,1), the destination address (C,1), and some control bits indicating that this is a connection request. The LAN delivers this frame to C, which, if it is free, returns a *connection-accepted* frame. Henceforth, all data from X will be assembled into a frame by A's LLC, which includes source (A,1) and destination (C,1) addresses. Incoming frames addressed to (A,1) will be rejected unless they are from (C,1); these might be acknowledgment frames, for example. Similarly, station C's printer is declared busy and C will only accept frames from (A,1).

Thus, a connection-oriented service is provided. At the same time, process Y could attach to (A,2) and exchange data with (B,1). This is an example of multiplexing. In addition, various other processes in A could use (A,3) to send datagrams to various destinations.

One final function of the link layer should be included to take advantage of the multiple access nature of the LAN:

- *Multicast, broadcast:* The link layer should provide a service of sending a message to multiple stations or all stations.

Addressing

The preceding discussion referred to both station and LLC addresses. A further elaboration of this point is warranted. To understand the function of addressing, we need to consider the requirements for exchanging data.

In very general terms, communication can be said to involve three agents: processes, hosts, and networks. *Processes* are the fundamental entities that communicate. One example is a file transfer operation. In this case, a file transfer process in one station is exchanging data with a file transfer process in another station. Another example is remote terminal access. In this case a user terminal is attached to one station and controlled by a terminal-handling process in that station. The user, through the terminal-handling process, may be remotely connected to a time-sharing system; data is exchanged between the terminal-handling process and the time-sharing process. Processes execute on *hosts* (computers), which can often support multiple simultaneous processes. Hosts are connected by a *network,* and the data to be exchanged is transmitted by the network from one host to another. From this point of view, the transfer of data from one process to another involves first getting the data to the host in which the process resides and then getting it to the process within the host.

These concepts suggest the need for at least two levels of addressing. To see this, consider Figure 2.4, which shows the overall format of data transmitted using the LLC and MAC protocols. User data is passed

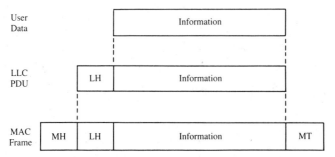

Figure 2.4. Local network protocol data units

down to LLC, which appends a header. This header contains control information that is used to manage the protocol between the local LLC entity and the remote LLC protocol entity. The combination of user data and LLC header is referred to as an LLC *protocol data unit* (PDU). After LLC has prepared a PDU, the PDU is then passed as data down to the MAC entity. The MAC entity appends both a header and a trailer, to manage the MAC protocol. The result is a MAC-level PDU. To avoid confusion with an LLC-level PDU, we will refer to the MAC-level object as a *frame;* this is the term used in the standards.

The MAC header must contain a destination address that uniquely identifies a station on the local network. This is needed as each station on the local network will read the destination address field to determine if it should capture the MAC frame. When a MAC frame is captured, the MAC entity strips off the MAC header and trailer and passes the LLC PDU up to the LLC entity. The link header must contain a destination SAP address so that LLC can determine to whom the data is to be delivered. Hence, two levels of addressing are needed:

- *MAC address:* Identifies a station on the local network.
- *LLC address:* Identifies an LLC user.

Figure 2.5 contrasts the two levels of addresses. The MAC address is associated with a physical attachment point on the network. The LLC SAP is associated with a particular user within a station. In some cases, the SAP corresponds to a host process. Another case relates to a common type of attached equipment, referred to as a network interface unit (NIU). Often, an NIU is used as a terminal concentration device. In this case each terminal port on the NIU has a unique SAP.

So far, we have discussed the use of addresses that identify unique entities. In addition to these *individual addresses,* group addresses are also employed. A *group address,* as the name implies, specifies a group of entities. For example, one might wish to send a message to all terminal

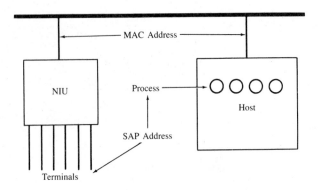

Figure 2.5. Local network addressing

users attached to a particular NIU, or all terminal users on the entire local network. Two types of group addresses are used:

- *Broadcast:* An address that refers to all entities within some context.
- *Multicast:* An address that refers to some subset of entities within some context.

Table 2.2 depicts the possible combinations. The first five combinations are straightforward. A specific user can be addressed. A group of users or all users at a specific station can be addressed. All users on some stations or all users on all stations can be addressed.

The last four combinations in Table 2.2 are less obvious. It should be clear that LLC addresses are unique only within a single station. It is only the LLC entity within a station that examines the LLC header and determines the user. It is possible to assign LLC values uniquely across all stations, but this is undesirable for several reasons:

- The total number of users on all stations would be limited by the SAP field length in the LLC header.
- Central management of SAP assignment would be required, no matter how large and heterogenous the user population.

On the other hand, it may be desirable to assign the same SAP value to entities in different stations. For example, a station management entity in a station may always be given a SAP value of 1. Or a group of management and control entities within a station may always be given the same multicast SAP address. When such a convention is followed, then it becomes possible to address data to one SAP address or a multicast SAP address in a group of stations or all stations. Appendix 2B discusses the assignment of specific addressing codes by IEEE.

Table 2.2. LOCAL NETWORK ADDRESSING

MAC Address	LLC User Address (Service Access Point)
Individual	Individual
Individual	Multicast
Individual	Broadcast
Multicast	Broadcast
Broadcast	Broadcast
Multicast	Individual
Multicast	Multicast
Broadcast	Individual
Broadcast	Multicast

2.4   IEEE 802 STANDARDS

Structure of the Standards

The key to the development of the LAN market is the availability of a low cost interface. The cost to connect equipment to a LAN must be much less than the cost of the equipment alone. This requirement, plus the complexity of the LAN protocols, dictate a VLSI solution. However, chip manufacturers will be reluctant to commit the necessary resources unless there is a high-volume market. A LAN standard would assure that volume and also enable equipment of a variety of manufacturers to inter-communicate. This is the rationale of the IEEE Project 802 [CLAN82], a committee established by the IEEE Computer Society in February of 1980 to prepare local area network standards. In 1985, the 802 committee issued a set of four standards, which were subsequently adopted in 1985 by the American National Standards Institute (ANSI) as American National Standards [IEEE85a-d]. These standards were subsequently revised and reissued as international standards by the International Organization for Standardization (ISO) in 1987, with the designation ISO 8802 [ISO87a-d].

The committee characterized its work in this way [IEEE88a]:

The LANs described herein are distinguished from other types of data networks in that they are optimized for a moderate size geographic area such as a single office building, a warehouse, or a campus. The IEEE 802 LAN is a shared medium peer-to-peer communications network that broadcasts information for all stations to receive. As a consequence, it does not inherently provide privacy. The local area network enables stations to communicate directly using a common physical medium on a point-to-point basis without any intermediate switching node being required. There is always need for an access sublayer in order to arbitrate the access to the shared

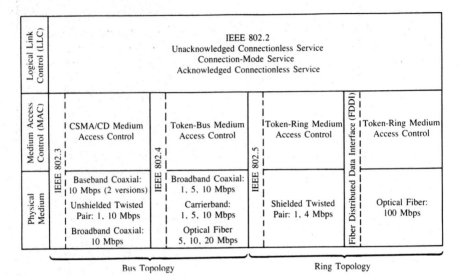

Figure 2.6. Local area network standards

medium. The network is generally owned, used, and operated by a single organization. This is in contrast to Wide Area Networks (WANs) that interconnect communication facilities in different parts of a country or are used as a public utility. These LANs are also different from networks, such as backplane buses, that are optimized for the interconnection of devices on a desk top or components within a single piece of equipment.

Two conclusions were quickly reached. First, the task of communication across the local network is sufficiently complex that it needs to be broken up into more manageable subtasks. Second, no single technical approach will satisfy all requirements.

The first conclusion is reflected in a "local network reference model," compared in Figure 2.1 to the better-known open systems interconnection (OSI) model.

The second conclusion was reluctantly reached when it became apparent that no single standard would satisfy all committee participants. There was support for both ring and bus topologies. Within the bus topology, there was support for two access methods (CSMA/CD and token bus) and two media (baseband and broadband). The response of the committee was to standardize all serious proposals rather than to attempt to settle on just one. Figure 2.6 illustrates the result.

Organization

The work of the IEEE 802 committee is currently organized into the following subcommittees:

- 802.1: High Level Interface
- 802.2: Logical Link Control
- 802.3: CSMA/CD Networks
- 802.4: Token Bus Networks
- 802.5: Token Ring Networks
- 802.6: Metropolitan Area Networks
- 802.7: Broadband Technical Advisory Group
- 802.8: Fiber Optic Technical Advisory Group
- 802.9: Integrated Voice and Data LAN Working Group
- 802.10: LAN Security Working Group

The High Level Interface subcommittee deals with issues related to network architecture, internetworking, and network management for local networks. The discussion in this chapter on architecture and addressing is based on the work of this subcommittee.

Work has been completed on LLC, CSMA/CD, token bus, and token ring for an initial set of standards. Work on new options and features continues in each subcommittee. The next four chapters examine these standards in detail. The presentation is based primarily on the 1987 ISO standards. These contain minor additions and modifications to the 1985 ANSI/IEEE standards, which will be pointed out as this book proceeds.

The work on metropolitan area networks (MANs) is just beginning to make progress. The subcommittee is attempting to develop a small number of reasonable alternatives for further study. Since the FDDI standard, described in Chapter 7, satisfies many of the requirements for a MAN, there has been less enthusiasm and less progress within 802.6 than might have otherwise been expected.

The purpose of 802.7 and 802.8 is to provide technical guidance to the other subcommittees on broadband and optical fiber technology, respectively. The Broadband Technical Advisory Group is producing a recommended practices document for broadband cabling systems. The Fiber Optic Technical Advisory Group is investigating the use of optical fiber as an alternative transmission medium for 802.3, 802.4, and 802.5. It is also considering installation recommendations and a tutorial on fiber optic standards and related information.

The Integrated Voice and Data (IVD) LAN Working Group was chartered in 1986. It is developing an architecture and an interface standard for desktop devices to 802 LANs and to Integrated Services Digital Networks (ISDNs), utilizing twisted-pair wiring to carry both voice and data.

The LAN Security Working Group was formed in 1988. It will address such issues as secure data exchange, encryption key management, security aspects of network management, and the application of the OSI security architecture to LANs.

2.5   FDDI STANDARDS

Work on high-speed local network standards has been performed primarily within a subcommittee of the ASC X3T9 technical committee on I/O interface standards. Figure 2.7 shows the scope of work of X3T9. The X3T9 committee's work is aimed at developing I/O interface standards for four main areas:

- *Backplane bus:* Internal computer bus connecting processors, memory, and I/O controllers.
- *Peripheral bus:* Connects a single host (computer, storage director, file server) to one or more peripherals, where the peripheral includes the device (e.g., disk drive) and associated controller.
- *Device interface:* Connects a "naked" device such as a floppy or rigid disk drive or a printer.
- *System bus:* Connects computers, peripheral subsystems, terminal concentrators, gateways, and file servers as peers.

The system bus applies to high-speed local networks (HSLNs). Because of the expertise within X3T9 related to high-speed I/O, it was felt that this organization was better suited to developing HSLN standards than the 802 committee.

An approach for an HSLN based on an optical fiber ring was originally proposed in early 1983, and was assigned to X3T9.5, a subcommittee of X3T9. The resulting set of standards [ANSI86a,b, ANSI87a,b] cover the physical and MAC layers. The IEEE 802 LLC standard is as-

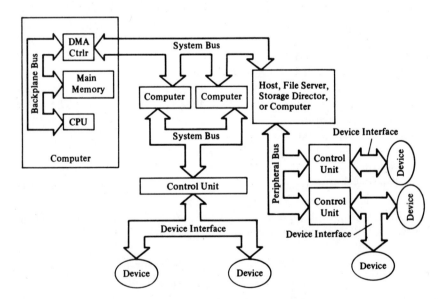

Figure 2.7.   Scope of work for ASC committee X3T9.5

sumed for use above the FDDI MAC. Chapter 7 deals with the FDDI standards.

APPENDIX 2A.   SERVICE PRIMITIVES AND PARAMETERS

Each layer of the OSI model is defined in two parts: the protocol between peer (at the same layer) entities in different open systems, and the services provided by one layer to the next higher layer in the same open system. The protocol is precisely defined in terms of the format of the PDUs exchanged between entities, the semantics of each field in each PDU, and the allowable sequencing of protocol actions.

The service provided by a layer is much less explicitly defined. The reason for this is that, generally, adjacent layers in the same open system reside on the same operating system and are implemented by the same vendor. The standards must leave the implementer free to implement adjacent layers and the interface between those layers in the most efficient manner possible. As the interaction between layers takes place within a single system, a precise and explicit standard is not needed. Accordingly, the service specification is presented in functional terms only.

The services to be provided across an interface between adjacent layers are expressed in terms of primitives and parameters. A primitive specifies the function to be performed, and the parameters are used to pass data and control information. The actual form of a primitive is implementation dependent. An example is a subroutine call.

Four types of primitives are used in ISO standards to define the interaction between adjacent layers in the architecture. These are defined in Table 2.3. The layout of Figure 2.8a suggests the time ordering of these

Table 2.3.   PRIMITIVE TYPES

REQUEST	A primitive issued by a service user to invoke some service and to pass the parameters needed to fully specify the requested service.
INDICATION	A primitive issued by a service provider either: 1. to indicate that a procedure has been invoked by the peer service user on the connection and to provide the associated parameters, or 2. to notify the service user of a provider-initiated action.
RESPONSE	A primitive issued by a service user to acknowledge or complete some procedure previously invoked by an indication to that user.
CONFIRM	A primitive issued by a service provider to acknowledge or complete some procedure previously invoked by a request by the service user.

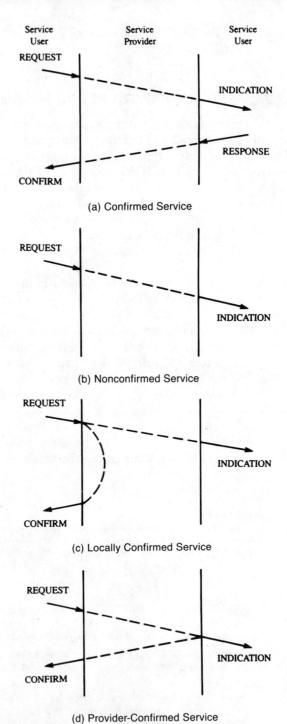

(a) Confirmed Service

(b) Nonconfirmed Service

(c) Locally Confirmed Service

(d) Provider-Confirmed Service

Figure 2.8.   Service primitives

events. For example, consider the transfer of data from a service user *A* to a peer entity *B* in another system. The following steps occur:

1. *A* invokes the services of the next lower layer with a Data.request primitive. Associated with the primitive are the parameters needed, such as the data to be transmitted and the destination address.
2. The service provider in *A*'s system prepares a protocol data unit (PDU) to be sent to its peer entity.
3. The destination peer entity delivers the data to *B* via a Data.indication, which includes the data and the source address as parameters.
4. If an acknowledgment is called for, *B* issues a Data.response to its service provider.
5. *B*'s service provider conveys this acknowledgment to *A*'s service provider in a PDU.
6. The acknowledgment is delivered to *A* via a Data.confirm.

This sequence of events is referred to as a *confirmed service,* as the initiator receives confirmation that the requested service has had the desired effect at the other end. If only request and indication primitives are involved (steps 1 through 3), then the service dialogue is a *nonconfirmed service* (Figure 2.8b); the initiator receives no confirmation that the action has taken place.

As we can see, then, in the ISO service primitive model, the generation of a confirm is always the result of a response from the distant service user. Unfortunately, this model was not adopted in the original IEEE 802 standards issued in 1985, nor in the FDDI standard. Instead the original IEEE and FDDI models make use of only the request, indication, and confirm primitives. In this model, the request and indication primitives have the same meanings as in the ISO model. There is no response primitive, however, and the confirm primitive is defined to be a service-provider confirmation only.

Two forms of service are possible with this latter model. In a *locally confirmed service* (Figure 2.8c), the confirm primitive indicates that the local entity providing service has been able to transmit a PDU and has, to the best of its knowledge, carried out the request. The confirm in this case does not indicate whether the data unit reached the other side, nor does it indicate whether the distant service user functioned properly and accepted the data. Consequently, no timing relationship is implied between the indication and confirm primitives; indeed, the confirm could be issued before the indication. It could be argued that this procedure is superior to the ISO unconfirmed service; even if the user does not expect confirmation from the other side, it is useful to receive timely notification as to whether the local service provider is able to respond to the request.

In the *provider-confirmed service* (Figure 2.8d), the confirm primitive indicates that the entire service provider functioned properly and that the data was delivered successfully to the distant service provider, who has issued an indication to present the data to the distant user. No guarantee is provided that the distant service user actually received the data, only that it was left on the door step. In the IEEE/FDDI model, the conveying of information about the actions of a distant service user should be handled as data by the service provider, and should not be a separate, distinguishable part of the service offered by the service provider.

Regardless of the relative merits of the ISO and IEEE/FDDI models of service provision, the fact is that virtually all international standards make use of the ISO model. Thus, for the sake of consistency, and to expedite the adoption of the IEEE 802 standards as international standards, the 1985 IEEE model has been abandoned in favor of the OSI model in the 1987 revision of the IEEE standards. This book is based on the 1987 version of the IEEE 802 standards, and hence, reflects this latest change. As of this writing, however, the latest version of the FDDI standard reflects the request-indication-confirm model, and this is presented in Chapter 7.

APPENDIX 2B   STANDARD ADDRESS FORMATS AND CODES

In Section 2.3, we discussed the use of two levels of addressing for LANs: the LLC address, known as the LLC service access point (LSAP), which identifies an LLC user; and the MAC address, which identifies a station on the LAN. The IEEE 802.2 standard specifies a format for LSAPs, and the various IEEE 802 and FDDI MAC layer standards specify a common format for MAC addresses. In addition, the IEEE has assigned certain specific addresses for universal use.

LLC Service Access Points

The LLC service access point (LSAP) specifies a user of LLC. Typically, the LLC user is a protocol at a higher layer than LLC. Within any station, multiple SAPs provide interface ports to support multiple higher layer users.

In terms of format, the IEEE 802.2 standard specifies the use of an 8-bit LSAP. The first (most significant) bit of the address is set to zero to indicate an individual address, and to one to indicate a group address. The remaining seven bits specify a specific user or group.

As a first step, IEEE distinguishes three types of LLC users, or protocols: standard, public, and private. A *standard protocol* is one that is in the public domain and its specification is controlled by a standards body such as ISO. Examples are the X.25 packet level and the ISO connectionless internetwork protocol [STAL89a]. A *public protocol* is one that is in the public domain, and may therefore be widely used, but whose specification is controlled by other than an international standards body. An example is the internet protocol (IP) issued by the U.S. Department of Defense [STAL89b]. Finally, a *private protocol* is one whose use and specification are controlled by a private organization. An example would be a proprietary protocol used by a computer vendor.

To accommodate multiple protocols in a single station as users of LLC, the IEEE 802 organization has published a set of address code assignments; these assignments should be honored in any network configuration. Table 2-4 lists these assignments. Note that the first bit after the individual/group bit divides the address space in two, with half of the space reserved for standard protocols and the other half for public and private protocols.

Several specific assignments are worth noting. If the last six bits are all zeros, then the address refers to an LLC network management entity. Protocols are being developed for LAN network management, and this address would be used for that purpose. Several LSAPs have been set aside for PROWAY, which is discussed in Appendix 5B, and one LSAP for the manufacturing messaging service, which is part of MAP (also discussed in Appendix 5B).

Private protocols can be accommodated in one of two ways. As was mentioned, half of the LSAP address space is available. LSAPs can be assigned by mutual agreement between correspondents using a private

Table 2.4.   LLC Service Access Point (LSAP) Code Assignments

Code	Interpretation
X1XXXXXX	Standard LSAP
X110XXXX	For use by national standards bodies to designate national network layer entities that are not recognized internationally
X0XXXXXX	User defined
00000000	Null LSAP
11111111	Global LSAP
01000000	Individual LLC sublayer management function
11000000	Group LLC sublayer management function
01111111	OSI network layer protocol; discrimination among specific OSI network layer protocols is performed using the OSI network layer protocol identification scheme that is part of all OSI network layer PDU formats
01110000	PROWAY network management and initialization; related to ISA-S72 PROWAY-LAN Industrial Data Highway
01110001	PROWAY active station list maintenance; related to ISA-S72 PROWAY-LAN Industrial Data Highway
01110010	Layer messaging service for factory automation; related to the EIA-RS 511 Manufacturing Message Service
01010101	Sub-network access protocol, SNAP
01100000	Department of Defense Internet Protocol, MIL-STD-1777

Protocol identification (40 bits)	Protocol Data ($8 \times N$ bits)

Figure 2.9.   Information field format for SNAP protocol data units

protocol. Another approach, which might support dynamic assignment of protocol identifiers, is to use a sub-network access protocol (SNAP). The SNAP is a concept developed as part of the OSI network layer [STAL89a]. The SNAP is a network-level protocol that provides for access to a network from a station; it is a useful concept in some communications architectures. To be able to discriminate among a variety of higher-level protocols, a SNAP can make use of a protocol identifier. In the case of IEEE 802.2, the protocol identifier is carried in the information field (Figure 2-4). In this case, the SNAP value is 01010101 and the information field has the format depicted in Figure 2-9; the first 40 bits are the protocol identifier, and the remaining octets are the data provided by the higher-layer user of LLC.

MAC Addresses

The MAC address field used in both the IEEE 802 standards (802.3, 802.4, 802.5) and FDDI follows the same formatting rules for all of these standards. The address may be either 16 bits or 48 bits in length; the formats are shown in Figure 2-10a and b, respectively. The first bit is set to zero to indicate an individual address and to one to indicate a group address. A group address of all ones is a broadcast address for all active stations on the LAN. All other group addresses designate a logical user group defined at configuration time or by a higher-layer convention.

For 48-bit addresses, the second bit is set to zero to indicate a universally administered address and to one to indicate a locally administered address. A *locally administered address* is set up by the LAN user or manager and has significance only for the purposes of that environment. A *universally administered address* is one assigned by the IEEE Standards Office on behalf of ISO. The concept of a universal address is based on the idea that all potential members of a communications environment need to have a unique identifier, in order to coexist and communicate with other members. The advantage of a universal address is that a station with such an address can be attached to any LAN in the world with an assurance that its address is unique. This 48-bit universal address scheme originated with Ethernet, and has been adopted by the IEEE 802, ISO 8802, FDDI, and other official LAN standards.

The universal address is based on the concept of an *organizationally unique identifier*. This is a 22-bit identifier that is assigned by IEEE to applying organizations. An organization can be a company, a government

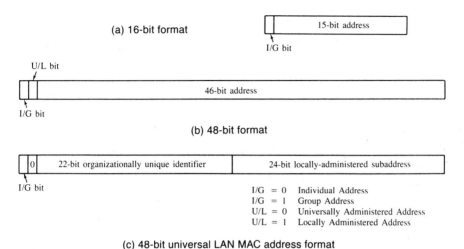

(a) 16-bit format

15-bit address

I/G bit

U/L bit

46-bit address

I/G bit

(b) 48-bit format

| 0 | 22-bit organizationally unique identifier | 24-bit locally-administered subaddress |

I/G bit

I/G = 0   Individual Address
I/G = 1   Group Address
U/L = 0   Universally Administered Address
U/L = 1   Locally Administered Address

(c) 48-bit universal LAN MAC address format

Figure 2.10.   MAC address formats

agency, or any other type of organization that intends to use LANs and wishes to develop unique addresses for both internal use and for communicating with stations on LANs outside the organization.

The format of the universal address is shown in Figure 2-10c. The first bit, as before, is the individual/group bit (although an organization may make an alternative use of this bit). The second bit is set to zero to indicate that this is a universally administered address. Next comes the organizationally unique identifier. The final 24 bits are assigned by the organization. Thus, IEEE does not directly assign unique addresses to stations. Rather, it assigns identifiers to organizations. The identifier becomes part of the MAC address, and the assignment of the remaining portion of the address is done by the organization.

3

IEEE 802.2 Logical
Link Control

Logical link control (LLC) is the highest layer of the local network communications architecture. It is used above all of the medium access control (MAC) standards specified by IEEE 802 and by FDDI. The primary purpose of this layer is to provide a means of exchanging data between LLC users across a MAC-controlled link. Different forms of the LLC service are specified to meet specific reliability and efficiency needs.

This chapter begins with a description of the LLC service; each of the three forms of this service is described. The next section deals with some of the key mechanisms of link control protocols. We are then in a position to examine the LLC protocols that support the various LLC services.

3.1 LLC SERVICES

In this section, we examine the services provided by LLC to the upper layers. The services that LLC expects from the MAC layer are also briefly examined. We use the specification developed for the ISO standard rather than those found in the original 1985 IEEE 802.2 standard (see Appendix 2A); the IEEE standard will soon be changed to conform to the ISO specification.

Forms of LLC Service

The LLC standard provides three forms of service to LLC users:

- Unacknowledged connectionless service
- Connection-mode service
- Acknowledged connectionless service

The first two forms are specified in the original 1985 standard. The third form was added later. All these services are defined in terms of the primitives and the parameters (Table 3.1) that are exchanged between the LLC

Table 3.1.   LOGICAL LINK CONTROL PRIMITIVES

UNACKNOWLEDGED CONNECTIONLESS SERVICE

DL-UNITDATA.request (source-address, destination-address, data, priority)
DL-UNITDATA.indication (source-address, destination-address, data, priority)

CONNECTION-MODE SERVICE

DL-CONNECT.request (source-address, destination-address, priority)
DL-CONNECT.indication (source-address, destination-address, priority)
DL-CONNECT.response (source-address, destination-address, priority)
DL-CONNECT.confirm (source-address, destination-address, priority)

DL-DATA.request (source-address, destination-address, data)
DL-DATA.indication (source-address, destination-address, data)

DL-DISCONNECT.request (source-address, destination-address)
DL-DISCONNECT.indication (source-address, destination-address, reason)

DL-RESET.request (source-address, destination-address)
DL-RESET.indication (source-address, destination-address, reason)
DL-RESET.response (source-address, destination-address)
DL-RESET.confirm (source-address, destination-address)

DL-CONNECTION-FLOWCONTROL.request (source-address, destination-address, amount)
DL-CONNECTION-FLOWCONTROL.indication (source-address, destination-address, amount)

ACKNOWLEDGED CONNECTIONLESS SERVICE

DL-DATA-ACK.request (source-address, destination-address, data, priority, service-class)
DL-DATA-ACK.indication (source-address, destination-address, data, prioriity, service-class)
DL-DATA-ACK-STATUS.indication (source-address, destination-address, priority, service-class, status)
DL-REPLY.request (source-address, destination-address, data, priority, service-class)
DL-REPLY.indication (source-address, destination-address, data, priority, service-class)
DL-REPLY-STATUS.indication (source-address, destination-address, data, priority, service-class, status)
DL-REPLY-UPDATE.request (source-address, data)
DL-REPLY-UPDATE-STATUS.indication (source-address, status)

entity providing the LLC service and the LLC users that are identified by LLC service access points (SAPs). In this subsection, we briefly define each service, and then offer a comparison. The details of the services are then presented.

Services Provided.   With the unacknowledged connectionless service, there is an a prior agreement between LLC users in different systems that allows them to exchange data. A single service access is required to initiate the transmission of a data unit. From the point of view of the LLC service provider, previous and subsequent data units are unrelated to the current data unit. The service provider does not guarantee that data presented by one user will be delivered to another user, nor does it inform the sender if the delivery attempt fails. Furthermore, if data units are delivered, there is no guarantee that they will be delivered in the same order in which they were sent. This service supports point-to-point (deliver to one user), multipoint (deliver a copy of the data unit to a number of users), and broadcast (deliver to all active users).

With the connection-mode service, a logical connection is established between two LLC users. Three phases occur (Figure 3.1):

- Connection establishment
- Data transfer
- Connection termination

During the connection-establishment phase, two LLC users agree to exchange data. One user issues a connection request to the other. If the

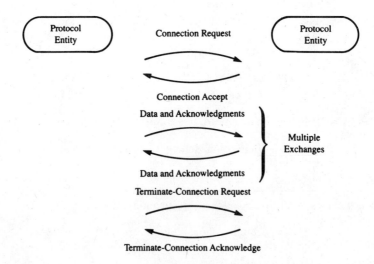

Figure 3.1.   The phases of a connection-oriented data transfer

service provider can provide the requested service and the other user is prepared to exchange data, then agreement has been reached and the logical connection is established. In essence, the existence of a logical connection means that the LLC service provider at each end of the connection will keep track of the data units being transmitted and those being received. During the data-transfer phase, LLC guarantees that all data units will be delivered and that they will be delivered in the order in which they were presented. Rarely, there may be a failure and this failure is reported to the user. Finally, one of the two users or the LLC service itself may wish to terminate the connection.

The acknowledged connectionless service is also connectionless but provides for the immediate acknowledgment of each transmitted data unit. The LLC service provider will only send data units one at a time; that is, each transmitted data unit must be acknowledged before the next one is transmitted. This service is only point-to-point.

Comparison of the Three Forms. The unacknowledged connectionless service requires minimum protocol complexity and is useful in two contexts:

- When higher layers (e.g., transport) provide any required error handling and ordered delivery services, or
- In applications where it is not necessary to guarantee the delivery of every data unit.

In many local network implementations, the end systems will implement protocols at layers 3 through 7 of the OSI model (see Appendix A) and will provide the needed connection mode service at layer 4. Thus, there is no need to duplicate these services at the LLC level. As for the second point above, there are instances in which the overhead of connection establishment and maintenance is unjustified or even counterproductive. Some examples, suggested in [CHAP82]:

- *Inward data collection:* Involves the periodic active or passive sampling of data sources, such as sensors, and automatic self-test reports from security equipment or network components. In a real-time monitoring situation, the loss of an occasional data unit would not cause distress, as the next report should arrive shortly.
- *Outward data dissemination:* Includes broadcast messages to network users, the announcement of a new mode or the change of address of a service, and the distribution of real-time clock values.
- *Request-response:* Application in which a transaction service is provided by a common server to a number of distributed users, and for which a single request-response sequence is typical. Use of the service is regulated at the application level, and lower-level connections are often unnecessary and cumbersome.

- *Real-time applications:* Such as voice and telemetry, involving a degree of redundancy and/or a real-time transmission requirement. These must not have connection-oriented functions that would result in long or variable delays, such as retransmission (described in Section 3.2).

The benefits of the connection-mode service are more obvious than those of the other two services. The connection-mode service provides for ordered delivery and error control, and hence can relieve higher layers of this burden. With connection-mode service, it is possible for the users and the LLC service to agree on certain characteristics that will remain valid for the duration of the connection, such as the priority of data units on this connection relative to those on other connections. These characteristics are well suited to applications that involve lengthy exchanges of data, such as file transfer and remote access from a terminal to a time-sharing system.

The acknowledged connectionless service is useful in several contexts [FIEL86]. Consider that with connection-mode service, the LLC entity must maintain a state table for each active connection. If the user needs guaranteed delivery, but there are a large number of destinations for data, then the connection-mode service may be impractical because of the large number of state tables required. An example is a process control or automated factory environment where a central site may need to communicate with a large number of processors and programmable controllers. Another use of this service is to provide a mechanism for polling with a guaranteed response. Again, in a process control or automated factory environment, it may be required to obtain information from sensor equipment with very little processing capability. The implementation of the acknowledged connectionless service is simpler than that of the connection-mode service, and therefore, is a better choice for such equipment. A final example of the use of this service can also be expressed in terms of the requirements of the factory environment, in which certain alarm or control signals may be very important and time-critical. Because of their importance, an acknowledgment is needed so that the sender can be assured that the signal got through. Because of the urgency of a signal, the user might not want to take the time to first establish a logical connection and then send the data.

Unacknowledged Connectionless Service

The unacknowledged connectionless service provides for only two primitives across the interface between the next higher layer and LLC (Table 3.1). DL-UNITDATA.request is used to pass a data unit down to LLC for transmission. DL-UNITDATA.indication is used to pass a data unit up from LLC upon reception. The time sequence diagram is shown in Figure 3.2.

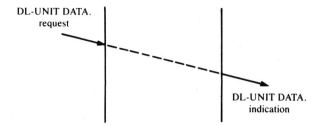

Figure 3.2. Unacknowledged connectionless service

Four parameters are included with the DL-UNITDATA.request. The source-address and destination-address parameters specify the local and remote LLC users, respectively. Each of these parameters is logically equivalent to the combination of the LLC SAP and the MAC address. The destination-address parameter may specify either an individual or a group address. The data parameter is the block of data exchanged between LLC and its user. The priority parameter specifies the priority desired for the data unit transfer. This parameter is passed through the LLC entity to the MAC entity, which has the responsibility of implementing a priority mechanism. Token bus (802.4), token ring (802.5), and FDDI are capable of this, but the CSMA/CD (802.3) protocol is not. The LLC standard does not specify the range of the priority value; this is dictated by the MAC protocol, and must be known by the LLC user. LLC simply passes the parameter down to MAC in a MAC service primitive.

The same parameters appear in a DL-UNITDATA.indication. As before, the destination address may be an individual or a group address. The priority parameter indicates the priority that had been requested for this data transfer. If the MAC protocol is CSMA/CD, however, that priority has not been provided.

Connection-Mode Service

The connection-mode service provides a means to establish, maintain, and terminate a logical connection between two users at different SAPs.

Connection Establishment.   Connection establishment begins with a user request, contained in a DL-CONNECT.request primitive. The primitive specifies the source and destination addresses, and the desired priority. If the connection is established, the priority is assigned to the connection as a whole, and may be used to determine the relative resources allocated by the LLC entity to each active connection. In addition, the priority will be passed down to the MAC entity for each data unit transferred over the logical connection.

Following the issuance of a DL-CONNECT.request, a variety of

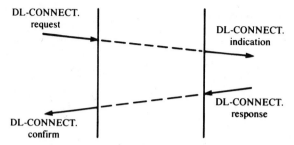

(a) Successful Connection Establishment

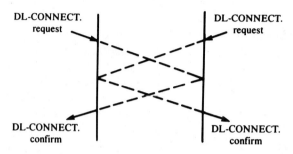

(b) Simultaneous Connection Request

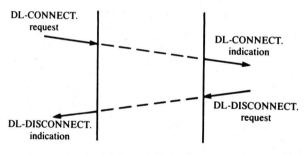

(c) Remote Rejection

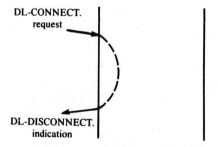

(d) Provider Rejection

Figure 3.3.   Connection-mode service: connection establishment

results can occur. The most common of these are indicated in Figure 3.3. Figure 3.3a is the most straightforward sequence. A DL-CON-NECT.indication is delivered to the destination LLC user, who responds with a DL-CONNECT.response, indicating acceptance of the connection. The priority parameter in the response primitive may be less than or equal to the priority parameter in the corresponding indication primitive (which is the same as that in the corresponding request primitive). The priority specified in the response primitive becomes the priority provided on this connection. This is reported to the original requester in a DL-CONNECT.confirm.

Alternatively, two LLC users may request a connection to each other at about the same time, and the LLC entities provide a confirmation to both (Figure 3.3b). Again, the lower requested priority becomes the provided priority.

Figure 3.3 illustrates two ways in which a connection request may be rejected. The remote user may refuse the connection by issuing a DL-DISCONNECT.request in response to a DL-CONNECT.indication (Figure 3.3c). This is reported to the requesting user in a DL-DISCON-NECT.indication. Alternatively, the connection may be refused by the LLC service (Figure 3.3d). Examples of reasons for this latter event:

- The remote LLC entity never replied to the connection request. The local LLC entity will attempt to set up the connection a number of times before giving up and reporting failure.
- The local LLC entity is unable to set up the connection (e.g., buffer storage, local network malfunction).

The reason parameter in the DL-DISCONNECT.indication primitive is used to specify the reason for the connection rejection.

Data Transfer.   Once a connection is set up between two LLC users at two LLC SAPs, data may be exchanged using the DL-DATA primitives. Note that there are only request and indication primitives for DL-DATA; the sequence of events is the same as that depicted in Figure 3.2. The reason that there is no need for a confirmation back to the user that sent the data is that the connection-mode service guarantees to deliver all data in the proper order, with no losses. Thus, normally, the user needs no form of acknowledgment. If something goes wrong, the user is informed by means of the reset or disconnect functions, described later.

A flow control service is provided for use during the data transfer phase. The DL-CONNECTION-FLOWCONTROL.request primitive is passed from the LLC user to the LLC entity (Figure 3.4a) to control the flow of data from the LLC entity on a particular connection. The indication primitive independently controls the flow in the opposite direction (Figure 3.4b). The amount parameter specifies the amount of data that

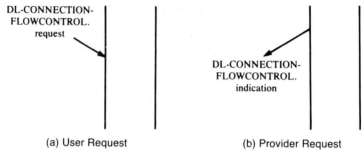

DL-CONNECTION-
FLOWCONTROL.
request

DL-CONNECTION-
FLOWCONTROL.
indication

(a) User Request   (b) Provider Request

Figure 3.4. Connection-mode service: flow control

may be passed, and is dynamically updated by each request or indication. If amount is specified as zero, then the associated flow on that connection is stopped.

While in the data transfer phase, the LLC entities on both sides of the connection keep track of the data units flowing in both directions so that they can assure that each data unit is successfully delivered in the proper order. At any time, the LLC service provider (i.e., the two LLC entities) or either of the LLC users may reset the logical connection. This means that the logical connection is reinitialized and some data units may be lost. That is, some data units may have been sent by one LLC entity but have not yet been acknowledged by the other LLC entity, and these data units may not be delivered. A service provider may need to perform a reset if for some reason it becomes out of synchronization with the other side. A user may need to perform a reset because it wishes to abort the current exchange without losing the connection; for example, if a terminal user is receiving a stream of data from a host computer, he or she may wish to abort the flow of data to the screen but maintain the connection to the host.

Figures 3.5a and 3.5b show resets successfully requested by the user, and Figure 3.5c illustrates a provider-invoked reset. In all of these cases, the reason parameter in the DL-RESET.indication is used to indicate who initiated the reset. A value of remote indicates that the reset was initiated by the remote LLC entity or the remote LLC user. A value of local indicates that the reset was initiated by the local LLC entity. Finally, a reset attempt may fail, leading to a termination of the connection. This can happen either because the remote user refused the reset (Figure 3.5d) or because the remote LLC entity did not respond (Figure 3.5e).

Disconnect Phase. At any time, the LLC service provider (i.e., the two LLC entities) or either of the LLC users may terminate the logical connection. This means that the logical connection is destroyed and some outstanding data units may be lost. A service provider may need to perform a disconnect if for some reason it experiences an unrecoverable failure.

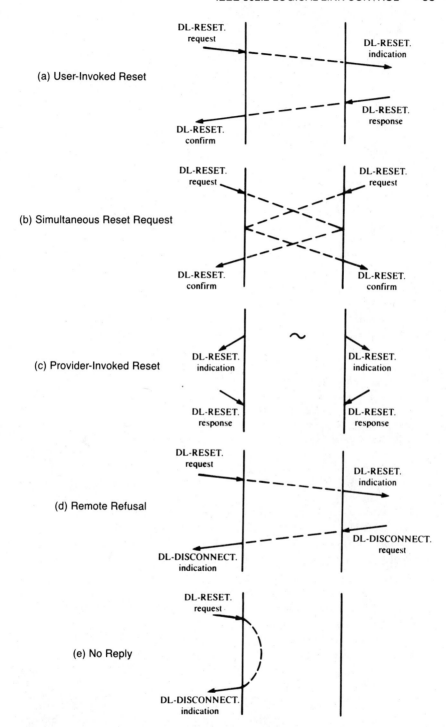

Figure 3.5. Connection-mode service: reset

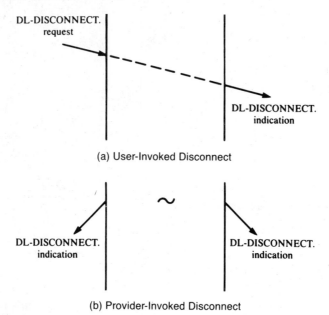

(a) User-Invoked Disconnect

(b) Provider-Invoked Disconnect

Figure 3.6.   Connection-mode service: disconnect

Figure 3.6 illustrates possible disconnection scenarios. The reason parameter in the indication primitive indicates whether the disconnect was requested by the other user or was initiated by the service provider.

Acknowledged Connectionless Service

The acknowledged connectionless service actually consists of two related but independent services. The DL-DATA-ACK service is a guaranteed delivery service, in which data is sent from an originating LLC user, and acknowledged. The DL-REPLY service is essentially a poll with a guaranteed response; it enables a user to request a previously prepared data unit from another user or to exchange data units with another user. For both of these services, no prior connection is set up.

DL-DATA-ACK Service.   This service enables an LLC user to send data to a remote user and receive an immediate confirmation of the receipt or nonreceipt of the data (Figures 3.7a and 3.7b). The service-class parameter specifies whether or not an acknowledge capability in the MAC layer is to be used for the data unit transmission. So far, only the 802.4 standard supports this capability (see Chapter 5 for a discussion). The DL-DATA-ACK-STATUS.indication primitive includes a status parameter that indicates that the data unit was successfully received by the peer LLC entity or it indicates failure. Failure may be at the local or remote entity and includes such causes as inability to transmit and no response from the other side.

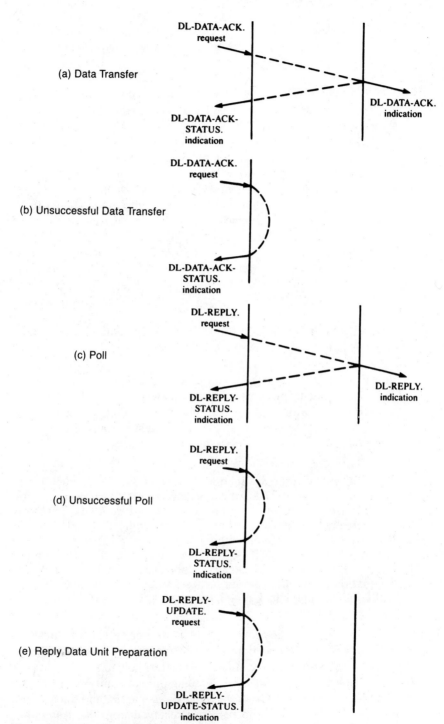

Figure 3.7. Acknowledged connectionless service

The LLC entity enforces a discipline that only one data unit at a time may be outstanding, and must be acknowledged before transmission of the next data unit.

DL-REPLY Service.   The DL-REPLY service enables a user to solicit data from a remote user and, optionally, transmit data at the same time. To begin, we assume that an LLC user has data to send, but that it will wait until it is polled before sending it. The DL-REPLY-UPDATE.request primitive (Figure 3.7e) passes a data unit to the LLC entity to be held and sent out at a later time, when requested to do so by some other user. The LLC entity associates this data unit with the SAP of the user and will transmit it to other users as often as requested; a subsequent DL-REPLY-UPDATE.request serves to replace the currently associated data unit with a new one. When the LLC entity receives a DL-REPLY-UP-DATE.request, it responds with a DL-REPLY-UPDATE-STATUS. indication. The status parameter indicates success if the data unit has been associated with this SAP. A failure status indicates that the association could not be made (e.g., because of inability to access a shared data area).

We can now describe this service, which is invoked with a DL-REPLY.request and may be issued with or without user data. If the LLC entity receiving the request (the source LLC entity) is unable to transmit the request to the intended destination LLC entity (e.g., because of protocol or buffer capacity problems), it immediately issues a DL-REPLY-STATUS.indication with a status parameter that indicates the failure (Figure 3.7d). Otherwise (Figure 3.7c), this request is transmitted to the destination LLC entity and results in the following actions:

- The LLC entity at the destination issues a DL-REPLY.indication to the destination user. This indicates that a request has been made by another user. If the request was accompanied by a data unit, it is also delivered to the destination user in the indication primitive.
- If a data unit is associated with the destination SAP as a result of a previous DL-REPLY-UPDATE.request, this data unit is transmitted back to the source LLC entity. If there is no such data unit, the destination LLC entity sends a message back to the source LLC entity indicating the lack of a data unit.

When the resulting message is received by the source LLC entity, it issues a DL-REPLY-STATUS.indication. If the corresponding request has been completely successful, then the status parameter indicates complete success and there is a data parameter containing the data unit obtained from the destination LLC entity. Otherwise, the status parameter indicates the nature of the failure, such as no response received from the destination LLC entity, or no data unit available at the remote LLC entity.

Table 3.2.   IEEE 802.2 MAC SERVICE PRIMITIVES AND PARAMETERS

MA-UNITDATA.request (source-address, destination-address, data, priority, service-class)

MA-UNITDATA.indication (destination-address, source-address, data, reception-status, priority, service-class)

MA-UNITDATA-STATUS.indication (destination-address, source-address, transmission-status, provided priority, provided-service-class)

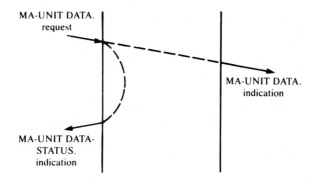

(a) Without MAC acknowledgement

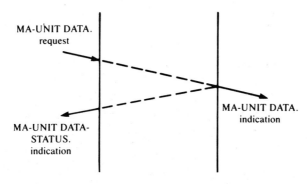

(b) With MAC acknowledgement

Figure 3.8.   MAC service expected by LIC

MAC Service Specification

The LLC standard includes a specification of the services expected from the MAC layer. Table 3.2 lists the primitives and the parameters that define this service, and Figure 3.8 illustrates the interaction. The MA-UNITDATA.request primitive is used by LLC to transmit all forms of LLC PDUs (described in Section 3.3). The source and destination address parameters specify MAC addresses. The destination address may be an individual or a group address. The data parameter contains the LLC

PDU. The priority parameter specifies the desired priority for this data unit transfer. The service-class parameter specifies whether an acknowledge capability in the MAC layer is to be used for the data unit transmission.

Data transmitted via an MA-DATA.request are delivered by an MA-DATA.indication. The reception-status parameter indicates the success or failure of the incoming frame. For example, if an error is detected in an incoming frame, that fact is reported to LLC, which may make use of this information in its error control protocol described later in this chapter.

The MA-UNITDATA-STATUS.indication primitive is passed from the MAC entity to the LLC entity to confirm the success or failure of the service provided for the previous associated MA-UNITDATA.request. If the requested service class is without acknowledgment (the usual case), the indication primitive is passed immediately after the transmission attempt, and only indicates that the local MAC entity has or has not succeeded in transmitting a frame. If the requested service class is with acknowledgment, then the indication primitive is passed when an acknowledgment is received from the peer MAC entity, or when the allowed number of transmission retries has occurred, or upon local failure.

The transmission status parameter is used to pass status information back to the local requesting LLC entity. The types of status that can be associated with this primitive are dependent on the particular implementation as well as the type of MAC protocol that is used (e.g., excessive collisions may be a status returned by a CSMA/CD MAC entity).

3.2   LINK CONTROL PROTOCOL MECHANISMS

Before examining the particular protocols defined for the LLC standard, it will be useful to describe two of the most important mechanisms used in link control protocols: flow control and error control. Flow control and error control mechanisms are used in both the connection-oriented and the acknowledged connectionless protocols.

Flow Control

Flow control is a technique for assuring that a transmitting entity does not overwhelm a receiving entity with data. The receiving entity will typically allocate a data buffer with some maximum length. When data are received, it must do a certain amount of processing (e.g., examine the header and strip it off the PDU) before passing the data to a higher-layer user. In the absence of flow control, the receiver's buffer may fill up and overflow while it is processing old data.

The simplest form of flow control, known as *stop-and-wait,* supports the acknowledged connectionless LLC service, and works as follows. A source entity transmits a data unit. After reception, the destination entity indicates its willingness to accept another data unit by sending back an acknowledgment to the data unit just received. The source entity must wait until it receives the acknowledgment before sending the next data unit. The destination station can thus stop the flow of data by simply withholding acknowledgment.

This procedure works fine, and indeed can hardly be improved on, when a message is sent as one contiguous block or PDU of data. However, it is often the case that a transmitter will break a large block of data up into smaller blocks and send these one at a time. This is done for one or more of the following reasons:

- The longer the transmission, the more likely that there will be an error, necessitating retransmission of the entire block. With smaller blocks, errors are less likely per block, and fewer data need be retransmitted.
- On a multipoint line, it is usually desirable not to permit one station to occupy the line for very long, thus causing long delays at the other stations.
- The buffer size of the receiver may be limited.

With the use of multiple PDUs for a single message, the stop-and-wait technique may be inadequate. The essence of the problem is that only one PDU at a time can be in transit. In situations where the bit length of the link is greater than the PDU length, serious inefficiencies result. The obvious solution is to allow multiple PDUs to be in transit at one time. This technique, known as *sliding-window,* supports the connection-mode LLC service.

Let us examine how this might work for two stations. *A* and *B*, connected via a full-duplex link. Station *B* allocates seven buffers for reception instead of the one discussed above. Thus *B* can accept seven PDUs, and *A* is allowed to send seven PDUs without waiting for an acknowledgment. To keep track of which PDUs have been acknowledged, each is labeled with a sequence number in the range 0 to 7 (modulo 8). *B* acknowledges a PDU by sending an acknowledgment that includes the sequence number of the next PDU expected. Thus, if *B* returns the sequence number 5, this acknowledges receipt of PDU number 4, and says that *B* is now expecting PDU number 5. This scheme can be used to acknowledge multiple PDUs. For example, *B* could receive PDUs 2, 3, and 4, but withhold acknowledgment until PDU 4 arrives. By then returning sequence number 5, *B* acknowledges PDUs 2, 3, and 4 at one time. *A* maintains a list of sequence numbers that it is allowed to send, and *B* maintains a list of sequence numbers that it is prepared to receive. Each of these lists can be thought of as a *window* of PDUs.

An example of operation is shown in Figure 3.9. Initially, A and *B* have windows for seven PDUs. After transmitting three PDUs with no acknowledgment, *A* has shrunk its window to four PDUs. When PDU 2 is acknowledged, *A* is back up to seven PDUs.

So far, we have discussed transmission in one direction only. If two

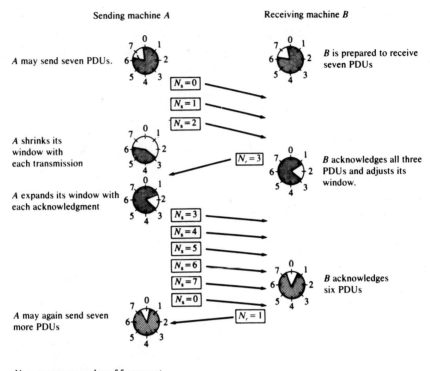

Sending machine A   Receiving machine B

A may send seven PDUs.   B is prepared to receive
                                                          seven PDUs

$N_s = 0$
$N_s = 1$
$N_s = 2$

A shrinks its
window with
each transmission $N_r = 3$ B acknowledges all three
                                                          PDUs and adjusts its
A expands its window with   window.
each acknowledgment

$N_s = 3$
$N_s = 4$
$N_s = 5$
$N_s = 6$ B acknowledges
$N_s = 7$ six PDUs
$N_s = 0$

A may again send seven $N_r = 1$
more PDUs

N_s = sequence number of frame sent
N_r = sequence number of next frame expected
Shaded part designates window

Figure 3.9. Example of a sliding-window protocol

stations exchange data, each needs to maintain two windows: one for transmit and one to receive, and each side needs to send both data and acknowledgments to the other. To provide efficient support for this requirement, a feature known as *piggybacking* is part of the flow control protocol. Each data PDU includes a field that holds the sequence number used for acknowledgment. Thus, if a station has data to send and an acknowledgment to send, it sends both together in one PDU, thus saving communication capacity. Of course, if a station has an acknowledgment but no data to send, it sends a separate ACK PDU. Note that if a station has data to send but no acknowledgment to send, it must repeat the last acknowledgment that is sent. This is because the data PDU includes a field for the acknowledgment number and some value must be put into that field. The station that receives duplicate ACKs simply ignores them.

Error Control

The most common data link control techniques for error control, and those used by LLC, are based on two functions:

- *Error detection:* The receiver detects errors and discards PDUs that are in error. This function is actually performed by the MAC layer, and is described in Appendix C. Thus, PDUs that contain detectable errors never reach the destination LLC entity.
- *Automatic repeat request (ARQ):* This error control technique involves positive acknowledgment of PDUs and automatic retransmission of unacknowledged PDUs. These concepts are explained in what follows.

The use of error detection and ARQ results in the conversion of an unreliable data link into a reliable one. Two versions of ARQ are employed in the LLC standard: stop-and-wait ARQ, used to support the acknowledged connectionless service, and go-back-N ARQ, used to support the connection-mode service.

Stop-and-Wait ARQ. Stop-and-wait ARQ is based on the stop-and-wait flow control technique outlined previously, and is depicted in Figure 3.10.

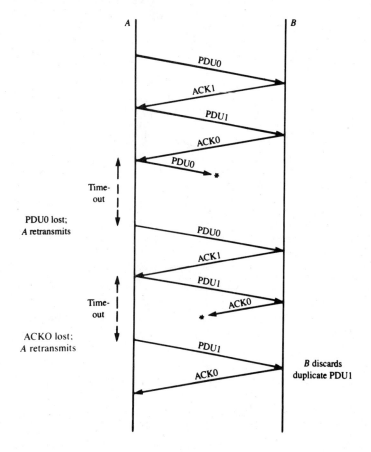

Figure 3.10. Stop-and-wait ARQ

The source station transmits a single PDU and then must await an acknowledgment. No other data PDUs can be sent until the destination station's reply arrives at the source station.

Two sorts of errors could occur. First, the PDU that arrives at the destination could be damaged. The receiver detects this by using the error detection technique referred to earlier and simply discards the PDU. To account for this possibility, the source station is equipped with a timer. After a PDU is transmitted, the source station waits for an acknowledgment. If no acknowledgment is received by the time that the timer expires, then the same PDU is sent again. Note that this system requires that the transmitter maintain a copy of a transmitted PDU until an acknowledgment is received for that PDU.

The second sort of error is a damaged acknowledgment. Consider the following situation. Station *A* sends a PDU. The PDU is received correctly by station *B*, which responds with an acknowledgment (ACK). The ACK is damaged in transit and is not recognizable by *A*, which must resend the same PDU. This duplicate PDU arrives and is accepted by *B;* *B* has, therefore, accepted two copies of the same data unit as if they were separate. To avoid this problem, PDUs are alternately labeled with 0 or 1 and positive acknowledgments are of the form ACK0 or ACK1. In keeping with the sliding-window convention, an ACK0 acknowledges receipt of a PDU numbered 1 and indicates that the receiver is ready for a PDU numbered 0.

The reader may note the loss of time due to the discard of a PDU in error and the timeout operation, and wonder about the use of a negative acknowledgment to speed things up. That is, if *B* receives a damaged PDU, it could immediately return a negative acknowledgment (NAK0 or NAK1), indicating that the last PDU was in error. This is in fact done, in some cases, on point-to-point links. On a local network, however, if a received PDU contains an error, there is no way for the station to be sure that the address field is correct, and therefore, no way to be sure that the PDU is addressed to itself.

Go-Back-N ARQ.   The principal advantage of stop-and-wait ARQ is its simplicity. Its principal disadvantage is that of the underlying stop-and-wait flow control technique: it is inefficient. However, just as the stop-and-wait flow control technique can be used as the basis for error control, so too can the sliding-window flow control technique be adapted. The form of error control based on sliding-window flow control that is used to support the connection-oriented LLC service is known as go-back-N ARQ (Figure 3.11).

In go-back-N ARQ, a station may send a series of PDUs sequentially numbered modulo some maximum value. The number of unacknowledged PDUs outstanding is determined by window size. The receiving station has the option of acknowledging each incoming PDU or providing a cumulative acknowledgment of some number of PDUs. Consider that

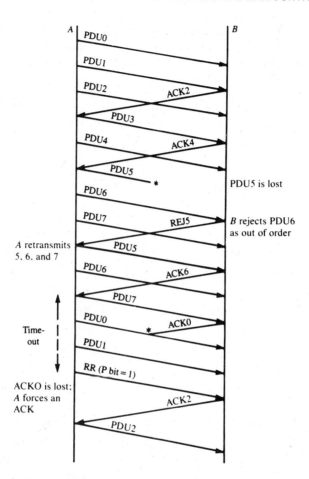

Figure 3.11.   Go-back-N ARQ

station *A* is sending a sequence of PDUs to station *B*. The error control techniques takes into account the following contingencies:

1. Damaged PDU. There are two subcases:
   a. *A* transmits a PDU and sets an Acknowledgment Timer for that PDU. *B* receives a damaged version of the PDU and does not acknowledge. If the timer expires without an acknowledgment, *A* transmits a *receive ready* (RR) command. This command causes *B* to send an ACK indicating the next PDU that it expects. *A* clears the timer and retransmits any unacknowledged PDUs.
   b. *A* transmits a sequence of PDUs, one of which is damaged in transit. *B* receives a sequence of correct PDUs, then a damaged PDU that it discards, then more PDUs. Because of the discarded PDU, there is a gap in the sequence numbers. *B* will not accept PDUs out of order, and so sends back a *reject*

(REJ), indicating the number of the next PDU expected. *A* must retransmit not only the PDU that was rejected, but all subsequent PDUs. Note that *A* must, therefore, maintain a copy of all unacknowledged PDUs.

2. Damaged ACK. Again, there are two subcases.
   a. Since ACKs are cumulative (e.g., ACK6 means that all PDUs through 5 are acknowledged), it may be that *A* will receive a subsequent acknowledgment to a subsequent PDU that will do the job of the lost ACK, before the timer that *A* has associated with that PDU expires.
   b. *A* times out and transmits an RR command as in Case 1a. It sets another timer, called the P-bit Timer (terminology explained later). If *B*'s acknowledgment to the RR command is damaged, then *A*'s timer will expire. At this point, *A* will try again by issuing a new RR command and restarting the P-bit timer. This procedure is tried for a number of iterations. If *A* fails to obtain an acknowledgment, it initiates a resetting procedure, as described later.

One final point worth noting is the relationship between the sequence number range and the window size. If the sequence number field in the PDU is *n* bits, then the sequence number range is $2^n - 1$, because of the interaction of error control and acknowledgment. To see this, consider that if data are being exchanged in both directions, station *B* must send a piggybacked acknowledgment to station *A*'s PDUs in the PDUs being transmitted by *B*, even if the acknowledgment has already been sent. As we have mentioned, this is because *B* must put some number in the acknowledgment field of its data PDUs. (This has the side benefit that in case the first ACK gets lost, the second ACK may get through.) Now consider a 3-bit sequence number size. Suppose a station sends PDU0 and gets back an ACK1, and then sends PDUs 1, 2, 3, 4, 5, 6, 7, 0 and gets another ACK1. This could mean that all eight PDUs were received correctly and the ACK1 is a cumulative acknowledgment. It could also mean that all eight PDUs were damaged in transit and the receiving station is repeating its previous ACK1. The problem is avoided if the window size is limited to 7 ($2^n - 1$).

3.3 LLC PROTOCOLS

The LLC protocols are modeled after the balanced mode of high-level data link control (HDLC) [ISO84a, b, c], and have similar formats and functions. This is especially true of the connection-oriented protocol.

LLC Types and Classes

There are three LLC protocols (referred to as types of operation) defined in the standard, one for each of the three forms of service:

Table 3.3.   LLC CLASSES

		Class of LLC			
		I	II	III	IV
Types of	1	X	X	X	X
Operation	2		X		X
Supported	3			X	X

- *Type 1 operation:* Supports unacknowledged connectionless service.
- *Type 2 operation:* Supports connection-mode service.
- *Type 3 operation:* Supports acknowledged connectionless service.

It is possible for a single station to support more than one form of service, and hence employ more than one of the types of protocols. The combination of services supported is given by the *station class.* Table 3.3 indicates the allowable station classes. Note that all allowable classes support Type 1. This ensures that all stations on a LAN will have a common service form that can be used for management operations. Beyond that, each station supports only those services needed by its users, and thus the implementation size is minimized.

If a station supports more than one form of service, then individual LLC SAPs may be activated for one or more of the available services. This is a configuration function beyond the scope of the standard. Although it is not explicitly stated in the standard, it is implied that some mechanism exists for dealing with received PDUs according to the type of operation [FIEL86]. If a destination LLC SAP is activated for a particular form of service, incoming PDUs for the corresponding type of operation are given to the appropriate LLC service entity for processing. That service entity will use the appropriate service primitives to interact with a user at a particular SAP. If a SAP has not been activated for a particular service, then all PDUs for that service are discarded.

LLC Protocol Data Units

All three LLC protocols employ the same PDU format (Figure 3.12a), which consists of four fields. There are two 8-bit address fields: the destination service access point (DSAP) field and the source service access point (SSAP) field. Each address field consists of a 7-bit address and a control bit. In the DSAP field, the control bit indicates whether this is an individual address or a group address. A group address specifies a group of service access points at a particular station to which data is to be sent;

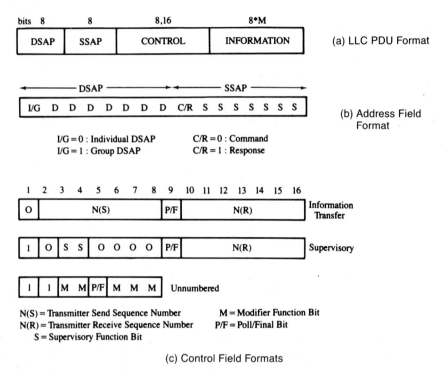

Figure 3.12. LLC protocol data unit formats

it can only be used in type 1 (unacknowledged connectionless) operation. A group address of all 1s is predefined to be the global DSAP address; this address designates all active DSAPs being serviced by the underlying MAC address. In the SSAP field, the control bit indicates whether this PDU is a command or a response (these terms are explained later); this bit is used by the LLC entity to determine the significance of certain bits in the control field. See Appendix 2B for a discussion of specific SAP assignments.

The control field identifies the particular PDU and specifies various control functions. It is 8 or 16 bits long, depending on the identity of the PDU. PDUs can be characterized in two dimensions: A PDU is either a command or a response, and is either an information transfer, supervisory, or unnumbered PDU. Table 3.4 lists the PDUs used in all three LLC protocols.

Finally, the information field consists of zero or more octets. It is used to carry user or management data.

Type 1 Operation

Type 1 operation supports the unacknowledged connectionless service, using three unnumbered PDUs: UI, XID, and TEST. The identity of the PDU is specified by the modifier function bits (Figure 3.12c).

Table 3.4. LLC PROTOCOL DATA UNITS

Format	Control Field Encoding	Commands	Responses
a. Unacknowledged Connectionless Service			
Unnumbered	1100*000 1111*101 1100*111	UI Unnumbered Information XID Exchange Identification TEST Test	XID Exchange Identification TEST Test
b. Connection-Mode Service			
Information Supervisory	0-N(S)--*-N(R)-- 1000000*-N(R)-- 10100000*-N(R)-- 10010000*-N(R)--	I Information RR Receive Ready RNR Receive Not Ready REJ Reject	I Information RR Receive Ready RNR Receive Not Ready REJ Reject
Unnumbered	1111*110 1100*010 1100*110 1111*000 1110*001	SABME Set Asynchronous Balanced Mode Extended DISC Disconnect	UA Unnumbered Acknowledgment DM Disconnected Mode FRMR Frame Reject
c. Acknowledged Connectionless Service			
Unnumbered	1110*110 1110*111	AC0 Acknowledged Connectionless Information, Sequence 0 AC1 Acknowledged Connectionless Information, Sequence 1	AC0 Acknowledged Connectionless Acknowledgment, Sequence 0 AC1 . Acknowledged Connectionless Acknowledgment, Sequence 1

* = P/F bit

The UI PDU is used to send user data. When a user issues a DL-UNITDATA.request, the data parameter is transmitted to the destination in the information field of the UI PDU. When this PDU is received, the information field is passed up to the destination user as the data parameter in a DL-UNITDATA.indication. There is no acknowledgment, flow control, or error control. However, there is error detection and discard at the MAC level. Thus, there is no guarantee that a UI PDU will be successfully received.

Use of the remaining two PDUs is not triggered by an LLC user service request. These PDUs are intended to support management functions associated with all three types of operation. Both PDUs are used in exchanges that operate in the following fashion. An LLC entity may issue a command (C/R bit set to 0) XID or TEST. When this is received, the destination LLC entity issues an XID or a TEST response. The information field contains management information relating to the operation of the PDU. Although a station is not required to issue XID or TEST commands, it is required to return an XID or TEST response when the corresponding command is received.

The XID PDU is used to exchange two types of information: types of operation supported and window size. If the XID includes a null DSAP and SSAP, then the XID PDU indicates which class of service is sup-

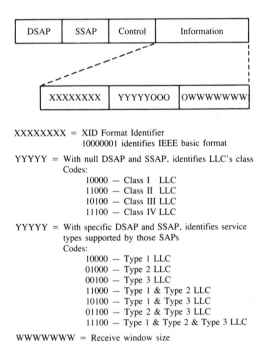

XXXXXXXX = XID Format Identifier
   10000001 identifies IEEE basic format

YYYYY = With null DSAP and SSAP, identifies LLC's class
   Codes:
      10000 — Class I   LLC
      11000 — Class II LLC
      10100 — Class III LLC
      11100 — Class IV LLC

YYYYY = With specific DSAP and SSAP, identifies service
   types supported by those SAPs
   Codes:
      10000 — Type 1 LLC
      01000 — Type 2 LLC
      00100 — Type 3 LLC
      11000 — Type 1 & Type 2 LLC
      10100 — Type 1 & Type 3 LLC
      01100 — Type 2 & Type 3 LLC
      11100 — Type 1 & Type 2 & Type 3 LLC

WWWWWWW = Receive window size

Figure 3.13. XID information field

ported by the LLC entity at the sending station. In the case of operation type, if the XID includes a specific DSAP and SSAP (either individual or group), then the XID PDU indicates which types of operation are supported by the sending LLC entity for that particular SSAP. For a SAP that supports type 2 operation, and for a particular connection (determined by the SSAP, DSAP pair), the XID includes the receive window size. This is the amount of credit extended to the other side with each acknowledgment. That is, when an acknowledgment is sent using the N(R) variable, then the window size is the number of frames that may be transmitted beginning with N(R).

All of the XID information is carried in the information field of the LLC PDU. Figure 3.13 shows the format.

The TEST PDU is used to conduct a loop-back test of the transmission path between two LLC entities. Upon receipt of a TEST command, the addressed LLC entity issues (presents to MAC for transmission) a TEST response as soon as possible.

With all of the type 1 PDUs, the P/F bit of the control field has no particular significance. In the UI PDU, it is always set to zero. In the XID and TEST commands, it may be set to zero or one, and the same value is used in the corresponding response.

Type 2 Operation

Type 2 operation supports the connection-mode service. It makes use of three PDU formats:

- *Information transfer:* Used to transfer user information.
- *Supervisory:* Used for acknowledgment, flow control, and error control.
- *Unnumbered:* Used for connection establishment, connection termination, and other control functions.

Connection Establishment.   Connection establishment is attempted by the type 2 protocol in response to a DL-CONNECT.request from a user. The LLC entity receiving the request issues a SABME PDU. (Note: this stands for Set Asynchronous Balanced Mode (ABM) Extended; it is used in HDLC to choose the ABM mode, which involves two peer entities, and to select extended sequence numbers of seven bits. Both ABM and 7-bit sequence numbers are mandatory in type 2 operation.) The peer LLC entity receives the SABME PDU and passes up a DL-CONNECT.indication to the user at the designated DSAP. If the LLC user identified by the DSAP accepts the connection request, by issuing a DL-CONNECT.response, then the destination LLC entity returns a UA PDU to the source LLC entity. When the UA is received, signifying acceptance, the LLC entity passes a confirm to the source user (Figure 3.14a).

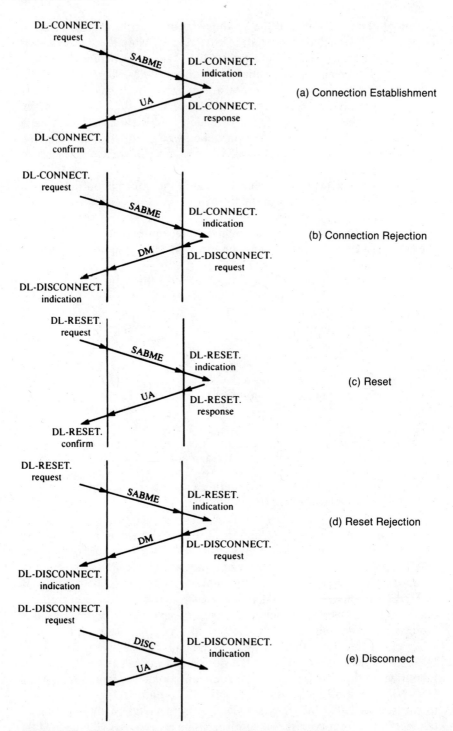

(a) Connection Establishment

(b) Connection Rejection

(c) Reset

(d) Reset Rejection

(e) Disconnect

Figure 3.14. Type 2 operation: connection management examples

The connection is henceforth uniquely identified by the pair of user SAPs. If the destination LLC user rejects the connection request, its LLC entity returns a DM PDU, and the LLC entity informs its user of the rejection (Figure 3.14b).

Data transfer.   When the connection request has been accepted and confirmed, the connection is established. Both sides may then begin to send user data units in information (I) PDUs, using sequence numbers beginning with zero. The N(S) and N(R) fields of the I PDU are sequence numbers that support flow control and error control. An entity sending a sequence of I PDUs will number them sequentially, modulo 128, and place the number in N(S). N(R) is the piggybacked acknowledgment for PDUs received; it enables the LLC entity to indicate which number PDU it expects to receive next.

The supervisory PDUs are used for flow control and error control. RR is used to acknowledge the last PDU received by indicating the next PDU expected. The RR is used when there is no reverse traffic to carry a piggybacked acknowledgment. As we have seen, the RR command is also used to elicit an acknowledgment when a transmitted PDU remains unacknowledged for an extended period of time. RNR acknowledges a PDU, as with RR, but also asks the transmitting station to suspend transmission of I PDUs. When the destination station is again ready, it sends an RR PDU. REJ implements the go-back-N ARQ. It indicates that the I PDU with number N(R) is rejected and that it and any subsequently transmitted I PDUs must be sent again. The N(R) in a REJ PDU also acknowledges the receipt of I PDUs through N(R)-1. Figure 3.15 is an example of two-way data exchange using information and supervisory PDUs.

Mention should be made of the timing requirements for the transmission of acknowledgments. When an I PDU is received, if the receiving LLC entity has an I PDU to send, it will acknowledge the incoming PDU immediately with its next outgoing I PDU. If the LLC entity has no I PDUs to send, then it may take one of the following actions:

1. Immediately acknowledge the incoming I PDU with an RR. This is required if the P bit of the incoming PDU is set to 1.
2. Wait up to some threshold value of time before acknowledging. During that time, an I PDU may become available for transmission, with the piggybacked acknowledgment, thus saving the transmission of an RR. Also, during that time, additional I PDUs may arrive, allowing a cumulative acknowledgment of multiple I PDUs with a single RR.

The interval of time the receiver may defer the generation of an acknowledgment must be limited such that unnecessary retransmissions due

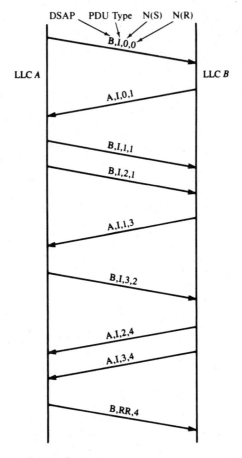

DSAP   PDU Type   N(S)   N(R)

LLC *A*

LLC *B*

B,I,0,0

A,I,0,1

B,I,1,1

B,I,2,1

A,I,1,3

B,I,3,2

A,I,2,4

A,I,3,4

B,RR,4

Figure 3.15. Two-way data exchange

to delayed acknowledgments are avoided. The threshold value may be static or dynamic (e.g., depending on the current traffic load). For a discussion of the performance implications of various acknowledgment strategies, see [BIER88].

Either LLC entity can request a reset, either on its own initiative or in response to a user's DL-RESET.request. An LLC entity requests a reset on a particular connection by sending a SABME PDU to the other LLC entity on the connection. The remote LLC entity passes on the request to the appropriate user in a DL-RESET.indication. The remote user has the choice of accepting the reset, which causes its LLC entity to reply with a UA, or rejecting it, which causes its LLC entity to reply with a DM (Figures 3.14c and 3.14d).

When a reset occurs, both sides reset their send and receive sequence numbers to zero. Any outstanding I PDUs may be lost and it is the responsibility of higher layers to recover.

Disconnect.   Either LLC entity can initiate a disconnect, either on its own initiative or in response to a user's DL-DISCONNECT.request. The entity initiates a disconnect on a particular connection by sending a DISC PDU to the other LLC entity on the connection. The remote entity must accept the disconnect by replying with a UA and issuing a DL-DISCON-NECT.indication to its user (Figure 3.14e). Again, no assumption can be made about outstanding I PDUs, and their delivery is the responsibility of higher layers.

Frame Reject.   The Frame Reject (FRMR) PDU is used to indicate that an improper PDU has arrived—one that somehow violates the protocol. The error is one that is not correctable by simply resending the identical PDU. The nature of the violation is reported in the information field of the FRMR, as illustrated in Figure 3.16. The reported information includes the control field of the rejected PDU, the current send and receive sequence numbers, and whether the rejected PDU was a command or response. In addition, five bits are used to specify particular types of errors, as shown in the figure.

Upon receipt of an FRMR, an LLC entity will attempt to reset the connection (by sending a SABME command PDU). It should be noted that the station that issued the FRMR could have simply issued a SABME to reset the connection. The purpose of the FRMR is to return status information that a management entity can log, and that may be of use in subsequent failure analyses.

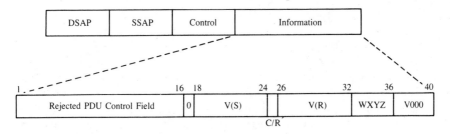

$V(S)$ = Current send sequence number
$V(R)$ = Current receive sequence number
C/R = 1 if the PDU that caused the FRMR was a response PDU
      0 if the PDU that caused the FRMR was a command PDU
  W = 1 if control field was invalid
  X = 1 if PDU contained an information field not permitted with this PDU
  Y = 1 if information field exceeded maximum length
  Z = 1 if $N(R)$ was invalid
  V = 1 if $N(S)$ was invalid

Figure 3.16. FRMR information field

The P/F Bit.   The P/F bit is referred to as the Poll bit in command PDUs and as the Final bit in response PDUs. The P bit is used to solicit a response from the other side. When an LLC entity issues a command with a P bit set to one, the receiving LLC entity must issue a response PDU with the F bit set to one as soon as possible. This bit provides a direct command/response linkage that is useful in maintaining a mutual understanding of the status of the connection. For example, suppose LLC entity A is sending I PDUs to entity B. At some point, A fails to receive a response to a PDU and times out. It may be that the last PDU sent by A was lost or that the last acknowledgment sent by B was lost. A can send a supervisory PDU (RR, RNR, REJ, depending on the local state) with the P bit set to one. This forces B to respond with an appropriate PDU (RR, RNR, REJ, or I) with the F bit set to one, and N(R) equal to the number of the next expected I PDU.

Type 3 Operation

With type 3 operation, each transmitted PDU is acknowledged. Two new unnumbered PDUs are defined: Acknowledged Connectionless, Seq. 0 (AC0) and Acknowledged Connectionless, Seq. 1 (AC1); when the distinction is unimportant, both are referred to as ACn. The encodings of the two PDUs differ only in one bit position (located in the eighth bit of the control field; see Table 3.4c). As we shall see, this bit functions as a 1-bit sequence number. Unlike the other PDUs used in LLC, the ACn PDUs are not defined in HDLC.

User data is sent in an ACn command PDU and must be acknowledged using an ACn response PDU. To guard against lost PDUs, the sender alternates the use of AC0 and AC1 in its command PDUs, and the receiver responds with an ACn PDU with the opposite number of the corresponding command. Stop-and-wait flow control and stop-and-wait ARQ error control are used.

For the DL-DATA-ACK service, the P/F bit is always set to zero. The ACn command contains user data and the ACn response does not. For the DL-REPLY service, the P/F bit is always set to one. The ACn command may or may not contain user data. The ACn response contains user data if it is available; otherwise it does not and this signals the other side that the reply has failed.

For both the DL-DATA-ACK service and the DL-REPLY service, the ACn response includes an 8-bit code in the information field that indicates the status associated with this response, as illustrated in Figure 3.17. The code returned in the CCCC part of the status field indicates the success or failure of the information passage in the corresponding command PDU. The RRRR part of the field indicates the success or failure of information passage in the response PDU; this part is meaningful only

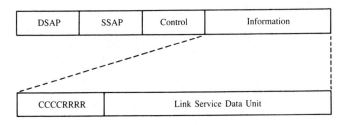

(a) Format

CCCC	Mnemonic	Category	Description
0000	OK	Success	Command accepted
1000	RS	Permanent error	Unimplemented or inactivated service
1010	UE	Permanent error	LLC user interface error
0110	PE	Permanent error	Protocol error
1110	IP	Permanent error	Permanent implementation dependent error
1001	UN	Temporary error	Resources temporarily unavailable
1111	IT	Temporary error	Temporary implementation dependent error

(b) CCCC codes

RRRR	Mnemonic	Category	Description
0000	OK	Success	Response LSDU present
1000	RS	Permanent error	Unimplemented or inactivated service
1100	NE	Permanent error	Response LSDU never submitted
0010	NR	Success	Response LSDU not requested
1010	UE	Permanent error	LLC user interface error
1110	IP	Permanent error	Permanent implementation dependent error
1001	UN	Temporary error	Resources temporarily unavailable
1111	IT	Temporary error	Temporary implementation dependent error

(c) RRRR codes

Figure 3.17.   ACn response information field

for the DL-REPLY service. The category of *temporary error* indicates that a temporary and self-correcting condition at the responding LLC prevented the performance of the requested action, and retrying the request is likely to result in success. The category of *permanent error* indicates that a programming or hardware error occurred and retrying is not likely to result in success.

4

IEEE 802.3 CSMA/CD

The IEEE 802.3 standard defines the carrier sense multiple access with collision detection (CSMA/CD) medium access control (MAC) protocol for bus topology. It also defines a variety of physical layer transmission medium and data rate options. We begin with an overview of the scope of the 802.3 standard. This is followed by a look at the MAC protocol and service specifications, and finally a description of the various physical layer specifications.

4.1 SCOPE OF THE IEEE 802.3 STANDARD

As with IEEE 802.4, IEEE 802.5, and FDDI, the IEEE 802.3 standard encompasses both the MAC layer and the physical layer. Figure 4.1 depicts the architecture of the 802.3 standard in more detail. It can be seen to consist of four parts:

- MAC service specification
- MAC protocol
- Medium-independent physical specification
- Medium-dependent physical specification

The MAC service specification defines in functional terms the service provided by IEEE 802.3 to LLC or any other higher-level user. This

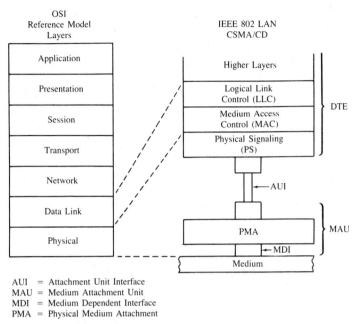

Figure 4.1. IEEE 802.3 architecture

service specification includes facilities for transmitting and receiving PDUs, and provides per-operation status information for use by higher-layer error recovery procedures. It is assumed that the higher-level user will be LLC, but, because of the adherence of the 802 standards to the principle of layering, this is not strictly necessary. In any case, this service specification hides the details of the MAC and physical layers from the MAC user. In particular, the use of a variety of transmission media should not be visible to the user except as it affects performance.

The MAC protocol is the heart of the 802.3 standard, which is often referred to simply as the CSMA/CD standard. The specification defines the frame structure and the interactions that take place between MAC entities.

The physical layer is divided into two parts. The medium-independent part specifies the interface between the MAC and the physical layers. The interface includes facilities for passing a pair of serial bit streams between the two layers and for the timing functions needed by the MAC algorithm. In addition, the standard anticipates that, in many cases, stations will be located a short distance from the physical medium of the LAN. In this configuration, a small amount of circuitry will exist in a medium attachment unit (MAU) directly adjacent to the LAN medium, whereas the majority of the hardware and all of the software will be placed within the station. The standard specifies an attachment unit interface (AUI) between the station and the MAU. The specification includes the transmission medium between the station and the MAU and the signaling technique to be used across the interface. This interface is not a requirement of the standard, but is useful in many cases. It allows the MAC logic and part of the physical layer logic to be integrated with the station and reduced to silicon while at the same time providing flexibility concerning the relative locations of stations and LAN medium.

The medium-dependent part of the standard is mandatory and specifies the interface to the LAN medium and the signals exchanged with the medium. This part of the standard offers a variety of options in terms of medium type, signaling mode (analog or digital), and data rate.

The IEEE 802.3 standard is based on the Ethernet specification (see Appendix 4A). The standard states that it is intended for use in commercial and light industrial environments. Use in home or heavy industrial environments, although not precluded, is not considered within the scope of the standard.

4.2 MAC PROTOCOL

CSMA/CD

The most commonly used MAC technique for bus/tree topologies is carrier sense multiple access with collision detection (CSMA/CD). The original baseband version of this technique was developed and patented by Xerox [METC77] as part of its Ethernet local network [SHOC82]. The original broadband version was developed and patented by MITRE [HOPK80] as part of its MITREnet local network [HOPK79].

Before examining this technique, we look at some earlier schemes from which CSMA/CD evolved.

Precursors.   All of the techniques discussed in this section, including CSMA/CD, can be termed *random access* or *contention* techniques. They are designed to address the problem of how to share a common broadcast transmission medium—the "Who goes next?" problem. The techniques are random access in the sense that there is no predictable or scheduled time for any station to transmit; station transmissions occur randomly. They are contending in the sense that no control is exercised to determine whose turn it is—all stations must contend for time on the network.

The earliest of these techniques, known as *ALOHA,* was developed for ground-based packet radio broadcasting networks [ABRA70]. However, it is applicable to any transmission medium shared by uncoordinated users. ALOHA, or *pure ALOHA* as it is sometimes called, is a true free-for-all. Whenever a station has a frame to send, it does so. The station then listens for an amount of time equal to the maximum possible round-trip propagation time on the network (twice the time it takes to send a frame between the two most widely separated stations). If the station hears an acknowledgment during that time, fine; otherwise, it resends the frame. After repeated failures, it gives up. A receiving station determines the correctness of an incoming frame by examining the checksum (see Appendix C). If the frame is valid, the station acknowledges immediately. The frame may be invalid, due to noise on the channel or because another station transmitted a frame at about the same time. In the latter case, the two frames may interfere with each other so that neither gets through; this is known as a *collision*. In that case, the receiving station simply ignores the frame. ALOHA is as simple as can be, and pays a penalty for it. Because the number of collisions rises so rapidly with increased load, the maximum utilization of the channel is only about 18 percent.

To improve efficiency, a modification of ALOHA [ROBE75] was developed in which time on the channel is organized into uniform slots whose size equals the frame transmission time. Some central clock or other technique is needed to synchronize all stations. Transmission is permitted only to begin at a slot boundary. Thus frames that do overlap will do so totally. This increases the maximum utilization of the system to about 37 percent. The scheme is known as *slotted ALOHA*.

Both ALOHA and slotted ALOHA exhibit poor utilization. They fail to take advantage of one of the key properties of both packet radio and local networks, which is that the propagation delay between stations is usually very small compared to frame transmission time. Consider the following observations. If the station-to-station propagation time is large compared to the frame transmission time, then, after a station launches a frame, it will be a long time before other stations know about it. During that time, one of the other stations may transmit a frame; the two frames may interfere with each other, and neither gets through. Indeed, if the distances are great enough, many stations may begin transmitting, one after the other, and none of their frames gets through unscathed. Suppose, however, that the propagation time is extremely small compared to frame transmission time. In that case, when a station launches a frame, all the other stations know it almost immediately. So, if they had any sense, they would not try transmitting until the first station was done. Collisions would be rare as they would occur only when two stations began to transmit almost simultaneously. Another way of looking at it is that the short delay time provides the stations with better feedback about the state of the system; this information can be used to improve efficiency.

The foregoing observations led to the development of a technique known as carrier sense multiple access (CSMA), or listen before talk (LBT). With this technique, a station wishing to transmit first listens to the medium to determine if another transmission is in progress. If the medium is in use, the station backs off some period of time and tries again. On the other hand, if the medium is idle, the station may transmit. Now, it may happen that two or more stations attempt to transmit at about the same time. If this happens, there will be a collision. To account for this, a station waits a reasonable amount of time after transmitting for an acknowledgment, taking into account the maximum round-trip propagation delay, and the fact that the acknowledging station must also contend for the channel in order to respond. If there is no acknowledgment, the station assumes that a collision has occurred and retransmits.

One can see how this strategy would be effective for systems in which the frame transmission time is much longer than the propagation time. Collisions can occur only when more than one user begins transmitting within a short time (within the period of propagation delay). If a station begins to transmit, and there are no collisions during the time it takes for the leading edge of the frame to propagate to the farthest station, then the station has seized the channel and the remainder of the frame will be transmitted without collision. The maximum utilization achievable using CSMA can far exceed that of ALOHA or slotted ALOHA.

With CSMA, an algorithm is needed to specify what a station should do if the medium is found to be busy. In one such algorithm, a station wishing to transmit listens to the medium and obeys the following rules:

1. If the medium is idle, transmit. Otherwise, go to step 2.
2. If the medium is busy, continue to listen until the medium is sensed idle; then transmit immediately.
3. If there is a collision (determined by a lack of acknowledgment), wait a random amount of time and repeat step 1.

Description of CSMA/CD. CSMA, although more efficient than ALOHA or slotted ALOHA, still has one glaring inefficiency. When two frames collide, the medium remains unusable for the duration of transmission of both damaged frames. For long frames, compared to propagation time, the amount of wasted bandwidth can be considerable. This waste can be reduced if a station continues to listen to the medium while it is transmitting. The rules can be stated as follows:

1. If the medium is idle, transmit (after a brief interframe delay to provide recovery time for other MAC entities and for the physical medium). Otherwise, go to step 2.
2. If the medium is busy, continue to listen until the medium is sensed idle; then transmit immediately.
3. If a collision is detected during transmission, transmit a brief jamming signal to assure that all stations know that there has been a collision and then cease transmission.
4. After transmitting the jamming signal, wait a random amount of time, then attempt transmitting again (go to step 1).

The above procedure raises several timing issues, all of which depend on a single parameter called the *slot time*. This single parameter describes four important aspects of collision handling:

- It is an upper bound on the time it takes to detect a collision, and hence on the amount of wasted bandwidth.
- It is an upper bound on the acquisition time of the medium (i.e., the time beyond which the transmission will not suffer a collision).
- It is an upper bound on the length of a frame fragment generated by a collision.
- It is the scheduling quantum for retransmission.

To fulfill all of these functions, the slot time is defined to be larger than the sum of the physical layer round-trip propagation time (twice the time it takes for a signal to travel from one end of the medium to the other) and the MAC layer jam time. This time depends on the details of the physical layer.

To understand the slot time, let us consider the first point above, namely, how long it takes to detect a collision. Figure 4.2 illustrates the answer for a baseband system. Consider the worst case of two stations that are as far apart as possible. As can be seen, the amount of time it takes to detect a collision is twice the propagation delay. For broadband bus, the wait is even longer. Figure 4.3 shows a dual-cable system. This time, the worst case is two stations close together and as far as possible from the head end. In this case, the time required to detect a collision is four times the propagation delay from the station to the head end. The results would be the same for a midsplit system.

Both figures indicate the use of frames long enough to allow CD before the end of transmission. In most systems that use CSMA/CD in-

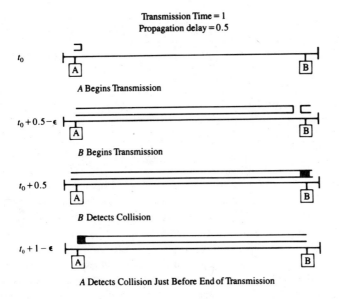

Figure 4.2. Baseband collision detection timing

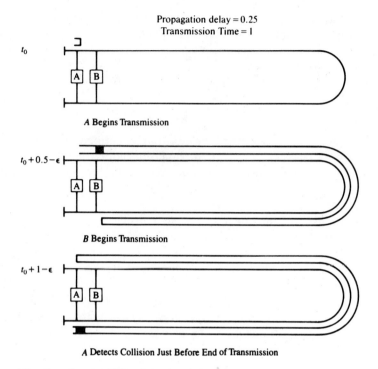

Figure 4.3.   Broadband collision detection timing

cluding the 802.3 standard, it is required that all frames be at least this long. Otherwise, the performance of the system is the same as the less efficient CSMA protocol, since collisions are not detected. Thus, the slot time is used to determine the minimum MAC frame length. It also comes into play in the retransmission algorithm. Consider that if a collision occurs and the two stations involved back off an equal amount of time and then try again, there will be another collision. To avoid this, each station backs off a random amount of time taken from a uniform probability distribution. Furthermore, it should be observed that collisions generate additional traffic. As the medium becomes busier, it is important not to clog the network with retransmissions, which lead to more collisions, which lead to more retransmission, and so on. Accordingly, when a station experiences repeated collisions, it backs off for longer periods of time to compensate for the extra load on the network.

The rule, known as *truncated binary exponential backoff,* is as follows. The backoff delay is an integral number of slot times. The number of slot times to delay before the nth retransmission attempt is chosen as a uniformly distributed random integer r in the range $0 < r < 2^k$ where $k = \min(n, 10)$. After a user-defined number of attempts, the MAC entity assumes that some problem exists, gives up, and reports failure to LLC. More formally,

$$while \text{ attempts} < \text{backOffLimit}$$
$$k := \text{Min(attempts, 10)}$$
$$r := \text{Random}(0,2^k)$$
$$\text{delay} := r^* \text{slotTime}$$

The truncated binary expotential backoff algorithm approximates the ideal algorithm where the probability of transmission of a packet is $1/Q$, with Q representing the number of stations attempting to transmit and with truncation occurring when Q equals the number of stations [SHOC82]. One unfortunate effect of the backoff algorithm is that it has a last-in, first-out effect; stations with no or few collisions will have a chance to transmit before stations that have waited longer.

MAC Frame

Figure 4.4 depicts the format of the frame generated by the IEEE 802.3 protocol. It consists of the following fields:

- *Preamble:* A 7-octet pattern used by the receiver to establish bit synchronization. The pattern is an alternating sequence of 1s and 0s, with the last bit being a zero. The nature of the pattern is such that, for Manchester encoding (see Appendix B), it appears as a periodic square wave on the medium.
- *Start frame delimiter (SFD):* Is the sequence 10101011. This indicates the actual start of the frame and enables the receiver to locate the first bit of the frame.
- *Destination address (DA):* Specifies the station(s) for which the frame is intended. It may be a unique physical address (one station), a multicast-group address (a group of stations), or a global address (all stations on the local network). The choice of a 16- or 48-bit address is an implementation decision, and must be the same for all stations on a particular LAN.
- *Source address (SA):* Specifies the station that sent the frame. The SA size must equal the DA size.
- *Length:* Specifies the number of LLC octets that follow.
- *LLC data:* Data unit supplied by LLC.
- *Pad:* Octets added to ensure that the frame is long enough for proper collision-detection operation. The frame must be at least long enough to require one slot time to transmit.
- *Frame check sequence (FCS):* A 32-bit cyclic redundancy check (see Appendix C), based on all fields except preamble, SFD, and FCS.

The address field formats are shown in Figure 2.10.
As we have mentioned, a minimum frame size is enforced to assure

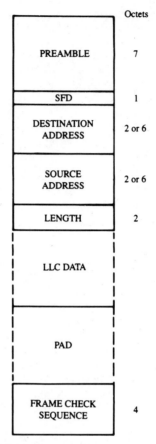

	Octets
PREAMBLE	7
SFD	1
DESTINATION ADDRESS	2 or 6
SOURCE ADDRESS	2 or 6
LENGTH	2
LLC DATA	
PAD	
FRAME CHECK SEQUENCE	4

Figure 4.4. IEEE 802.3 frame format

the proper functioning of the collision detection mechanism. In addition, a maximum frame size is also specified. Motivations for this include:

- Limit buffer size requirements at transmitting and receiving stations
- Prevent one station from tying up the medium with a very long transmission

As with the minimum frame size, the maximum frame size depends on the characteristics of the physical layer.

Functional Model and Specification

The IEEE 802.3 standard provides a narrative description of the CSMA/CD MAC algorithm. Because the standard is intended to give detailed implementation guidance, it also contains a more formal description. This includes a functional model and a Pascal specification of the algorithm.

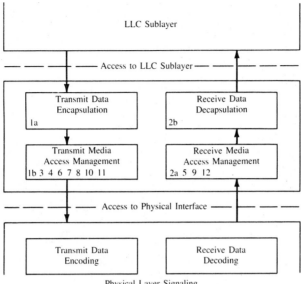

Note: Numbers refer to functions listed in Table 4.1

Figure 4.5. Functional block diagram of IEEE 802.3 MAC layer

Table 4.1 lists the functional capabilities of the MAC layer, and Figure 5.6 suggests how these functions may be organized. Transmit and receive operations are independent of each other, and each consists of functions oriented toward the LLC layer and functions oriented toward the physical layer. We have touched on all of the functions in the list except for the use of an interframe gap. The purpose of this is to provide interframe recovery time for other MAC entities and for the physical medium.

After this functional description, the standard provides a Pascal specification of the algorithm. Figure 4.6 is a flowchart that follows that specification and summarizes the control flow for both transmission and reception.

4.3 MAC SERVICES

The services provided by the MAC layer allow the local LLC entity to exchange LLC data units with peer LLC entities. Table 4.2 lists the primitives and parameters that define the IEEE 802.3 MAC service.

The IEEE 802.3 service specification is a close but not exact match to that expected in the LLC standard (see Section 3.1). It is probable that the minor discrepancies will be resolved in a later version of the standard.

Table 4.1. IEEE 802.3 MAC FUNCTIONS [IEEE 85b]

(1) For frame transmission
    (a) Accepts data from the LLC sublayer and constructs a frame
    (b) Presents a bit-serial data stream to the physical layer for transmission on the medium
NOTE: Assumes data passed from the LLC sublayer are octet multiples.
(2) For frame reception
    (a) Receives a bit-serial data stream from the physical layer
    (b) Presents to the LLC sublayer frames that are either broadcast frames or directly addressed to the local station
    (c) Discards or passes to Network Management all frames not addressed to the receiving station
(3) Defers transmission of a bit-serial stream whenever the physical medium is busy
(4) Appends proper FCS value to outgoing frames and verifies full octet boundary alignment
(5) Checks incoming frames for transmission errors by way of FCS and verifies octet boundary alignment
(6) Delays transmission of frame bit stream for specified interframe gap period
(7) Halts transmission when collision is detected
(8) Schedules retransmission after a collision until a specified retry limit is reached
(9) Enforces collision to ensure propagation throughout network by sending jam message
(10) Discards received transmissions that are less than a minimum length
(11) Appends preamble, Start Frame Delimiter, DA, SA, length count, and FCS to all frames, and inserts pad field for frames whose LLC data length is less than a minimum value
(12) Removes preamble, Start Frame Delimiter, DA, SA, length count, FCS and pad field (if necessary) from received frames

Because it is IEEE 802.3 and not IEEE 802.2 that defines the functions of the MAC layer, the service specification in the 802.3 document should take precedence. The comments in Section 3.1 concerning the meaning and the timing of the MAC service primitives apply here. Only the differences are noted in this section.

In the MA-UNITDATA.request primitive, the service class parameter is ignored by the MAC entity, which can only provide one level of priority. The parameter is included for the sake of commonality with the other specifications.

When a MAC frame is received with an address match, the MAC entity will issue an MA-UNITDATA.indication. The reception-status parameter takes on one of the following values:

- *receiveOK:* The received data is passed in the m-sdu parameter.
- *lengthError:* The value in the length field is inconsistent with the size of the received frame.

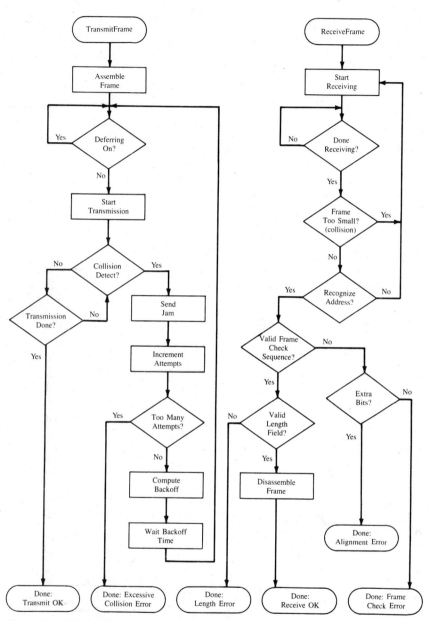

Figure 4.6. Control flow summary

Table 4.2. CSMA/CD MAC SERVICE PRIMITIVES AND PARAMETERS

MA-DATA.request (destination-address, m-sdu, service-class)

MA-DATA.indication (destination-address, source-address, m-sdu, reception-status)

- *frameCheckError:* Bits of incoming frame do not generate a CRC identical to the one in the FCS field.
- *alignmentError:* The received frame was damaged (invalid FCS) and, in addition, its length was not an integral number of octets.

4.4   PHYSICAL LAYER SPECIFICATIONS

As was discussed in Section 4.1, the IEEE 802.3 physical layer specification is divided into a number of parts. In terms of chapter organization, the standard is organized as follows:

- Physical Signaling Service Specifications (Chapter 6)
- Physical Signaling and Attachment Unit Interface Specifications (Chapter 7)
- Medium Attachment and Medium Specifications (Chapters 8, 10, 11, 14)
- Physical Signaling, Medium Attachment, and Baseband Medium Specification for 1-Mbps system (Chapter 12)
- Repeater Unit (Chapter 9)

Chapter 6 covers medium-independent and data-rate-independent aspects of IEEE 802.3. Chapter 7 covers medium-independent aspects for 10-Mbps implementations. Chapters 8, 10, 11, and 12 specify the characteristics of and attachment to alternative media. To distinguish implementations using these alternative media, the following notation is used:

<data rate in Mbps><medium type><maximum segment length (* 100m)>

For example, Chapter 8 deals with 10BASE5, which is a 10-Mbps, baseband medium with a maximum segment length of 500 m. The defined alternatives are:

- 10BASE5 (Chapters 7 and 8)
- 10BASE2 (Chapters 7 and 10)
- 10BROAD36 (Chapters 7 and 11)
- 1BASE5 (Chapter 12)
- 10BASET (Chapter 14)

Chapter 9 specifies repeater units that can be used to connect separate IEEE 802.3 10BASE5 and 10BASE2 segments.

The original 1985 IEEE standard includes Chapters 1 through 9, and is similar in basic concept to the Ethernet specification (see Appendix 4A). The remaining chapters have been added to accommodate a variety of requirements. As of this writing, Chapters 10 through 12 have been approved by IEEE, and work on Chapter 14 has progressed to the final

IEEE Standards Board voting level. The description here should closely reflect the final version of Chapter 14.

Physical Signaling (PLS) Services

As always, the services provided by the physical layer are defined in terms of primitives and parameters, and these are shown in Table 4.3.

The PLS-DATA primitives support the transfer of data from a single MAC entity to all other MAC entities contained within the same local network defined by the medium. That is, data transmitted by one MAC entity using PLS-DATA.request is received by all other MAC entities with a PLS-DATA.indication. The OUTPUT-UNIT parameter takes on one of three values: ONE, ZERO, or DATA-COMPLETE. This allows a MAC entity to request the transmission of a bit of data and to signify that MAC has no more data to output. The physical layer encodes and transmits each bit of data.

Each active station attached to the medium receives the transmitted bits. As each bit is received, the physical layer generates a PLS-DATA.indication with a parameter value of ONE or ZERO.

The remaining two primitives provide information needed by the local MAC entity to perform the medium access function. PLS-CARRIER.indication transfers the status of the activity on the physical medium. A parameter value of CARRIER-OFF indicates that the medium is idle, and a value of CARRIER-ON indicates that there is signal activity and that input is being received. This primitive is issued whenever the status changes.

The PLS-SIGNAL.indication primitive is issued with a parameter value of SIGNAL-ERROR when an improper signal or collision is first detected by the physical layer. A primitive with parameter value of NO-SIGNAL-ERROR is issued when the error condition is over.

It must be emphasized that the specification associated with Table 4.3 is an abstract description of services and does not imply any particular implementation. It does serve to illustrate that the MAC layer is substantially independent of the characteristics of the physical medium.

Table 4.3.   IEEE 802.3 PHYSICAL SIGNALING SERVICE PRIMITIVES AND PARAMETERS

PLS-DATA.request (OUTPUT-UNIT)
PLS-DATA.indication (INPUT-UNIT)
PLS-CARRIER.indication (CARRIER-STATUS)
PLS-SIGNAL.indication (SIGNAL-STATUS)

Physical Signaling and Attachment Unit Interface

The IEEE 802.3 standard anticipates that it may be desirable to locate stations at some distance from their actual attachment point to the medium. The typical configuration would place a minimum of electronics at the point at which the medium is tapped, and the bulk of the hardware and software at the station. That portion that is colocated with the tap is referred to in the standard as the medium attachment unit (MAU); in the Ethernet specification, it is referred to as the transceiver. The remainder of the logic required to perform the physical layer functions is in the station. The interface between station and MAU is referred to as the attachment unit interface (AUI). There are several advantages to this approach:

- The LAN can be installed with minimum path length and without worrying about the specific placement of equipment to be added later.
- The bulk of the IEEE 802.3 logic, which is colocated with the station, can be placed on one or more chips and integrated with the station to minimize cost.
- The MAU only contains those functions that must be performed at the medium. It is desirable to minimize the complexity of the MAU as, in many cases, the MAU may be located in an inaccessible location so that maintenance and repair are difficult and expensive.
- The AUI can be standardized, so that the station implementation is independent of the physical medium.

It is not necessary that the LAN be configured in such a way that there is a visible AUI. In fact, we will see that the 10BASE2 specification was developed primarily for products without this interface. In many cases, however, the AUI is desirable and is provided in IEEE 802.3-based products.

The specification assumes that the MAU performs the following functions:

- Transmit signals on the medium.
- Receive signals from the medium.
- Recognize the presence of a signal on the medium.
- Recognize a collision.

Physically, the attachment unit interface consists of four or five shielded twisted pairs:

- *Data Out:* Used for transmission of data from station to MAU.
- *Data In:* Used for transmission of data from MAU to station.

- *Control In:* Used for transmission of control signals from MUA to station.
- *Control Out (optional):* Used for transmission of control signals from station to MAU.
- *Voltage:* Used to supply power from the station to the MAU.

The shielded twisted pairs are bundled together in a single overall shield. A maximum length of 50 m is supported.

The standard specifies that Manchester signaling is to be used to transmit data signals across the interface. For the reader unfamiliar with this form of signal encoding, Appendix B describes Manchester signaling and summarizes its benefits. The data rate to be used across the interface is the same as that to be used on the medium. Hence, no buffering in the MAU is required.

The control-in circuit is used to carry one of three messages:

- *mau-available:* MAU is ready to output data. This is represented by an idle line (IDL).
- *mau-not available (optional):* MAU is not ready to output data. This is represented by a periodic square wave pattern of frequency equal to half the bit rate (CS1).
- *signal-quality-error:* Sent in response to one of three possible conditions, described below. This is represented by a periodic square wave pattern of frequency equal to the bit rate (CS0).

The signal-quality-error message is sent when the MAU detects: (1) an improper signal (the exact nature of the improper signal is medium dependent. Typically, this might be caused by a malfunctioning MAU somewhere on the LAN or by a break or short in the medium.); (2) a collision; or (3) at the completion of output, to confirm that the collision-signaling circuitry is functioning properly.

The control-out circuit also carries one of three signals:

- *normal:* Instructs the MAU to enter or remain in normal mode, that is, able to transmit and receive. Encoded as IDL.
- *mau-request:* Requests that the MAU should be made available; the station wishes to transmit data. Encoded as CSI.
- *isolate:* Instructs the MAU to enter or remain in monitor mode, which allows the station to perform local management functions. Encoded as CS0.

The reader should be able to see that the two data circuits, plus the two control circuits with their accompanying control signals, are sufficient to support the physical layer services defined earlier in this section.

10BASE5 Medium Specification

The 10BASE5 medium specification in the IEEE 802.3 is the original specification (the only one included in the original 1985 IEEE/ANSI standard), and is based on Ethernet [SHOC82]. Table 4.4 lists the key parameters of 10BASE5, as well as the other IEEE 802.3 medium specifications.

The medium employed is a 50-ohm coaxial cable. This a special-purpose coaxial cable that is usually used for baseband LANs in preference to the standard CATV 75-ohm cable. These values refer to the *characteristic impedance* of the cable. This parameter is sometimes referred to as the complex resistance of the cable. It defines the ratio of electromagnetic wave voltages to currents at every point along the conductor. Roughly speaking, impedance is a measure of how much voltage must be applied to the cable to achieve a given signal strength. It is also a criterion for the matching of the line; that is, if a cable is exactly terminated by a resistance equal to its characteristic impedance, or, if the line connected to it has the same characteristic impedance, then the oscillation (wave) arriving at the end of the first line is not reflected. For digital signals, the 50-ohm cable suffers less intense reflections from the insertion capacitance of the taps, and provides better immunity against low-frequency electromagnetic noise than the 75-ohm cable.

With any transmission system, there are engineering tradeoffs involving data rate, cable length, number of taps, and electrical characteristics of the medium and the transmit and receive components. For example, the lower the data rate, the longer the cable can be. This is true for the following reason: when a signal is propagated along a transmission medium, the integrity of the signal suffers due to attenuation, noise, and other impairments. The longer the propagation path, the greater the effect, increasing the probability of error. At a lower data rate, however, the individual pulses of a digital signal last longer and can be recovered in the presence of impairment more easily than higher-rate, shorter pulses.

10BASE5 specifies the 50-ohm coaxial cable and a data rate of 10 Mbps using digital signaling with Manchester encoding. With these parameters, the maximum length of the cable is set at 500 meters. Stations attach to the cable by means of a tap, with the distance between any two taps being a multiple of 2.5 meters; this spacing ensures that reflections from adjacent taps do not add in phase [YEN83]. A maximum of 100 taps is allowed.

The length of the network can be extended by the use of repeaters. In essence, a repeater consists of two MAUs joined together and connected to two different segments of coaxial cable. The repeater passes digital signals in both directions between the two segments, amplifying and regenerating the signals as they pass through. A repeater is transpar-

Table 4.4. IEEE 802.3 PHYSICAL LAYER ALTERNATIVES

Parameter	10BASE5	10BASE2	1BASE5	10BASET	10BROAD36
Transmission medium	Coaxial cable (50 ohm)	Coaxial cable (50 ohm)	Unshielded twisted pair	Unshielded twisted pair	Coaxial cable (75 ohm)
Signaling technique	Baseband (Manchester)	Baseband (Manchester)	Baseband (Manchester)	Baseband (Manchester)	Broadband (DPSK)
Data rate (Mbps)	10	10	1	10	10
Maximum segment length (m)	500	185	500	100	1800
Network span (m)	2500	925	2500	500	3600
Nodes per segment	100	30	—	—	—
Node spacing (m)	2.5	0.5	—	—	—
Cable diameter (mm)	10	5	0.4–0.6	0.4–0.6	—

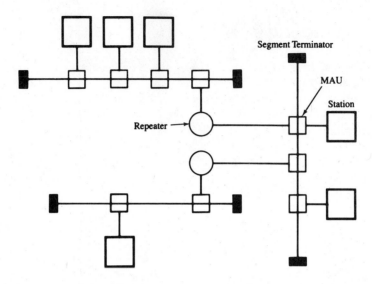

Figure 4.7. 10BASE5 configuration with three segments

ent to the rest of the system; as it does no buffering, it does not isolate one segment from another. So, for example, if two stations on different segments attempt to transmit at the same time, their transmissions will collide. To avoid multipath interference and looping, only one path of segments and repeaters is allowed between any two stations. The standard allows a maximum of four repeaters in the path between any two stations, extending the effective length of the cable to 2.5 kilometers. Figure 4.7 is an example of a network with three segments and two repeaters.

In a baseband system, a collision should produce substantially higher voltage swings than those produced by a single transmitter. Accordingly, the standard specifies that a transmitting MAU will detect a collision if the signal on the cable at the MAU exceeds the maximum that could be produced by the MAU alone. For a nontransmitting MAU, a collision is detected if the signal strength equals or exceeds that which could be produced by two MAU outputs. Because frames cross repeater boundaries, collision conditions must cross as well. Hence, if a repeater detects a collision on either cable, it must transmit a jamming signal on the other side.

10BASE2 Medium Specification

To provide a low-cost system for personal computer local networks, the first addition to the IEEE 802.3 standard was 10BASE2, which has been dubbed "Cheapernet" [METC83, FLAT84, JONE85]. Table 4.4 lists the parameters of this specification. As with 10BASE5, 10BASE2 uses 50-ohm coaxial cable and Manchester signaling at a data rate of 10 Mbps.

The determining difference between the two specifications is the use of a thinner cable in 10BASE2. This thinner cable, which is used in products such as public address systems, is more flexible; this makes it easier to bend around corners and bring to a workstation cabinet rather than installing the cable in the wall and having to provide a drop cable to the station. The cable is easier to install and the electronics may be contained within the station. On the other hand, the thinner cable suffers greater attenuation and lower noise resistance. Thus, it supports fewer taps over a shorter distance.

The cost saving in 10BASE2 comes about in two ways. First, the thinner cable is cheaper than the thicker cable. Second, because of the flexibility and ease of use of the cable, the cable physically comes to the station, connects to the MAU circuitry within the station, and goes to the next station (Fig. 4.8). This kind of connection, known as a "T" connector, allows all of the physical layer components to be integrated into the station, eliminating the AUI cables and interface logic. The segment is built up by a simple daisy-chaining of stations. However, the use of AUI cables and external MAUs is allowed.

The 10BASE2 specification employs the same collision detection scheme as 10BASE5. It also allows for extending the length of the network by using repeaters, with a limit of four repeaters in a path between any two stations. Because they have the same data rate, it is possible to mix 10BASE5 and 10BASE2 segments in the same network, by using a repeater that conforms to 10BASE5 on one side and 10BASE2 on the other side. The only restriction is that a 10BASE2 segment should not be used to bridge two 10BASE5 segments, because a "backbone" segment should be as resistant to noise as the segments it connects.

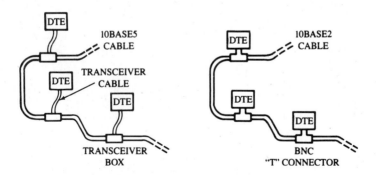

Figure 4.8. Comparison of 10BASE5 and 10BASE2

10BROAD36 Medium Specification

The next medium specification added to the IEEE 802.3 standard was 10BROAD36. This broadband specification makes use of the same AUI as the 10BASE5 specification [ABRA86, RUBY88]. This confers two benefits. First, it becomes relatively easy for users who already have a 10BASE5 system to change to a broadband network; only the MAUs and the cable need to be replaced. Second, the large base of products that conform to 10BASE5 means that the broadband system can immediately make use of low-cost components already developed.

The medium employed in 10BROAD36 is the standard 75-ohm CATV coaxial cable. Either dual-cable or split-cable configuration is allowed. The maximum length of an individual segment, emanating from the headend, is 1800 meters; this results in a maximum end-to-end span of 3600 meters (two 1800-meter segments emanating from the headend). To maintain AUI compatibility with 10BASE5, the data rate is 10 Mbps.

As with the 10BASE5 configuration, the MAU of the 10BROAD36 configuration performs the following functions:

- Transmit signals on the medium
- Receive signals from the medium
- Recognize the presence of a signal on the medium
- Recognize a collision

The transmission and the reception of signals involve several steps, as depicted in Figure 4.9. The station transmits data to the MAU across the AUI using Manchester-encoded digital signals. The MAU first converts this to a simple NRZ signal (see Appendix B for a discussion of Manchester and NRZ). Next the data is scrambled. This gives the data a pseudorandom nature that helps the receiver extract bit-timing information (see Appendix 4B). It also improves the spectral characteristics of the signal, giving it a more uniform power distribution, as opposed to the potentially strong discrete spectral lines in nonscrambled data. However, this scrambling process must take into account the IEEE 802.3 frame structure. Recall that a frame begins with a 56-bit preamble, which is an alternating string of 1s and 0s, and which is used by the receiver to detect and synchronize on the beginning of the frame. Clearly, it would not do to scramble this pattern. Therefore, the frame encoding rules are as follows:

- Up to 5 bits of the incoming (from the AUI) data stream may be dropped for detection and Manchester decoding purposes.
- Beginning with a zero, 20 bits of zero–one pattern shall be sent unscrambled to permit receiver synchronization and clock recovery.

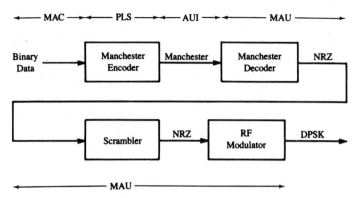

Figure 4.9.   10BROAD36 transmit functions

- The next two bits (zero–one) in the incoming pattern are set to zero. This is the unscrambled mode delimiter (UMD), which indicates the beginning of the scrambled part of the frame.
- All of the remaining bits in the preamble, the start-of-frame delimiter, and the other frame fields are scrambled.
- An unscrambled postamble consisting of a zero followed by 22 ones follows the end of the frame.

Finally, the scrambled data, which is still in digital form, is modulated onto an analog carrier using differential phase-shift keying (DPSK). In ordinary PSK, a binary zero is represented by a carrier with a particular phase, and a binary one is represented by a carrier with the opposite phase (180-degree difference). DPSK makes use of differential encoding, in which a change of phase occurs when a zero occurs, and there is no change of phase when a one occurs. The advantage of differential encoding is that it is easier for the receiver to detect the presence or absence of a change of phase than it is to determine the phase itself. Appendix B provides a further discussion.

The characteristics of the modulation process are specified so that the resulting 10 Mbps signal fits into a 14-MHz bandwidth. On reception, the incoming analog signal is taken through the reverse process of demodulation, descrambling, and Manchester encoding.

The collision detection function for 10BROAD36 differs significantly from that of the baseband media. With broadband, we can take advantage of the fact that there is a delay between a station's transmission and its reception of its own transmission. Three different events that can be detected by the MAU are used as indications of a collision:

- A transmitting MAU attempts to detect the UMD in the received signal. If a timer expires before detection of the UMD, a collision is assumed.

- After detection of the UMD, a transmitting MAU does a bit-by-bit comparison of the transmitted and received scrambled bits up through the last bit of the source address. A mismatch indicates a collision.
- If a MAU begins to receive a data transmission from its AUI while it is receiving a signal from the cable, a collision is detected.

At least one of the MAUs participating in a collision will detect it through one of the three indications listed previously. The station detecting the collision generates a constant-amplitude radio-frequency (RF) signal, known as the *collision enforcement signal,* on a dedicated band to notify all the MAUs on the network.

Collision enforcement is necessary because RF data signals from different MAUs on the broadband cable system may be received at different power levels. As an example of the problem, consider that MAUs *A* and *B* are transmitting and that *A*'s signals are received by both *A* and *B* at a significantly higher power level than *B*'s signals. At both modems, the frame from *A* is demodulated error free; the overlapping signal from *B* appears as a small amount of noise. *A* does not detect the collision, and therefore, assumes that its frame reached the destination. *B* detects the collision by means of the bit-by-bit comparison, and uses the collision enforcement signal to notify *A* (and all other MAUs).

Each 14-MHz data channel is provided with a dedicated 4-MHz collision enforcement channel. Thus, on a dual-cable system, each channel requires 18 MHz, and on a split-cable system, each channel requires 36 MHz. For split-cable systems, the highsplit system is recommended but not required. The midsplit system is allowed for compatibility with some existing systems.

1BASE5 Medium Specification

The 1BASE5 specification is intended to provide a very low cost system for personal-computer local networking. It provides a significantly lower data rate than the other IEEE 802.3 versions and a correspondingly lower cost. The network defined by the specification is referred to as "StarLAN" [GAND85, PARL85]. Table 4.4 lists the parameters of this specification. This is a baseband system and, as with the others, uses Manchester encoding. The data rate is only 1 Mbps, and the medium specified is unshielded twisted pair.

Single Hub. The intended configuration of 1BASE5 is a star-shaped topology. Figure 4.10 shows the simplest example. At the center of the star is the hub. Each station is connected to the hub by two twisted pairs (transmit and receive). The hub performs two major functions: signal regeneration/retiming (repeating) and collision detection/notification. When a single station transmits, the hub repeats the signal, compensating for

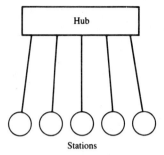

Figure 4.10. Single-hub 1BASE5

amplitude and phase distortion, and broadcasts it to all stations. When more than one station transmits, the hub will detect activity on more than one input and hence detect a collision. It then generates a collision presence (CP) signal, which it broadcasts instead of the originally transmitted signals. The hub continues to send as long as activity is sensed on any of the input lines.

Let us look at some of the details of this scheme. First, note that although the arrangement is physically a star, it is logically a bus: a transmission from any one station is received by all other stations, and if two stations transmit at the same time, there will be a collision. Thus the IEEE 802.3 MAC algorithm (CSMA/CD) will function properly.

The maximum station-to-hub distance is 250 meters. Thus the maximum station-to-station distance for two stations attached to the same hub is 500 meters. The standard does not specify a minimum or maximum number of stations to be connected to a given hub; this is an implementation and installation detail.

With a 250-meter radius, a star-topology LAN can be laid out with the hub in a wiring closet and individual stations scattered in various offices. This approach has a number of advantages:

1. It lends itself to prewiring of the building. The layout is a regular one and conforms to normal installation practice in office buildings. Furthermore, most existing buildings are prewired with excess unshielded twisted pair.
2. The system can be easily expanded simply by patching additional cables into the network at the wiring closet.
3. Servicing and maintenance are easier. Diagnosis of problems can be performed from centralized points. Faults can be isolated easily by patching cables out of the network.

Collision detection in the hub can be performed by simple digital logic, as all of the potential input signals are available at the same place. When a collision is detected, the hub broadcasts a collision presence signal. The signal is a repeating sequence of 1 bit-time LO, ½ bit-time HI, 1 bit-time LO, 1 bit-time HI, ½ bit-time LO, and 1 bit-time HI. Figure 4.11 shows two examples of this pattern, representing a shift of ½ bit time in the receiver's timing. The signal looks very much like a valid Manchester signal except for missing mid-bit transitions at periodic intervals. The station will detect this code violation and assume a collision.

Multiple Hubs.   Up to five levels of hubs can be cascaded in a hierarchical configuration. Figure 4.12 illustrates a two-level configuration. In a multiple-hub configuration, there is one header hub (HHUB) and one or more intermediated hubs (IHUB). Each hub may have a mixture of stations and other hubs attached to it from below. The maximum distance between adjacent hubs is 250 meters. Hence, the maximum span of the network (five levels) is 2500 meters. This topology again fits well with building wiring practices. Typically, there is a wiring closet on each floor of an office building, and a hub can be placed in each one. Each hub could service the stations on its floor.

Figure 4.13 shows an abstract representation of the intermediate and header hubs. The header hub performs all the functions described previously for a single-hub configuration. In addition, the header hub may receive a collision presence signal from one of its subordinate hubs (upstream). This signal is broadcast on all of its output (downstream) lines. An intermediate hub has an upstream and a downstream signal processing unit and is connected to each subordinate station or hub by one upstream and one downstream line. The upstream unit receives signals from subordinate stations and hubs and repeats these to its superior hub. If an intermediate node detects a collision among upstream inputs or if it re-

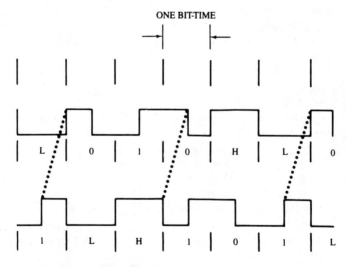

Figure 4.11.   Collision presence signal

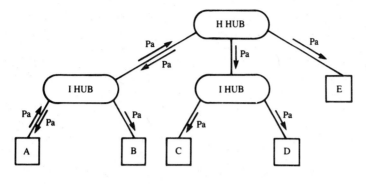

(a) *A* Transmitting

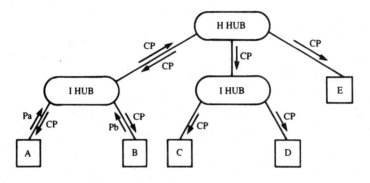

(b) *A* and *B* Transmitting

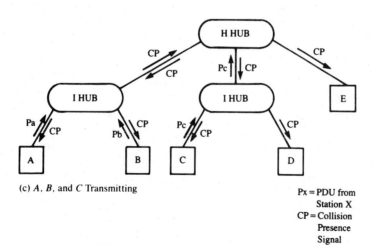

(c) *A*, *B*, and *C* Transmitting

Px = PDU from
    Station X
CP = Collision
    Presence
    Signal

(c) *A*, *B*, and *C* Transmitting

Figure 4.12.   Operation of two-level 1BASE5 configuration

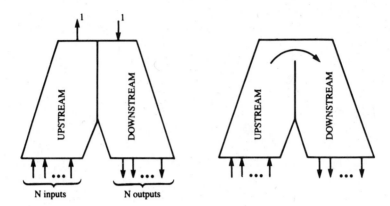

Figure 4.13. Intermediate and header hubs

ceives a collision presence signal from one of its subordinate hubs, it signals collision presence on its upstream output. The downstream unit is connected the other way. A data signal or collision presence signal from its superior hub is repeated on all its downstream lines.

Figure 4.12 shows several examples of the operation of a multiple-hub network. In the first example, a frame transmitted from station A propagates up to HHUB and is eventually received by all stations in the network. In the second example, a collision is detected by IHUB. The collision presence signal propagates up to A's HHUB and is rebroadcast down to all stations. The third example shows the result of a three-way collision.

10BASET Medium Specification

The attraction of the 1BASE5 specification is that it allows the use of inexpensive unshielded twisted pair wire, which is ordinary telephone wire. Such wire is often found prewired in office buildings as excess telephone cable, and can be used for LANs. Of course, the disadvantage of this specification is the rather low data rate of 1 Mbps. By sacrificing some distance, it is possible to develop a 10-Mbps LAN using the unshielded twisted pair medium. Such an approach is specified in the latest physical medium addition to the 802.3 family, the 10BASET specification [STIX88]. Table 4.4 lists the parameters of this specification.

As with the 1BASE5 specification, the 10BASET specification defines a star-shaped topology. The details of this topology differ slightly from those of 1BASE5. In both cases, a simple system consists of a number of stations connected to a central point. In both cases, stations are connected to the central point via two twisted pairs. The central point accepts input on any one line and repeats it on all of the other lines. In the case of the 10BASET specification, the central point is referred to as a multiport repeater.

Stations attach to the multiport repeater via a point-to-point link. Ordinarily, the link consists of two unshielded twisted pairs. The data rate is 10 Mbps using Manchester encoding. Because of the high data rate and the poor transmission qualities of unshielded twisted pair, the length of a link is limited to 100 meters. As an alternative, an optical fiber link may be used. In this case, the maximum length is 500 meters. The details of the fiber link are the same as those for the inter-repeater fiber link, discussed in a later section.

The distinction between a 1BASE5 hub and a 10BASET multiport repeater becomes clear when we consider a multi-star arrangement. Figure 4.14 shows a sample configuration for 10BASET. Note that the connection between one repeater and the next is a link that appears the same as an ordinary station link. In fact, the repeater makes no distinction between a station and another repeater. Recall that in the 1BASE5 system, there is a distinction between intermediate hubs and header hub, and that the handling of data signals and collision presence signals differs for the two types of hubs. In the 10BASET system, all multiport repeaters function in the same manner, and indeed function in the same manner as an ordinary repeater on a 10BASE5 or 10BASE2 system:

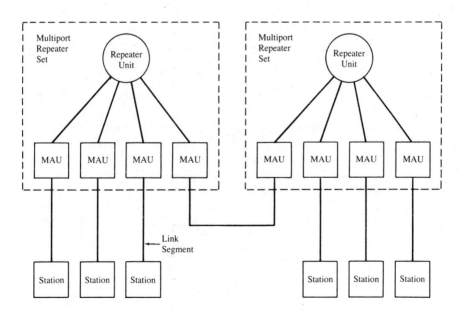

Figure 4.14.   Simple 10BASET configuration

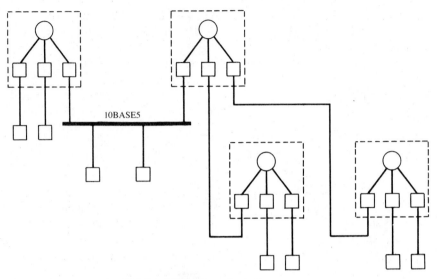

Figure 4.15. Mixed 10BASET, 10BASE5 configuration

- A valid signal appearing on any input is repeated on all other links.
- If two inputs occur, causing a collision, a collision enforcement signal is transmitted on all links.
- If a collision enforcement signal is detected on any input, it is repeated on all other links.

One advantage of the use of repeaters and the use of a data rate of 10 Mpbs is that the 10BASET system can mixed with 10BASE2 and 10BASE5 systems. All that is required is that the medium access unit (MAU) conform to the appropriate specification. Figure 4.15 shows a configuration that contains four 10BASET systems and one 10BASE5 system.

Table 4.5 summarizes the allowable connections. The maximum transmission path permitted between any two stations is five segments and four repeater sets. A segment is either a point-to-point link segment, or a coaxial cable 10BASE5 or 10BASE2 segment. The maximum number of coaxial cable segments in a path is three.

Table 4.5.   ALLOWABLE CONNECTIONS TO A 10BASET MULTIPORT REPEATER

Transmission Medium	Number of Attached Device	Maximum Length (meters)
Two unshielded twisted pair	2	100
Two optical fiber	2	500
Coaxial cable (10BASE2)	30	185
Coaxial cable (10BASE5)	100	500

Repeaters

In addition to specifying the various transmission media, the 802.3 physical layer standard includes specifications for repeaters. Two types of repeaters have now been specified:

- A single repeater that directly connects two cables
- Two repeaters connected by a point-to-point inter-repeater link

Both dual port and multiport repeaters have been specified. The latter are used in the 10BASET system. Figure 4.16 illustrates the two dual-port alternatives.

On one or both sides, depending on configuration, a repeater attaches to a 10BASE2 or 10BASE5 coaxial cable. This attachment is the same as with an ordinary station. That is, the repeater attachment obeys the 10BASE2 or 10BASE5 specification. Attachment may be through an attachment unit interface (AUI), consisting of two twisted pair, and a medium attachment unit (MAU). Alternatively, the MAU electronics may be integrated with the repeater unit.

The basic function of the repeater is to accept a frame transmitted on one cable and to repeat it, bit by bit, on the other cable. For a repeater that directly connects two cables via AUIs, the maximum delay, not including MAU delay, must be less than or equal to 8 bit times; at 10 Mbps,

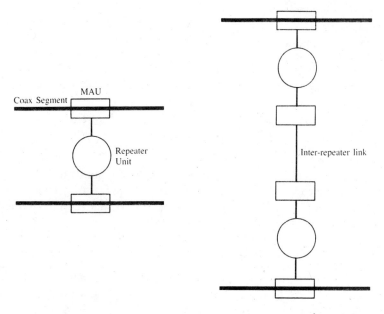

(a) Coax-to-coax repeater   (b) Two repeaters with inter-repeater link

Figure 4.16.   Repeater configurations

Table 4.6. IEEE 802.3 PARAMETERIZED VALUES

Parameters	Values
slotTime	512 bit times
interFrameGap	9.6 μsec at 10 Mbps; 96 μsec at 1 Mbps
attemptLimit	16
backoffLimit	10
jamSize	32 bits
macFrameSize	1518 octets
minFrameSize	512 bits (64 octets)

this works out to 0.8 μsec. For a repeater set with internal MAUs on both ports, the maximum delay must be less than or equal to 18 bit times. With an inter-repeater link configuration, the delays of two repeaters are allowed.

If a collision is detected on either of its ports, the repeater will transmit a brief jamming signal on the other port. The jamming signal can be any pattern, beginning with 62 bits of alternating ones and zeros.

So far, the only inter-repeater link that has been specified is a fiber optic link operating at 10 Mbps. The link consists of two optical fibers, one for transmission in each direction. The characteristics of the link are as follows:

- Maximum length: 1000 meters
- Center wavelength: 790 to 860 nanometers
- Optical modulation: on-off keying

For purposes of modulation, the Manchester signal from the cable is fed directly into the optical transmitter. A high voltage is transmitted as a pulse of light, a low voltage is transmitted as the absence of light.

MAC Compatibility Considerations

As part of the 802.3 MAC specification, certain parameters are defined that are to some extent medium-dependent. Thus they are, strictly speaking, part of the physical layer specification. Table 4.6 lists the parameters and the values that have been defined.

APPENDIX 4A. ETHERNET

The IEEE 802.3 MAC specification and 10BASE5 physical layer specification are based on Ethernet concepts. In this appendix, we examine the differences between the two specifications.

Ethernet is still perhaps the most widely known type of local network [SHOC82]. An experimental version of Ethernet was developed in the mid-1970s by Xerox Corporation [METC76, METC77]. The network used the CSMA/CD protocol on a 3-Mbps baseband coaxial cable. Xerox's announced purpose for this system was to develop a de facto industry standard for local networks. Xerox strengthened its hand by enlisting Digital Equipment Corporation and Intel to participate in the development of specifications and components. In 1980, Version 1.0 of the Ethernet specification was jointly published by the three participants [DIX80]; its principal difference from the experimental system was the use of a 10-Mbps data transfer rate. In 1982 a slightly revised specification, known as Version 2.0, was released [DIX82]. This later version incorporates changes and enhancements at the physical layer introduced during the elaboration of the IEEE 802.3 standard.

There are several differences among Ethernet 1.0, Ethernet 2.0, and IEEE 802.3 10BASE5 [MIER83]. The major differences are as follows:

- *Electrical functions:* Ethernet 2.0 and 802.3 include a "heartbeat" function. This is a signal sent from the MAU (Ethernet transceiver) to the station that confirms that the MAU collision signaling is working and connected to the station. In Section 4.4, this was referred to as the signal-quality-error signal. Without this signal, the station is unsure whether the frame was actually sent without a collision, or whether a defective MAU failed to report properly a collision. Eth-

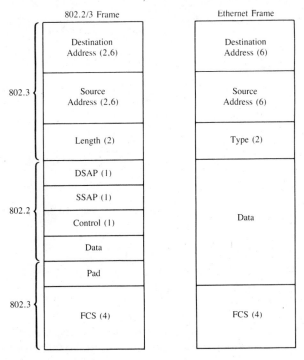

Figure 4.17. Comparison of 802.2/3 and Ethernet formats

ernet 1.0 does not have this function. In addition, both 802.3 and Ethernet 2.0 have a *jabber* function. This is a self-interrupt capability that allows a MAU to inhibit transmit data from reaching the medium if the transmission occurs for longer than the maximum frame size.

- *Frame format:* The Ethernet (both versions) format differs significantly from the IEEE 802.2/3 format. Figure 4.17 compares the two. Ethernet does not include a length field, and therefore, expects some higher layer to do the padding. The Ethernet type field is used to determine which client protocol the frame is for. This is a similar concept to the service access point (SAP). Ethernet provides what amounts to LLC type 1 operation, and therefore, does not need a control field.

APPENDIX 4B.   SCRAMBLING AND DESCRAMBLING

For some digital data encoding techniques, a long string of zeros or ones in a transmission can degrade system performance. For example, in the differential phase shift keying technique used in the 10BROAD36 standard, a phase shift occurs only when the input is a zero bit. If there is a long string of ones, it is difficult for the receiver to maintain synchronization with the transmitter. Also, other transmission properties are enhanced if the data are more nearly of a random nature rather than constant or repetitive [BELL82]. A technique commonly used with modems to improve signal quality is scrambling and descrambling. The scrambling process tends to make the data appear more random.

The scrambling process consists of a feedback shift register, and the matching descrambler consists of a feedforward shift register. An example is shown in Fig. 4.18. In this example, the scrambled data sequence may be expressed as follows:

$$B_m = A_m \oplus B_{m-3} \oplus B_{m-5}$$

where $\oplus$ indicates exclusive-or. The descrambled sequence is

$$C_m = B_{m-3} \oplus B_{m-5}$$
$$= (A_m \oplus B_{m-3} \oplus B_{m-5}) \oplus B_{m-3} \oplus B_{m-5} = A_m$$

As can be seen, the descrambled output is the original sequence.

We can represent this process with the use of polynomials. Thus, for this example, the polynomial is $P = 1 + x^{-3} + x^{-5}$. The input is divided by this polynomial to produce the scrambled sequence. At the receiver, the received scrambled signal is multiplied by the same polynomial to reproduce the original input. Figure 4.19 is an example using the polynomial P and an input of 101010100000111. The scrambled transmission, produced by dividing by P (100101) is 101110001101001. When this number is multiplied by P, we get the original input. Note that the

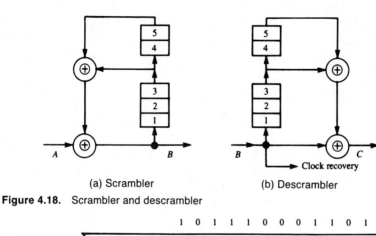

(a) Scrambler   (b) Descrambler

Figure 4.18.   Scrambler and descrambler

```
                              1 0 1 1 1 0 0 0 1 1 0 1 0 0 1 ◄B
P►1 0 0 1 0 1 ) 1 0 1 0 1 0 1 0 0 0 0 0 1 1 1 - - - - - -◄A
                1 0 0 1 0 1
                ─────────
                  1 1 1 1 1 0
                  1 0 0 1 0 1
                  ─────────
                    1 1 0 1 1 0
                    1 0 0 1 0 1
                    ─────────
                      1 0 0 1 1 0
                      1 0 0 1 0 1
                      ─────────
                        1 1 0 0 1 1
                        1 0 0 1 0 1
                        ─────────
                          1 0 1 1 0 1
                          1 0 0 1 0 1
                          ─────────
                            1 0 0 0 0 0
                            1 0 0 1 0 1
                            ─────────
                              1 0 1 0 0 0
```

(a) Scrambling

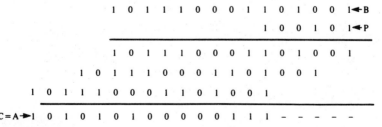

```
              1 0 1 1 1 0 0 0 1 1 0 1 0 0 1 ◄B
                                1 0 0 1 0 1 ◄P
              ─────────────────────────────
              1 0 1 1 1 0 0 0 1 1 0 1 0 0 1
            1 0 1 1 1 0 0 0 1 1 0 1 0 0 1
        1 0 1 1 1 0 0 0 1 1 0 1 0 0 1
      ─────────────────────────────────
C=A►1 0 1 0 1 0 1 0 0 0 0 0 1 1 1 - - - - - -
```

(b) Descrambling

Figure 4.19.   Example of scrambling and descrambling with $P(x) = 1 + x^{-3} + x^{-5}$

input sequence contains the periodic sequence 10101010 as well as a long string of zeros. The scrambler effectively removes both patterns.

For the 10BROAD36 specification, the following polynomial is used:

$$1 + x^{-1} + x^{-18} + x^{-19} + x^{-23} + x^{-24}$$

This polynomial is designed to give good performance over a wide range of potential input patterns.

A final note: the scrambler starts each transmission with a randomly generated seed to preclude the rare situation in which the pattern going through the scrambler might produce a long string of zeros.

5

IEEE 802.4 Token Bus

The IEEE 802.4 standard defines the token bus medium access control (MAC) protocol for bus topology. It also defines several physical layer transmission medium and data rate options, all of which make use of analog signaling. We begin with an overview of the scope of the 802.4 standard. This is followed by a look at the MAC protocol and service specifications, and finally a description of the various physical layer specifications.

5.1 SCOPE OF THE IEEE 802.4 STANDARD

As with IEEE 802.3, IEEE 802.5, and FDDI, the IEEE 802.4 standard encompasses both the MAC and the physical layer. Figure 5.1 depicts the architecture of the 802.4 standard in more detail. It is viewed as having five parts:

- MAC service specification
- MAC protocol
- Physical layer'service specification
- Physical layer entity specification
- Medium specification

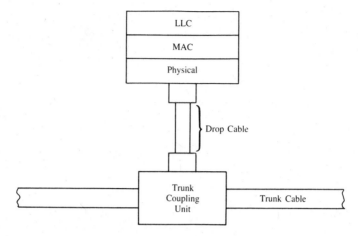

Figure 5.1. IEEE 802.4 architecture

The MAC service specification defines in functional terms the service provided by IEEE 802.4 to logical link control (LLC) or any other higher-level user. It includes facilities for transmitting and receiving higher-level data units, and provides per-operation status information for use by higher-layer error recovery procedures. Typically, the higher-level user will be LLC, but, because of the adherence of the 802 standards to the principle of layering, this is not strictly necessary. In any case, this service specification hides the details of the MAC and physical layers from the MAC user. In particular, the use of different transmission media is not visible to the user except as it affects performance.

The MAC protocol is the heart of the 802.4 standard, which is often referred to simply as the token bus standard. The specification defines the frame structure and the interactions that take place between MAC entities.

The physical service specification defines in functional terms the service provided by the physical layer to the token bus MAC layer. It is medium-independent.

The physical layer specification is divided into two parts for each medium alternative: a physical layer entity specification and a medium specification. Each physical layer entity specification includes the functional, electrical, and mechanical characteristics needed to transmit and receive signals over a particular medium. Corresponding to each physical layer entity specification is a physical medium specification. This specifies the characteristics of the transmission medium, the taps and other components on the medium, and the drop cables used to attach stations to the medium.

Unlike the case of IEEE 802.3, the IEEE 802.4 standard does not specify intended applications. However, the 802.4 standard is designed to be applicable not only in office environments, but also in factory and other industrial environments, and military environments.

5.2 MAC PROTOCOL

Token Bus

Token bus is a relatively new MAC technique, inspired by the token ring technique discussed in Chapter 6. For this technique, the stations on the medium form a logical ring; that is, the stations assume an ordered sequence, with the last member of the sequence followed by the first. Each station knows the identity of the stations preceding and following it. The physical ordering of the stations on the medium is irrelevant and independent of the logical ordering.

A control frame known as the *token* regulates the right of access. The token frame contains a destination address. The station receiving the token is granted control of the medium for up to some maximum time and may transmit one or more frames. The station must pass control of the medium when one of the following conditions occurs:

- The station has no data frames to send.
- The station sends all of the data frames that it has queued for transmission.
- The station's time expires.

When any of these conditions is met, the station passes the token to the next station in logical sequence. This receiving station now has permission to transmit. Hence steady-state operation consists of alternating data transfer and token transfer phases.

Figure 5.2 gives an example. At any given time, a certain number of stations are active on the network and may receive frames. Of these active stations, a subset (which may be all of the active stations) of stations is allowed to initiate transmission. This subset consists of all of the stations in the logical ring. The ordering within the logical ring is structured as follows. Each participating station knows the address of its predecessor (the station that transmitted the token to it), referred to as Previous Station (PS). It knows its successor (which station the token should be sent to next), referred to as Next Station (NS). And of course it knows its own address, referred to as This Station (TS). The predecessor and successor addresses are dynamically determined to maintain a single logical ring, in a manner described later in this section.

This scheme is significantly more complex than CSMA/CD. It re-

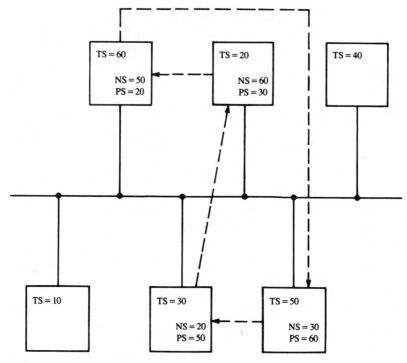

Figure 5.2. Token bus

quires considerable maintenance. The following functions, at a minimum, must be performed by one or more stations on the bus:

- *Ring initialization:* When the network is started up, or after the log-ical ring has broken down, it must be initialized. Some cooperative, decentralized algorithm is needed to sort out who goes first, who goes second, and so on.
- *Addition to ring:* Periodically, nonparticipating stations must be granted the opportunity to insert themselves in the ring.
- *Deletion from ring:* A station must be able to remove itself from the ring by splicing together its predecessor and successor.
- *Recovery:* A number of errors can occur. These include duplicate token (two stations think it is their turn) and lost token (no station thinks that it is its turn).
- *Priority:* The token bus scheme lends itself to the use of capacity allocation techniques.

The first three items listed can be grouped into the category of member-ship control. We examine this set of functions next. After that, we look at the techniques specified in the standard for fault control and priority control. A description of the MAC frame format completes our basic description of the 802.4 MAC specification. The section then concludes with a description of a mechanism known as immediate response.

Membership Control

Membership control comprises three functions: ring initialization, addition of a node to the logical ring, and deletion of a node from the logical ring. It is best to explain these in reverse order.

Node Deletion. If a station fails or shuts down, it is removed from the ring by the fault recovery mechanism, which is described later. Therefore, an active station can remove itself from the logical ring at any time by simply choosing not to respond to a token passed to it, allowing the fault recovery mechanism to patch it out.

There is a simpler (from the point of view of the network) and more efficient mechanism. To understand this, we need to know that the token frame contains not only a destination MAC address but also the source MAC address, and that when a station receives a token it automatically updates its PS variable. If a station wishes to drop out of the logical ring, it waits until it receives the token and then does the following:

1. Transmit any data frames up to the maximum time allowed.
2. Send a control frame, known as the set-successor frame (Table 5.1), to its predecessor (the station that transmitted the token to it) containing the address of its successor.
3. Send the token as usual to its successor.

Table 5.1. IEEE 802.4 CONTROL FRAMES

Claim-token	Used to create a new token if the old token is lost.
Solicit-successor-1	Used to invite stations to enter the ring. Invited stations are those whose addresses are between the token holder and its current successor.
Solicit-successor-2	Used to invite stations to enter the ring. Invited stations are those whose addresses are not between the current successor and the token holder.
Who-follows	Used to identify the successor of the successor of a station on the logical ring.
Resolve-contention	Used to resolve contentions among multiple stations based on address.
Token	Permission to transmit.
Set-successor	Requests a node to change the identity of its successor. Used to drop out of or enter the logical ring.

When a station receives a set-successor frame, it updates its NS variable accordingly. On the next token rotation, the former predecessor of the exited node sends the token to the former successor of the exited node, which updates its PS variable. Thus, the exited station is spliced out of the logical ring. For example, in Figure 5.2, station 50 can exit the ring by sending a set-successor frame to station 60 with an address of 30. The next time that station 60 gets the token, it will pass it on to station 30.

Node Addition.   Each station in the ring has the responsibility of periodically granting an opportunity to new stations to enter the ring, through a controlled contention process. To explain this process, we first need to note that the logical ring is created and maintained in such a way that the stations are logically arranged in numerically descending order of station address, except that the station with the lowest address passes the token to the station with the highest address in the logical ring (Figure 5.3). Now, consider that a station other than the one with the lowest address holds the token and attempts to add a station to the ring. To initiate this process, the token-holding station issues a *solicit-successor-1* frame that invites stations with an address between itself and the next station in logical sequence to request entrance. The token-holding station then waits

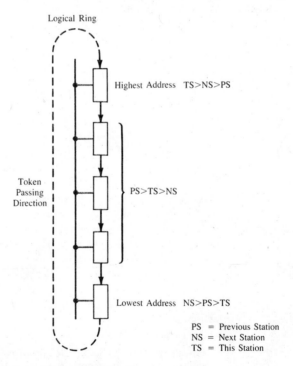

Figure 5.3.   Numerical relationship in IEEE 802.4 logical ring

for one *response window,* or slot time (equal to twice the end-to-end prop-agation delay of the medium plus the station delay). One of four events can occur (Figure 5.4).

1. *No response:* Nobody wants in. The token holder transfers the to-ken to its successor as usual.
2. *A set-successor frame:* The token holder hears a *set-successor* frame. The token holder sets its NS variable to the address of the requesting station and transmits the token to it. The node receiving the token sets its linkages (PS, NS) accordingly and proceeds.
3. *Garbled response:* The token holder will detect a garbled response (collision) if more than one node requests entrance. The conflict is resolved by an address-based contention scheme. The token holder transmits a *resolve-contention* frame and waits four response win-dows. Each contending station can respond with a set-successor frame that begins in one of these windows, based on the first two bits of its address (e.g., 00-stations respond immediately, 01-stations wait one response window, etc.). If a contending station hears any-thing before its window comes up, it refrains from transmitting. If the token holder receives a valid set-successor frame, it proceeds as in step 2. Otherwise, it tries again (by sending another resolve-con-tention frame), and only those stations that transmitted the first time are allowed to transmit this time, now based on the second pair of bits in their addresses. This process continues until a valid set-successor frame is received, no response is received, or the end of the address bits is reached. In the latter two cases, the token holder gives up and passes the token.
4. *Invalid response:* If the token holder hears a frame other than set-successor, it assumes that something has gone wrong in the proto-col. To avoid conflict, the station reverts to a listen state.

The other case to consider is that in which the station in the logical ring with the lowest address holds the token (e.g., station 20 in Figure 5.2) and attempts to add a station to the ring. In this case, the token-holding sta-tion sends a *solicit-successor-2* frame, and waits for the duration of two response windows. Stations with an address less than that of the token-holder may respond (with a set-successor frame) in the first response win-dow. If a station has an address greater than that of the token holder's successor and wishes to respond, it must wait one response window. If it hears nothing, it may then respond; otherwise, it may not respond to this invitation. In all other respects, the process proceeds as outlined in the four points previously mentioned.

One more detail needs to be explained: the timing that determines when each station in the ring invites other stations in the ring to enter. A station that holds the token and is ready to pass the token must determine

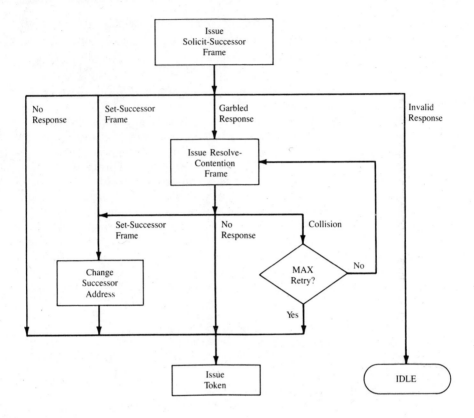

Figure 5.4. Addition of a node

whether to first perform the solicit-successor function. Two factors determine the decision.

1. When a station passes the token, it starts a ring-maintenance timer that continues to run until the station is ready to pass the token again. Thus, this timer measures one complete rotation of the token. When the station is again ready to pass the token, if the measured time exceeds a maximum set by station management, known as *target-rotation-time (ring maintenance)*, the station does not perform the solicit–successor function. This places an upper bound on the maximum token rotation time.

2. Another management-defined variable is *max-inter-solicit-count*, which is set in the range from 16 to 255. Normally, a station will perform the solicit–successor function before every Nth pass of the token, where N = max-inter-solicit-count. The function is not performed if the timer mentioned previously exceeds the threshold; that is, the function is not performed when the ring is heavily loaded.

Ring Initialization.   Logical *ring initialization* occurs when one or more stations detect a lack of bus activity of duration longer than a time-out value: the token has been lost. This can be due to a number of causes, such as the network has just been powered up, or a token-holding station fails. Once its time-out expires, a node will issue a *claim-token* frame. Contending claimants are resolved in a manner similar to the response-window process. Each claimant issues a claim-token frame padded by 0, 2, 4, or 6 slots based on the first two bits of its address. After transmission, a claimant listens to the medium and if it hears anything, drops its claim. Otherwise, it tries again, using the second pair of its address bits. The process repeats. With each iteration, only those stations who transmitted the longest on the previous iteration try again, using successive pairs of address bits. When all address bits have been used, a node that succeeds on the last iteration considers itself the token holder. The ring can now be rebuilt by the response window process described previously.

Fault Control

Fault control by the token holder covers a number of contingencies [PHIN83], listed in Table 5.2. First, while holding the token, a node may hear a frame indicating that another node has the token. If so, it immediately drops the token by reverting to the listener mode. In this way, the number of token holders drops immediately to 1 or 0, thus overcoming the multiple-token problem (which could be caused by two nodes having the same address). The next three conditions listed in the table are manifested during token passing. Upon completion of its turn, the token holder will issue a token frame to its successor. The successor should immediately issue a data or token frame. Therefore, after sending a token, the token issuer will listen for one slot time to make sure that its successor is active. This precipitates a sequence of events (Figure 5.5):

1. If the successor node is active, the token issuer will hear a valid frame and revert to listener mode.
2. If the token issuer hears a garbled transmission, it waits four time slots. If it hears a valid frame, it assumes that its token got through.

Table 5.2.   TOKEN BUS ERROR HANDLING

Condition	Action
Multiple token	Defer/drop to 1 or 0
Unaccepted token	Retry
Failed station	"Who follows" process
Failed receiver	Drop out of ring
No token	Initialize after time-out

If it hears nothing further, it assumes its token was garbled and reissues the token.

3. If the issuer does not hear a valid frame, it reissues the token to the same successor one more time.

4. After two failures, the issuer assumes that its successor has failed and issues a *who-follows* frame, asking for the identity of the node

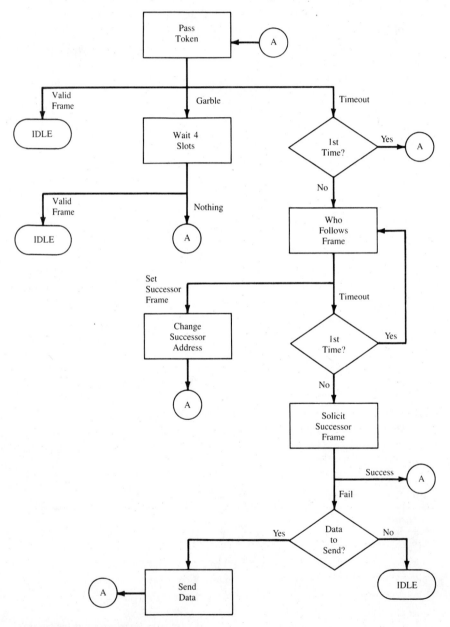

Figure 5.5.   Token passing

that follows the failed node. The issuer should get back a set-successor frame from the second node down the line. If so, the issuer adjusts its linkage and issues a token (back to step 1).

5. If the issuing node gets no response to its who-follows frame, it tries again.
6. If the who-follows tactic fails, the node issues a solicit–successor-2 frame with its address as destination and source address (every node is invited to respond). If this works, a two-node ring is established.
7. If the solicit–successor tactic fails, it assumes that some major fault has occurred; either all other stations have failed, all stations have left the logical ring, the medium has broken, or the station's own receiver has failed. At this point, if the station has any more data to send, it sends that data and tries passing the token again. If not, it drops the token, ceases transmission, and listens to the bus.

Priority Control

As an option, a token bus system can include *classes of service* that provide a mechanism of prioritizing access to the bus. Four classes of service are defined, in descending order: class 6, 4, 2, 0. Any station may have data in one or more of these classes to send. The object of the priority mechanism is to allocate network capacity to the higher priority frames and only send lower priority frames when there is sufficient capacity. To explain, let us define the following variables:

- THT = token holding time: the maximum time that a station can hold the token to transmit class 6 data.
- TRT4 = token rotation time for class 4: maximum time that a token can take to circulate and still permit class 4 transmission.
- TRT2 = token rotation time for class 2: as above.
- TRT0 = token rotation time for class 0: as above.

When a station receives the token, it can transmit classes of data according to the following rules (Figure 5.6):

1. It may always transmit class 6 data for a time THT. Hence for an n-station ring, during one circulation of the token, the maximum amount of time available for class 6 transmission is $n \times$ THT.
2. After transmitting any class 6 data, it may transmit class 4 data only if the amount of time for the last circulation of the token (including any class 6 data just sent) is less than TRT4, and then only for the time allowed by TRT4.
3. The station may next send class 2 data only if the amount of time for the last circulation of the token (including any class 6 and 4 data just sent) is less than TRT2, and then only for the amount of time allowed by TRT2.
4. The station may next send class 0 data only if the amount of time for the last circulation of the token (including any class 6, 4, and 2 data just sent) is less than TRT0, and then only for the amount of time allowed by TRT0.

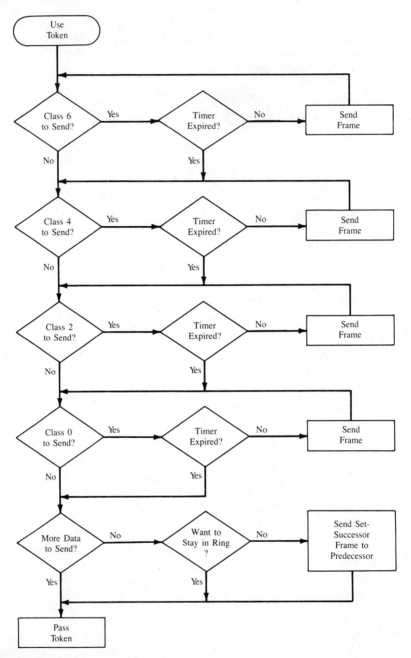

Figure 5.6. Token bus priority scheme

This scheme, within limits, gives preference to frames of higher priority. More definitively, it guarantees that class 6 data may have a certain portion of the bandwidth. Two cases are possible. If $n \times$ THT is greater than

MAX[TRT4, TRT2, TRT0], the maximum possible token circulation time is $n \times$ THT, and class 6 data may occupy the entire cycle to the exclusion of other classes. If $n \times$ THT is less than MAX[TRT4, TRT2, TRT0], the maximum circulation time is MAX[TRT4, TRT2, TRT0], and class 6 data are guaranteed $n \times$ THT amount of that time. This analysis ignores the time it takes to transmit the token and any other overhead, such as the reaction time at a station upon receipt of a token. However, these overhead quantities will generally be small compared to data transmission time.

Figure 5.7, which is adapted from one in [JAYA87], illustrates the average behavior of the 802.4 capacity-allocation scheme. That is, the plots ignore temporary load fluctuations, instead depicting the steady-state performance. For convenience, we assume that TRT4 > TRT2 > TRT0 and that the load generated in each class of data is the same.

Figure 5.7a depicts the first case ($n \times$ THT > TRT4). At very low loads, the token circulation time is very short, and all of the data offered in all four classes is transmitted. As the load increases, the average token circulation time reaches TRT0. There is then a range, as indicated in the figure, in which the load continues to increase but the token circulation time remains at TRT0. In this range, the other classes of data increase their throughput at the expense of Class 0 data, whose throughput declines. At some point, the load is such that the token circulation time equals TRT0, but the amount of transmission in Classes 2, 4, and 6 uses up all of that time and no Class 0 data can be transmitted. Further increase in offered load results in renewed increase in the token circulation time. The same pattern repeats for Class 2 and Class 4 data. There is a period when the load increases at a constant token circulation time of TRT2, and during that period, Class 2 data is gradually crowded out. Class 4 data is similarly crowded out at a higher level of load. Finally, a situation is reached in which only Class 6 data is being transmitted, and the token circulation time stabilizes at $n \times$ THT.

For the second case just mentioned ($n \times$ THT < TRT4), we need to examine two subcases. Figure 5.7b shows the case in which $\frac{TRT4}{2} <$ ($n \times$ THT) < TRT4. As before, with increasing load, Class 0 and Class 2 traffic are eliminated and the token circulation time increases. At some point, the increasing load drives the token circulation time to TRT4. Using our simple example, when this point is reached, approximately half of the load is Class 4 data and the other half is Class 6. But, since $n \times$ THT $> \frac{TRT4}{2}$, if the load on the network continues to increase, the portion of the load that is Class 6 traffic will also increase. This will cause a corresponding decrease in Class 4 traffic. Eventually, a point is reached at

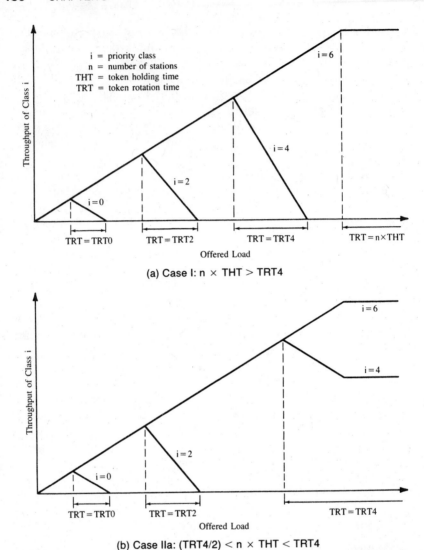

(a) Case I: $n \times$ THT $>$ TRT4

(b) Case IIa: (TRT4/2) $<$ n $\times$ THT $<$ TRT4

Figure 5.7.   Throughput of token bus priority classes

which all of the allowable Class 6 traffic is being handled during each token circulation. This will take an amount of time $n \times$ THT and still leave some time left over for Class 4 data. Thereafter, the total token circulation time remains stable at TRT4.

Finally, Figure 5.7c shows the case in which $n \times$ THT $< \dfrac{\text{TRT4}}{2}$. As before, increasing load eliminates Class 0 and Class 2 traffic. A point is reached at which the token circulation time is $2 \times n \times$ THT, with half of

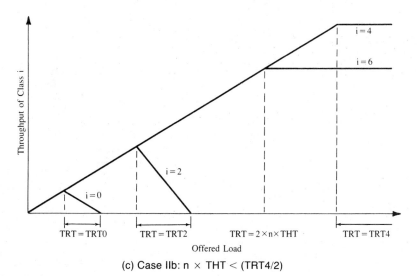

(c) Case IIb: n × THT < (TRT4/2)

Figure 5.7. *Continued*

	TS = 9 THT = 610	TS = 7 TRT = 1600	TS = 5 TRT = 1600	TS = 1 THT = 610
Token Rot.	**TRTC:XMIT**	**TRTC:XMIT**	**TRTC:XMIT**	**TRTC:XMIT**
1	76 3	460 3	1660 0	1660 2
2	2270 3	2270 0	1070 2	1782 2
3	1782 3	1782 0	1782 0	1070 2
4	1070 3	1070 2	1870 0	1870 2
5	1870 3	1870 0	1070 2	1782 2
6	1782 3	1782 0	1782 0	1070 2
7	1070 3	1070 2	1870 0	1870 2
8	1870 3	1870 0	1070 2	1782 1
9	1477 3	1477 1	1877 1	1165 1
10	1165 3	1165 2	1565 1	1921 1
11	1921 3	1921 0	1121 2	1477 1
12	1477 3	1477 1	1877 0	1165 1

Figure 5.8. Operation of a multiclass token bus protocol

the traffic being Class 4 and half being Class 6. This is a maximum throughput-per-token-circulation for Class 6. However, the amount of Class 4 data can continue to increase until the token circulation time is TRT4.

Figure 5.8 is a simplified example of a 4-station logical ring with THT = 610 and TRT4 = TRT2 = TRT0 = 1600. Time is measured in *octet times*. Station 9 always transmits three Class 6 frames of 128 octets each. Stations 7 and 5 send as many lower priority frames as possible, of lengths 400 and 356 octets, respectively. Station 1 transmits Class 6 frames of 305 octets each. Initially, Station 1 has two frames to transmit each time it gets the token, and later has only one frame to send per token possession. We assume that the time to pass the token is 19 octet times. In the figure, there are two columns of numbers under each station. The value in the left-hand column is the token circulation time observed at that station for the previous rotation of the token. The right-hand value is the number of frames that station transmits. Each row represents one rotation of the token.

The example begins after a period during which no data frames have been sent, so that the token has been rotating as rapidly as possible; thus each station measures a token circulation time of 76. In the first rotation, station 9 transmits all of its class 6 frames. When station 7 receives the token, it measures a rotation time of 460 since it last received the token ($3*128 + 4*19$). Thus it is able to send 3 of its frames before its TRT is exhausted. Station 5 measures a rotation time of 1660 ($3*400 + 3*128 + 4*19$) and thus is prevented from sending any data. Finally, station 1 sends 2 class 6 frames.

Note that rotations 5 through 7 repeat rotations 2 through 4, showing a stable bandwidth allocation: Stations 1 and 9 use 69 percent of the bandwidth for class 6 data and stations 5 and 7 share equally the remaining bandwidth for lower-priority data. Starting on the eighth rotation, station 1 reduces its use of the LAN. This reduces the bandwidth used for class 6 data to 52 percent, and lower priority data is allowed to fill in the unused bandwidth.

MAC Frame

Figure 5.9 depicts the format of the IEEE 802.4 frame. It consists of the following fields:

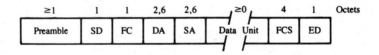

SD = Start Delimiter
FC = Frame Control
DA = Destination Address
SA = Source Address
FCS = Frame Check Sequence
ED = End Delimiter

Figure 5.9. General IEEE 802.4 frame format

- *Preamble:* A one or more octet pattern used by receivers to establish bit synchronization.
- *Start Delimiter (SD):* Indicates the start of frame. The SD consists of signaling patterns that are always distinguishable from data. It is coded as follows: NN0NN000, where N is a nondata symbol. The actual form of a nondata symbol depends on the signal encoding on the medium.
- *Frame Control (FC):* Indicates whether this frame contains LLC data or is a control frame. In the latter case, bits in this field control operation of the token bus MAC protocol. Figure 5.10 shows the specific formats.
- *Destination Address (DA):* Specifies the station(s) for which the frame is intended. It may be a unique physical address (one station), a multicast-group address (a group of stations), or a global address (all stations on the local network). The choice of a 16- or 48-bit address is an implementation decision, and must be the same for all stations on a particular LAN.
- *Source Address (SA):* Specifies the station that sent the frame. The SA length must equal the DA length.
- *Data Unit:* Contains LLC data or information related to a control operation.
- *Frame Check Sequence (FCS):* A 32-bit cyclic redundancy check (see Appendix C) based on all fields except preamble, SD, ED, and FCS.
- *End Delimiter (ED):* Indicates end of frame. It has the pattern NN1NN1IE. I is the intermediate bit; if set to one, it indicates that this is the last frame transmitted by the station. E is the error bit; this may be set to one by a repeater that detects an FCS error.

The address field formats are shown in Figure 2.10. The standard also recommends an optional address structure for locally administered addresses (Figure 5.11). A segment is used to identify multiple logical segments, with intermediate relay nodes interconnecting segments (e.g., multiple channels on a broadband cable). The stations of a single logical segment share a single token and form a single logical ring. Stations with different segment addresses can communicate only through the relay devices. The region address could be used to define multiple independent networks connected at a higher level.

Request-with-Response Mechanism

An additional facility, known as the request-with-response mechanism, is defined as an option in the standard. In the initial 1985 standard, this facility was designated for Trial Use, indicating that it had not received widespread review. This designation was subsequently dropped, and it is now simply listed as an option.

This mechanism is, in essence, an acknowledged connectionless mechanism, and works as follows. When a station has the token, it may

| Preamble | SD | 00000000 | DA | SA | arbitrary value, length = (0, 2, 4, 6) *slot-time octets | FCS | ED |

(a) Claim-token. The frame has a data-unit whose value is arbitrary and whose length in octets (between addresses and FCS exclusive) is 0, 2, 4, or 6 times the system's slot-time also measured in octets.

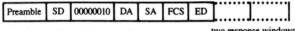

one response window

(b) Solicit-successor-1. The frame has a DA = the value of the station's NS and a null data unit. One response window always follows this frame.

two response windows

(c) Solicit-successor-2. The frame has DA = the value of the station's NS or TS and a null data unit. Two response windows always follow this frame.

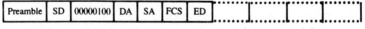

three response windows

(d) Who-follows. The frame has a data-unit = the value of the station's NS. The format and length of the data-unit is the same as a source address. Three response windows always follow this frame. (This gives receivers two extra slot-times to make a comparison with an address other than TS.)

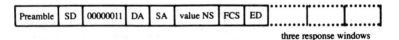

four response windows

(e) Resolve-contention. The frame has a null data-unit. Four response windows always follow this frame.

| Preamble | SD | 00000100 | DA | SA | FCS | ED |

(f) Token. The frame has DA = the value of the station's NS and has a null data-unit.

Figure 5.10. Specific IEEE 802.4 frame formats

Preamble	SD	00001100	DA	SA	new value of NS	FCS	ED

(g) Set-Successor. The frame has DA = the SA of the last frame received, and data-unit = the value of the station's NS or TS. The format and length of the data-unit is the same as that of a source address.

Preamble	SD	01MMMPPP	DA	SA	LLC-data-unit	FCS	ED

(h) LLC Data Frame Format. LLC data frames have a DA and data-unit specified by a station's LLC sublayer. A frame of this type with a nonnull data unit shall be passed to the receiving station's LLC sublayer.

Figure 5.10. *Continued*

temporarily delegate its right to transmit to another station by sending a *request-with-response data frame* instead of a normal data frame. A station hearing such a frame addressed to itself copies the data and responds with a *response data frame*. The response data frame causes the right to transmit to revert back to the station that sent the request-with-response data frame.

The station that responds is not required to be a member of the logical ring. If a valid response is not forthcoming, the station that requests the response will try a number of times, up to some predefined maximum, to elicit the response.

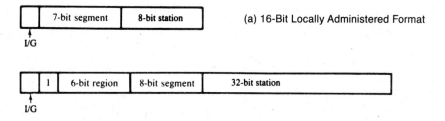

(a) 16-Bit Locally Administered Format

(b) 48-Bit Locally Administered Format

Figure 5.11.   IEEE 802.4 address field formats

5.3 MAC SERVICES

The services provided by the MAC layer allow the local LLC entity to exchange LLC data units with peer LLC entities. Table 5.3 lists the primitives and parameters that define the IEEE 802.3 MAC service, and Figure 5.12 shows the interaction.

Table 5.3.   TOKEN BUS MAC SERVICE PRIMITIVES AND PARAMETERS

MA-UNITDATA.request (destination-address, m-sdu, desired-quality)

MA-UNITDATA.indication (destination-address, source-address, m-sdu, quality)

MA-UNITDATA.STATUS.indication (destination-address, source-address, status, provided-quality)

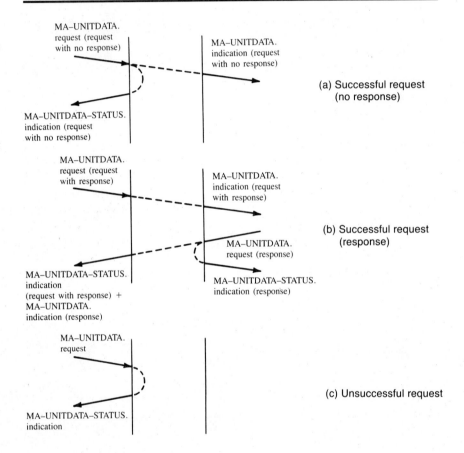

Figure 5.12.   IEEE 802.4 MAC service timing

The IEEE 802.4 service specification is a close but not exact match to that expected in the LLC standard (Section 3.1). It is probable that the minor discrepancies will be resolved in a later version of the standard. Because it is IEEE 802.4 and not IEEE 802.2 that defines the functions of the MAC layer, the service specification in the 802.4 document should take precedence. The comments in Section 3.1 concerning the meaning and the timing of the MAC service primitives apply here. Only the differences are noted in this section.

In the MA-UNITDATA.request primitive, the desired-quality parameter has two components. The first component specifies the requested priority. The second component takes on one of three values:

- *request-with-no-response:* The MAC layer is simply requested to transmit the data specified in m-sdu. The MAC service delivers the data in a MA-UNITDATA.indication with the same value in the quality parameter (Figure 5.12a).
- *request-with-response:* This requests that the remote MAC user respond to this transmission. The MAC service delivers the data in a MA-UNITDATA.indication with the same value in the quality parameter (Figure 5.12b).
- *response:* This action responds to an immediately prior MA-UNIT-DATA.indication that had a quality parameter of request-with-response. The MAC service delivers the data in a MA-UNIT-DATA.indication with the same value in the quality parameter (Figure 5.12b).

In MA-UNITDATA-STATUS.indication, the provided-quality parameter specifies the quality of service actually provided for the previous request. As before, the parameter has two components: priority and delivery confirmation service. The status parameter indicates the status of the service provided for a previous associated MA-UNITDATA.request. A failure indication is passed upon local failure. When the quality parameter of that request specifies request-with response, a failure indication is also passed if the allowed number or retries has occurred with no response. A success indication is passed when, to the best of the local MAC entity's knowledge, the request has been completed successfully. This would seem to imply the following: when the quality parameter of the corresponding request specifies request-with-no-response or response, the MA-UNITDATA-STATUS.indication is passed immediately after the transmission of the corresponding frame. When the quality parameter of that request specifies request-with response, then the MA-UNITDATA-STATUS.indication is passed when the requested response frame is received.

5.4 PHYSICAL LAYER SPECIFICATIONS

This section looks at the physical layer specification for the IEEE 802.4 standard. The current standard contains a single medium-independent physical layer service specification, and four medium-dependent physical layer specifications.

Physical Layer Services

As always, the services provided by the physical layer are defined in terms of primitives and parameters, and these are shown in Table 5.4.

The PHY-UNITDATA primitives support the transfer of data from a single MAC entity to all other MAC entities contained within the same

**Table 5.4. IEEE 802.4 PHYSICAL LAYER SERVICE PRIMITIVES AND
PARAMETERS**

PHY-UNITDATA.request (symbol)

PHY-UNITDATA.indication (symbol)

PHY-MODE.invoke (mode)

PHY-NOTIFY.invoke

local network defined by the medium. That is, data transmitted by one MAC entity using PHY-UNITDATA.request is received by all other MAC entities with a PHY-UNITDATA.indication. The symbol parameter can take on a value of binary one or zero, or a nondata symbol. The physical layer encodes and transmits each bit of data. Each active station attached to the medium receives the transmitted bits. As each bit is received, the physical layer generates a PHY-UNITDATA.indication.

The PHY-MODE primitive is used to cause the physical layer to select one of two modes of operation: originating or repeating. This primitive is useful in a station that is attached to more than one network segment. In repeating mode, an entity is attached to two or more segments, picking up transmissions from one segment and repeating them on other segments. If the station is to function as both an independent station and as a repeater, then the originating mode is entered to allow transmission from the attached station.

The PHY-NOTIFY primitive is used by the MAC entity to notify the physical layer entity that an end-of-frame delimiter has just been detected in the incoming data stream. The effect of this primitive is implementation dependent. It alerts the physical layer entity that the incoming transmission should have ceased.

It must be emphasized that the specification associated with Table 5.4 is an abstract description of services and does not imply any particular implementation. It does serve to illustrate that the MAC layer is substantially independent of the characteristics of the physical medium.

Phase-Continuous Carrierband

The IEEE 802.4 standard specifies four alternative physical media, whose characteristics are listed in Table 5.5. Two of these alternatives are known as carrierband, or single-channel broadband, systems. In a carrierband network, the entire spectrum of the cable is devoted to a single transmission path for analog signals. In general, a carrierband LAN has the following characteristics [KLEI86, RELC87]. Bidirectional transmission, using a bus topology, is employed. Hence, there can be no amplifiers, and there is no need for a headend. Some form of frequency-shift keying (FSK) is used, generally at a low frequency (a few MHz). This is an advantage as attenuation is less at lower frequencies.

Table 5.5. IEEE 802.4 PHYSICAL LAYER MEDIUM ALTERNATIVES

Parameter	Phase Continuous Carrierband	Phase Coherent Carrierband		Broadband			Optical Fiber		
Data rate (Mbps)	1	5	10	1	5	10	5	10	20
Bandwidth	N/A	N/A	N/A	1.5 MHz	6 MHz	12 MHz	270 nm	270 nm	270 nm
Center frequency	5 MHz	7.5 MHz	15 MHz	*	*	*	800–910 nm	800–910 nm	800–910 nm
Modulation	Manchester/ Phase continuous FSK	Phase coherent FSK		Multilevel duobinary AM/PSK			Manchester/on-off		
Topology	Omnidirectional bus	Omnidirectional bus		Directional bus (tree)			active or passive star		
Transmission Medium	Coaxial cable (75 ohm)	Coaxial cable (75 ohm)		Coaxial cable (75 ohm)			Optical fiber		
Scrambling?	No	No		Yes			No		

* = depends on channel
N/A = not applicable

Because carrierband is dedicated to a single data channel, it is not necessary to take care that the modem output be confined to a narrow bandwidth. Energy can spread over the cable's spectrum. As a result, the electronics are simple and inexpensive compared with those for broadband. This scheme would appear to give comparable performance, at a comparable price, to baseband. In this subsection, we look at the first of the two carrierband schemes incorporated into the 802.4 standard.

The lowest-cost alternative provided in the standard is the 1-Mbps phase-continuous FSK system. The distinguishing characteristic of this system is the use of phase-continuous FSK modulation. This is a particular form of FSK (see Appendix B for a discussion of FSK) in which the transition between signaling frequencies is accomplished by a continuous change of frequency, as opposed to the discontinuous replacement of one frequency by another, such as might be accomplished by a switch. This implementation of FSK results in a tighter bandwidth (more concentrated signal energy) and improved transmission and reception efficiency [OETT79].

The encoding that is used with this scheme is as follows. Two frequencies are defined, H = 6.25 MHz and L = 3.75 MHz. The signal on the line can be viewed as a carrier of 5 MHz that varies continuously between the two frequencies of H and L. Each zero bit is encoded as H L and each one bit as L H. Because the data rate is only 1 Mbps, there will be multiple periods of each signal in one bit time. Nondata symbols are always transmitted in pairs (see discussion of MAC frame) and are of the form L L H H. Note that the encoding of 0s and 1s effectively follows the Manchester encoding rules, translated into the analog realm.

This specification is intended to provide a low-cost, low-speed LAN that can be installed with flexible and/or semirigid coaxial cable. The system can use a variety of older cables already installed in buildings. The standard calls for the use of a single unbranched cable with very short (< 350 mm) drop cables. Nondirectional tee-connector taps are used so that a signal inserted onto the bus propagates in both directions. Table 5.6 shows typical maximum network lengths achieved with several commercially available cables. The number of taps is assumed to be between 2 and 30. To achieve longer distances and to support more taps, repeaters

Table 5.6. RECOMMENDED MAXIMUM CABLE LENGTHS FOR PHASE-CONTINUOUS CARRIERBAND

Cable Type	Outside Diameter (in)	Distance (km)
RG-59	0.242	1.28
RG-6	0.332	1.6
RG-11 (foam)	0.405	2.9
JT4412J	0.412	4.6
JT4750J	0.75	7.6

are used, as in IEEE 802.3 10BASE5 and 10BASE2. Once a system is installed, it is intended that future changes will be limited to adding extensions to the end of the cable, but not significantly increasing the size of the network.

Phase-Coherent FSK

The other carrierband technique standardized by 802.4 is phase-coherent FSK, at data rates of 5 and 10 Mbps. The phase-coherent modulation technique is a form of FSK in which the two signaling frequencies are integrally related to the data rate. This scheme is called phase-coherent because the zero crossing points are in phase at the beginning and end of each bit time. Proponents of this form of modulation, as opposed to phase-continuous, contend that it is preferable because a phase-coherent scheme is easier to implement digitally, and can thus provide a low-cost, single-chip solution [KLEI86].

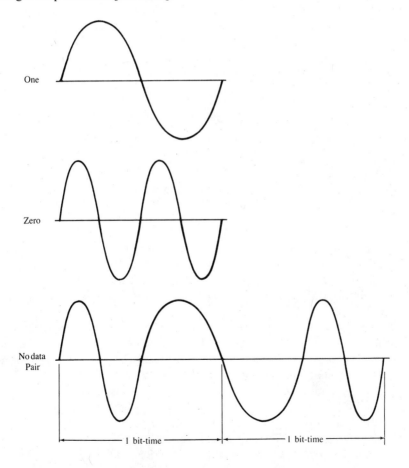

Figure 5.13. Phase-coherent encoding

The encoding that is used with this scheme is as follows. Again, two frequencies are defined: one with a frequency equal to twice the data rate, and one with a frequency equal to the data rate. Thus, for the 5-Mbps specification, the higher frequency is 10 MHz and the lower frequency is 5 MHz, and for the 10-Mbps specification, the higher frequency is 20 MHz and the lower frequency is 10 MHz. A data one is represented by a full cycle of the lower signaling frequency in one bit time, and a data zero by two cycles of the higher signaling frequency. A pair of nondata symbols is represented by one full cycle of the higher frequency, followed by one full cycle of the lower frequency, followed again by one full cycle of the higher frequency (Figure 5.13).

The phase-coherent specification is potentially more expensive and has a higher data rate than the phase-continuous specification, but is less expensive than a full-blown broadband system. When implemented with semirigid coaxial cable, this system may be converted to broadband by making relatively simple hardware changes. The principal application for phase-coherent carrierband is intended to be a factory environment in which the immense capacity of a full broadband is not needed, or at least is not needed immediately. To that end, there have been some minor changes [ALLA86, DOUG86], relating to signal level and noise tolerance, made to the standard to accommodate requirements put forth for the Manufacturing Automation Protocol (MAP). MAP is discussed in Appendix 5B.

Broadband

The third medium specification is for a full broadband system. These data rates are specified: 1, 5, and 10 Mbps, with bandwidths of 1.5, 6, and 12 MHz, respectively. The standard recommends the use of a single-cable mid-split system with a headend frequency translator. Other configurations, including dual cable, are permitted.

The frequency allocation is based on conventional North American channel definitions, as shown in Table 5.7. The recommended allocations are indicated in the table. For a 10-Mbps data rate, two channels are needed. For a 1-Mbps data rate, a 1.5-MHz subchannel is chosen within one of the recommended channels.

The modulation scheme used for the broadband specification is known as duobinary AM/PSK modulation [RATN83, DOUG86]. In this scheme, data is precoded and signaled as pulses in which both the amplitude and the phase may vary. The nature of the precoding is such that receivers can demodulate the modulated signal without having to recover the phase of the signal. In essence, the PSK component of the modulation is used to reduce the signal bandwidth, not to carry data.

In duobinary AM/PSK, a special narrow-bandwidth pulse is created that is used to amplitude-modulate an RF carrier. Such pulse is illustrated in Figure 5.14 for a 10-Mbps data rate; the pulse of opposite polarity is

**Table 5.7. USUAL NORTH AMERICAN 6 MHz MIDSPLIT CHANNELS—
NOMENCLATURE AND PAIRING**

Reverse channel	Frequency (MHz)		Forward channel	Frequency (MHz)
T10	23.75		J	216
T11	29.75		K	222
T12	35.75		L	228
T13	41.75		M	234
T14	47.75		N	240
2'	53.75		O	246
3'	59.75	*	P	252
4'	65.75	*	Q	258
4A'	71.75	*	R	264
5'	77.75	*	S	270
6'	83.75	*	T	276
FM1'	89.75	*	U	282
FM2'	95.75		V	288
FM3'	101.75		W	294

*These channel pairings are recommended for use with this standard.
'The primed reverse-direction channels are offset from the conventional forward-direction channels of the same (un-primed) name.

also used. Note that the pulse spreads over a number of bit times. Thus, pulses that are generated in nearby bit slots will overlap. However, the overlap is highly predictable: At each sample point, a pulse has a value of 0 or 1. Thus, at any sample point, a 0, 1, or 2 can be detected. To encode digital data, two pulses, one bit time apart are used. A binary one is represented by two consecutive pulses of the same polarity, which will produce a sample of $+2$ or -2, and a binary zero is represented by two consecutive pulses of opposite polarity, which produces a sample of 0. Each pulse participates in two bits; that is, each pulse is both the second pulse of one bit and the first pulse of the next bit.

As a refinement of duobinary AM/PSK, a third nondata symbol is added in the following manner. A pulse is normally sent every bit time. Depending on its polarity, it either doubles or cancels the second nonzero sampling level of the prior transmitted data pulse. It also leaves a second nonzero sampling level of its own that will work in concert with the next pulse. However, when one pulse is omitted, the line value at the sampling instant is $+1$ or -1, rather than the expected values of $+2$, -2, or 0. In addition, the leading edge of the pulse following the omitted pulse is also of unity amplitude. Normal levels are restored when one more pulse is sent. Thus adjacent pair of nondata bits are synthesized by omitting one pulse. The pulse follow-

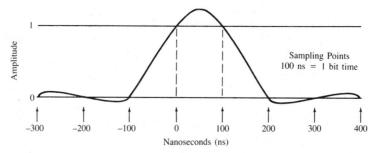

Figure 5.14.   Input pulse for duobinary AM/PSK at 10 Mbps

ing the omission can be of either polarity, but carries no information, as there is no previous data pulse with which it can work in concert.

As with the 802.3 10BROAD36 specification, the 802.4 broadband specification includes the use of scrambling. The polynomial used for 802.4 is $1 + x^{-6} + x^{-7}$. See Appendix 4B for a discussion of scrambling.

Optical Fiber

The most recent addition to the IEEE 802.4 physical layer standard is an optical fiber specification. Three data rates are specified: 5, 10, and 20 Mbps. In keeping with standard practice for optical fiber systems, the bandwidth and carrier are specified in terms of wavelength instead of frequency. For all three data rates, the bandwidth is 270 nm and the center wavelength is between 800 and 910 nm.

Data Encoding.   As discussed in Appendix B, digital data need to be encoded in some form for transmission as a signal. The type of encoding will depend on the nature of the transmission medium, the data rate, and other constraints, such as cost. Optical fiber is inherently an analog medium; signals can only be transmitted in the optical frequency range. Thus, as with carrierband and broadband, some sort of digital-to-analog encoding techniques must be used. We saw that the two carrierband systems use variants of frequency-shift keying (FSK), and that both the 802.3 and 802.4 broadband systems are based on variants of phase-shift keying (PSK). However, both PSK and FSK are difficult to do well at high data rates and optical frequencies; the optoelectronic equipment tends to be expensive to produce relatively high data rates [FREE81].

The alternative that is invariably used for optical transmission is based on a variant of amplitude-shift keying known as intensity modulation. Recall from Chapter 1 that the simplest form of intensity modulation encodes a binary one as a pulse of light and a binary zero as the absence of light. The disadvantage of this approach is its lack of synchronization. Because transitions on the fiber are unpredictable, there is no way for the receiver to synchronize its clock to that of the transmitter. The solution to this problem is to first encode the binary data to guarantee the presence of transitions and then to present the encoded data to the optical source for transmission.

For the 802.4 optical fiber specification, the precoding technique that is chosen is Manchester (see Figure B.1c). Thus a binary zero is transmitted as a pulse of light (H) followed by the absence of a pulse (L), in uniform time slots; and a binary one is transmitted as the absence of a pulse (L) followed by a pulse (H). Note that this doubles the effective signaling rate. Thus the data rates of 5, 10, and 20 Mbps require optical signaling rates of 10, 20, and 40 Mbaud (one baud = one signal element per second). Finally, nondata symbols are transmitted in pairs as the sequence (L L) (H H).

All of the above is similar to the scheme used for phase-continuous carrierband, except that ASK rather than FSK is the fundamental encoding technique.

Topology.   The 802.4 optical fiber specification can be used with any topology that is logically a bus. That is, a transmission from any one station is received by all other stations, and if two stations transmit at the same time, a collision occurs. At the present time, a simple bus system is impractical because of the high cost of low-loss optical taps. Instead, the standard recommends the use of active or passive stars.

For both the active and passive stars, each station attaches to a central node via two optical fibers, one for transmission in each direction. The active star operates in the same fashion as the star topologies used for 802.3. That is, a transmission on any one input fiber to the central node is retransmitted on all output fibers.

The passive star system is based on the use of a passive star coupler. Such schemes have been in use for 10 Mbps CSMA/CD systems for some time [SCHO88, KELL84, RAWS78]. The passive star coupler is fabricated by fusing together a number of optical fibers. The transmit fibers from all of the stations enter the coupler on one side, and all of the receive fibers exit on the other side. Any light input to one of the fibers on one side of the coupler will be equally divided among and output through all the fibers on the other side (Figure 5.15).

Two methods of fabrication of the star coupler have been pursued: the biconic fused coupler, and the mixing rod coupler. In the biconic fused coupler [STRA87], the fibers are bundled together. The bundled fibers are heated with an oxyhydrogen flame and pulled into a biconical tapered shape. That is, the rods come together into a fused mass that tapers into a conical shape and then expands back out again. The mixing rod approach [OHSH86] begins in the same fashion. Then, the biconical taper is cut at the waist and a cylindrical rod is inserted between the tapers and fused to the two cut ends. This latter technique allows the use of a less narrow waist and is easier to fabricate. The current 802.4 specification does not dictate which sort of coupler to use.

Commercially available passive star couplers can support a few tens of stations at a radial distance of up to a kilometer or more. Figure 5.16 shows the operating range of the two types of couplers. The limitations

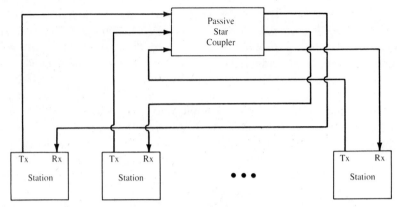

Figure 5.15. Optical fiber passive star configuration

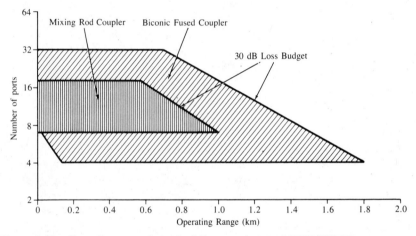

Figure 5.16. Operating range for optical fiber passive star LAN [SCHO88]

on number of stations and distances are imposed by the losses in the network. With today's equipment, the optical power loss between transmitter and receiver that can be tolerated is on the order of 25 to 30 dB. In Figure 5.16, the outer edge of each region is defined by a maximum end-to-end attenuation of 30 dB.

APPENDIX 5A.   A COMPARISON OF CSMA/CD AND TOKEN BUS

Both IEEE 802.3 and 802.4 define a MAC technique for bus/tree topology LANs. At present, CSMA/CD and token bus are the two principal contenders for MAC technique on bus/tree topologies. This appendix attempts to summarize the pros and cons of the two techniques. See also [STIE81] and [MILL82].

Let us look at CSMA/CD first. On the positive side, the algorithm is simple; good news for the very-large-scale integration folks, and also good news for the user, in terms of cost and reliability. The protocol has been widely used for a long time, which also leads to favorable cost and reliability. The protocol provides fair access—all stations have an equal chance at the bandwidth; good if you require only fair access. CSMA/CD exhibits quite good delay and throughput performance, at least up to a certain load (see [STAL87a]).

There are, unfortunately, quite a few cons for CSMA/CD. From an engineering perspective, the most critical problem is the collision detection (CD) requirement. To detect collisions, the differences in signal strength from any pair of stations at any point on the cable must be small; this is no easy task to achieve. Other undesirable implications flow from the CD requirement. Since collisions are allowed, it is difficult for diagnostic equipment to distinguish expected errors from those induced by noise or faults. Also, CD imposes a minimum frame size, which is wasteful of bandwidth in situations where there are a lot of short messages, such as may be produced in highly interactive environments.

There are some performance problems as well. For certain data rates and frame sizes, CSMA/CD performs poorly as load increases. Also, the protocol is biased toward long transmissions.

For token bus, perhaps its greatest positive feature is its excellent throughput performance. Throughput increases as the data rate increases and levels off but does not decline as the medium saturates. Furthermore, this performance does not degrade significantly as the cable length increases. A second pro for token bus is that, because stations need not detect collisions, a rather large dynamic receiver range is possible. All that is required is that each station's signal be strong enough to be heard at all points on the cable; there are no special requirements related to relative signal strength.

Another strength of token bus is that access to the medium can be regulated. If fair access is desired, token bus can provide this as well as CSMA/CD. Indeed, at high loads, token bus may be fairer: it avoids the last in, first-out phenomenon mentioned in Section 4.2. If priorities are required, as they may be in an operational or real-time environment, these can be accommodated. Token bus can also guarantee a certain bandwidth; this may be necessary for certain types of data, such as voice, digital video, and telemetry.

An advertised advantage of token bus is that it is *deterministic;* that is, there is a known upper bound to the amount of time any station must wait before transmitting. This upper bound is known because each station in the logical ring can hold the token for only a specified time. In contrast, with CSMA/CD, the delay time can only be expressed statistically. Furthermore, since every attempt to transmit under CSMA/CD can in principle produce a collision, there is a possibility that a station could be shut out indefinitely. For process control and other real time applications, this *nondeterministic* behavior is undesirable. Alas, in the real world, there is always a finite possibility of transmission error, which can cause a lost token. This adds a statistical component to token bus.

The main disadvantage of token bus is its complexity. The reader who made it through the description above can have no doubt that this is a complex algorithm. A second disadvantage is the overhead involved. Under lightly loaded conditions, a station may have to wait through many fruitless token passes for a turn.

APPENDIX 5B.   PROWAY AND MAP

Although LANs based on the IEEE 802.4 standard can be used in a wide variety of environments, a key motivation for this standard was to specify local networks that would be applicable to the needs of the factory and industrial environment. In this context, the work on IEEE 802.4 has been influenced by two other activities: PROWAY and MAP [CROW86].

PROWAY

In 1976, a technical committee of the Instrument Society of America began work on a local network standard, called the process data highway (PROWAY), for industrial control applications. The work was coordinated with the International Electrotechnical Commission, and the resulting standard has been adopted by both ISA and IEC [ISA85].

Industrial control systems differ from other on-line, real-time com-

Table 5.8.   PROWAY REQUIREMENTS

Application characteristics

The characteristics of the data highway should be such that they provide optimum features for use in industrial control systems and shall be applicable to both continuous and discrete processes. An industrial data highway is characterized by the following:

    a. Event driven communication that allows real-time response to events.
    b. Very high availability.
    c. Very high data integrity.
    d. Proper operation in the presence of electromagnetic interference and differences in earth potentials.
    e. Dedicated intraplant transmission lines.

Economic versus technical factors

To achieve broad applicability it is essential that industrial data highways should be economically viable in control systems under the following conditions:

    a. With low or high information transfer rate requirements.
    b. Within a control room and/or while exposed to the plant environment.
    c. In geographically small or large process plants.

The economic and technical factors may need to be reconciled to achieve a balance of transmission line length versus data signaling rate.

---

puter networks in that the control system's output causes material or energy to move. Table 5.8 is the requirements statement from the standard of PROWAY. The committee decided that a carrierband medium with a token-passing MAC best fit these requirements. The carrierband medium uses analog signaling and is, therefore, relatively immune (compared to baseband) to the low-frequency noise often found in the factory environment. Also, it is less expensive than full broadband, which in most cases would provide unnecessarily large capacity. Token passing is preferable to some sort of contention-based scheme, such as CSMA/CD, because of its deterministic nature and its ability to easily incorporate a priority mechanism. Both of these characteristics are important in the dynamic, real-time environment of the factory or process-control plant.

Since the inauguration of the IEEE 802.4 effort, the two groups have worked together to produce compatible specifications.

MAP

The Manufacturing Automation Protocol (MAP) is an effort begun by General Motors in 1982, and since transferred to the Society of Manufacturing Engineers [KAMI86]. The objective of MAP is to define a local network and associated communications architecture for terminals, computing resources, programmable devices, and robots within a plant or a complex. It sets standards for procurement and provides a specification for use by vendors who want to build networking products for factory use that are acceptable to MAP participants. The strategy has three parts:

1. For cases in which international standards exist, select those alternatives and options that best suit the needs of the MAP participants.
2. For standards currently under development, participate in the standards-making process to represent the requirements of the MAP participants.
3. In those cases where no appropriate standards exist, recommend interim standards until the international standards are developed.

Thus, MAP is intended to specify those standards and options within standards appropriate for the factory environment. This guarantees a large market for products that conform to those standards. To date, hundreds of companies have participated in the MAP effort.

For layers 1 and 2 of the OSI model, which correspond to the physical, MAC, and LLC layers of the IEEE 802 standard, the MAP document specifies the following:

- *Physical:* The IEEE 802.4 10-Mbps, midsplit broadband; or the IEEE 802.4 5-Mbps phase-coherent carrierband, as modified to reflect some of the medium specifications in the PROWAY standard.
- *Medium access control:* IEEE 802.4 token bus with 48-bit addresses; no options required.
- *Logical link control:* Unacknowledged connectionless service and acknowledged connectionless service.

6

IEEE 802.5 Token Ring

The IEEE 802.5 standard defines the token ring medium access control (MAC) protocol for ring topology. It also defines a physical layer based on shielded twisted pair and Differential Manchester signaling. We begin this chapter with an overview of the scope of the 802.5 standard. This is followed by a look at the MAC protocol and service specifications, and finally a description of the physical layer specification.

6.1 SCOPE OF THE IEEE 802.5 STANDARD

As with IEEE 802.3, IEEE 802.4, and FDDI, the IEEE 802.5 standard encompasses both the MAC and the physical layers. Figure 6.1 depicts the architecture of the 802.5 standard in more detail. It can be viewed as having four parts:

- MAC service specification
- MAC protocol
- Physical layer entity specification
- Station attachment specification

The MAC service specification defines in functional terms the service provided by IEEE 802.5 to logical link control (LLC) or any other

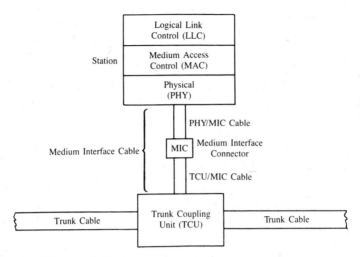

Figure 6.1. IEEE 802.5 architecture

higher-level user. The interface includes facilities for transmitting and receiving higher-level data units, and provides per-operation status information for use by higher-layer error recovery procedures. It is assumed that the higher-level user will be LLC, but, because of the adherence of the 802 standards to the principle of layering, this is not strictly necessary. In any case, this service specification hides the details of the MAC and the physical layers from the MAC user. In particular, the use of a variety of transmission media should not be visible to the user except as it affects performance.

The MAC protocol is the heart of the 802.5 standard, which is often referred to simply as the token ring standard. The specification defines the frame structure and the interactions that take place between MAC entities.

The physical layer specification is divided into two parts. The medium-independent part specifies the service interface between the MAC and the physical layers. The interface includes facilities for passing a pair of serial bit streams between the two layers. The medium-independent part of the standard also specifies the details of the signaling method, including symbol encoding and data rate.

The medium-dependent part of the standard specifies the functional, electrical, and mechanical characteristics of medium attachment. Figure 6.1 makes clear exactly what configuration is intended. It is assumed that each station attaches to the ring through a trunk coupling unit. The standard specifies the transmission medium and interface for connecting the station to the trunk coupling unit. The trunk coupling unit and the trunk medium itself are not part of the standard. We elaborate on this point in Section 6.4.

The standard originally did not specify the intended application environment. A revision of the standard states that it is intended for use in commercial and light industrial environments; use in home or heavy industrial environments, while not precluded, is not considered within the scope of the standard. These are the identical environments to that specified for IEEE 802.3.

6.2   MAC PROTOCOL

Token Ring

Token ring is probably the oldest ring control technique, originally proposed in 1969 [FARM69]. It has become the most popular ring access technique in the United States. This technique is the one ring access method selected for standardization by the IEEE 802 committee [PITT87a, DIXO87]. IBM's product and those of a number of competitors are compatible with this standard [DERF86, STRO87, DIXO83, BUX83, STRO83].

The token ring technique is based on the use of a particular bit pattern, called a *token,* that circulates around the ring when all stations are idle. A station wishing to transmit must wait until it detects a token passing by. It then seizes the token by changing one bit in the token, which transforms it from a token to a start-of-frame sequence for a frame. The station then appends and transmits the remainder of the fields needed to construct a frame (Figure 6.2).

There is now no token on the ring, so other stations wishing to transmit must wait. The frame on the ring will make a round trip and be purged by the transmitting station. The transmitting station inserts a new token on the ring when both of the following conditions have been met:

- The station has completed transmission of its frame.
- The leading edge of its transmitted frame has returned (after a complete circulation of the ring) to the station.

If the bit length of the ring is less than the frame length, the first condition implies the second. If not, a station could theoretically release a token after it has finished transmitting but before it begins to receive its own transmission; the second condition is not strictly necessary. However, use of the first condition alone might complicate error recovery, as several frames may be on the ring at the same time. In any case, the use of a token guarantees that only one station at a time may transmit.

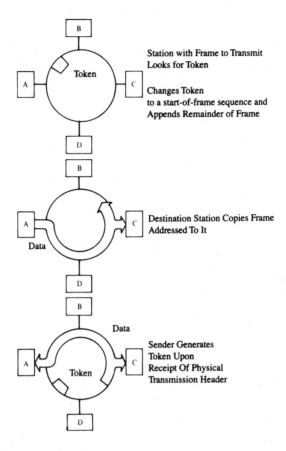

Figure 6.2. Token ring

When a transmitting station releases a new token, the next station downstream with data to send will be able to seize the token and transmit.

Several implications of the token ring technique can be mentioned. Note that under lightly loaded conditions, there is some inefficiency as a station must wait for the token to come around before transmitting. However, under heavy loads, which is where it matters, the ring functions in a round-robin fashion, which is both efficient and fair. To see this, refer to Figure 6.2. Note that after station *A* transmits, it releases a token. The first station with an opportunity to transmit is *D*. If *D* transmits, it then releases a token and *C* has the next opportunity, and so on. Finally, the ring must be long enough to hold the token. If stations are temporarily bypassed, their delay may need to be supplied artificially.

As with token bus, the token ring protocol contains mechanisms that support priority and ring maintenance. Before explaining these, we need to describe the frame formats used in IEEE 802.5.

MAC Frames

Figure 6.3 depicts the formats of the token and frames generated by the IEEE 802.5 protocol. The overall frame format consists of the following fields:

- *Starting delimiter (SD):* Indicates the start of token or frame. The SD consists of signaling patterns that are always distinguishable from data. It is coded as follows: JK0JK000, where J and K are

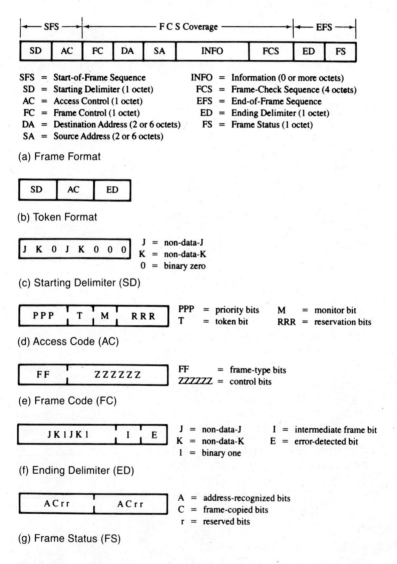

SFS = Start-of-Frame Sequence
SD = Starting Delimiter (1 octet)
AC = Access Control (1 octet)
FC = Frame Control (1 octet)
DA = Destination Address (2 or 6 octets)
SA = Source Address (2 or 6 octets)

INFO = Information (0 or more octets)
FCS = Frame-Check Sequence (4 octets)
EFS = End-of-Frame Sequence
ED = Ending Delimiter (1 octet)
FS = Frame Status (1 octet)

(a) Frame Format

(b) Token Format

J = non-data-J
K = non-data-K
0 = binary zero

(c) Starting Delimiter (SD)

PPP = priority bits   M = monitor bit
T = token bit   RRR = reservation bits

(d) Access Code (AC)

FF = frame-type bits
ZZZZZZ = control bits

(e) Frame Code (FC)

J = non-data-J   I = intermediate frame bit
K = non-data-K   E = error-detected bit
1 = binary one

(f) Ending Delimiter (ED)

A = address-recognized bits
C = frame-copied bits
r = reserved bits

(g) Frame Status (FS)

Figure 6.3. IEEE 802.5 frame format

nondata symbols. The actual form of a nondata symbol depends on the signal encoding on the medium.

- *Access control (AC):* Contains the priority and reservation bits, which are used in the priority mechanism, and the monitor bit, used in the ring maintenance mechanism (Table 6.1). The field also contains the token bit that indicates whether this is a token or a frame. If it is a token, the only additional field is ED (described later).
- *Frame control (FC):* Indicates whether this frame contains LLC data or is a MAC control frame. In the latter case, the control bits indicate the type of MAC frame (described later).
- *Destination address (DA):* Specifies the station(s) for which the frame is intended. It may be a unique MAC address (one station), a multicast-group address (a group of stations), or a global address (all stations on the ring). The choide of a 16- or 48-bit address is an implementation decision, and must be the same for all stations on a particular LAN.
- *Source address (SA):* Specifies the station that sent the frame. The SA size must equal the DA size.
- *Information.* Contains LLC data or information related to a control operation of the MAC protocol.
- *Frame check sequence (FCS):* A 32-bit cyclic redundancy check (see Appendix C), based on FC, DA, SA, and Information fields.
- *Ending delimiter (ED):* Contains nondata symbols to indicate the end of the frame. It also includes the I and E bits, with the meanings indicated in Table 6.1.

Table 6.1. IEEE 802.5 MAC FRAME CONTROL BITS

Bit	Description
Access control	
Priority (PPP)	Priority of the token
Token (T)	0 in a token; 1 in a frame
Monitor (M)	Used to prevent persistent data frame or persistent high-priority token
Reservation (R)	Used to request that the next token be issued at the requested priority
Frame control	
me type (FF)	MAC or LLC frame
Ending delimiter	
ermediate frame (1)	0 indicates last or only frame of the transmission; 1 indicates more frames to follow
ror detected (E)	Set by any station that detects an error (e.g., FCS error, nondata symbols)
Frame status	
ldress recognized (A)	Station recognizes its address
ame copied (C)	Station has copied frame

- *Frame status (FS):* Contains the A and C bits, with the meanings indicated in Table 6.1. Because the A and C bits are outside the scope of the FCS, they are duplicated to provide a redundancy check to detect erroneous settings.

Address Fields.   The address field formats are shown in Figure 2.10. Although the exact structure of the locally administered 15-bit or 46-bit address is not defined in the standard, 802.5 includes a recommended structure for further study. The general structure that is proposed is depicted in Figure 6.4. The structure provides for a LAN divided into multiple rings, with one or more relays, or bridges, interconnecting the rings. The hierarchical address format permits a bridge to recognize frames that require forwarding to other rings by examining the ring number portion of the address.

Two techniques are suggested for group addressing (Figure 6.5). One bit in the address indicates whether this is a bit-significant or a conventional group address. In the bit-significant mode, each bit in the station

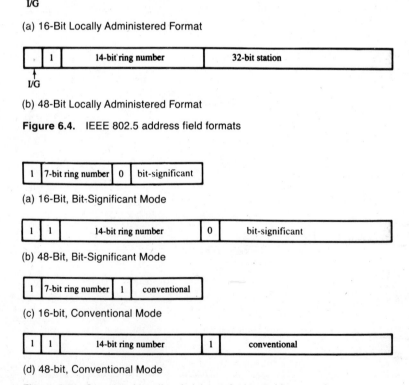

(a) 16-Bit Locally Administered Format

(b) 48-Bit Locally Administered Format

Figure 6.4.   IEEE 802.5 address field formats

(a) 16-Bit, Bit-Significant Mode

(b) 48-Bit, Bit-Significant Mode

(c) 16-bit, Conventional Mode

(d) 48-bit, Conventional Mode

Figure 6.5.   Suggested locally administered group address modes

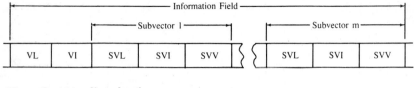

VL = (2 octets) = Vector Length
VI = (2 octets) = Vector Identifier
SVL = (1 octet) = Subvector Length
SVI = (1 octet) = Subvector Identifier
SVV = (n octets) = Subvector Value

Figure 6.6. MAC frame information field structure

address field refers to a different group. Thus a total of 7 or 31 different bit-significant groups can be defined. This technique has two advantages:

- A station can store its group membership with a simple bit-significant mask, which contains a 1-bit for each group that the station belongs to, and a 0-bit elsewhere. Checking an incoming group address then involves a simple logical AND operation.
- A frame can be multicast to more than one group by setting more than one bit in the station address field.

The advantage of conventional group addressing is that more groups can be defined.

MAC Frame Information Field.   In certain MAC frames, the information field is used to carry control information related to the particular control message. Figure 6.6 illustrates the format of this field. The contents of the field is referred to as a vector, and contains one or more subvectors, each of which is a parameter for the associated frame control function. The information field consists of the following subfields:

- *Vector length (VL):* The total length of the information field, in octets.
- *Vector identifier (VI):* Identifies the vector.
- *Subvector length (SVL):* Length of a subvector in octets.
- *Subvector identifier (SVI):* Identifies the subvector.
- *Subvector value (SVV):* The value of the subvector.

Basic Operation

Having described the IEEE 802.5 frame structure, we are now in a position to describe the MAC algorithm. To begin, we look at the basic operation, without the use of priority or ring maintenance functions.

A station that wishes to transmit waits until a token goes by, as indicated by the token bit in the access control (AC) field being set to zero. The station seizes the token by setting the token bit to 1, and appending the remaining fields (FC, DA, SA, INFO, FCS, ED, FS) to the SD and AC fields to form a complete transmitted frame. Meanwhile, the ED field of the captured token is absorbed and discarded by the station. The station may continue to transmit until it has no more data to transmit or until a token-holding timer expires. The station may transmit more than one frame contiguously by setting the I bit in the ED field to one on all but the last frame.

Other stations listen to the ring and repeat passing frames. Each station introduces into the ring approximately a one-bit delay as the time to examine, copy, or change a bit as necessary. Each station can check passing frames for errors and set the E bit if an error is detected. If a station detects its own address as the destination address, it sets the A bits to 1; if it has sufficient buffer space, it copies the frame, setting the C bits to 1. This allows the originating station to differentiate three conditions:

- Station nonexistent/nonactive
- Station exists but frame not copied
- Frame copied

The station that originates a frame is responsible for purging the frame from the ring. Each transmitted frame is absorbed as it returns to the originating station. The status bits (E, A, C) in the end-of-frame sequence are examined to determine the result of the transmission. However, if an error is reported, the MAC protocol does not attempt to retransmit the frame. This is the responsibility of LLC or some higher-layer protocol.

Priority Mechanism

In the IEEE 802.5 standard, the above scheme is augmented by a priority mechanism. The standard provides for eight levels of priority. It does this by providing two 3-bit fields in each data frame and token: a priority field and a reservation field. For clarity, let us define P_m = priority of message to be transmitted by a station; P_r = received priority; R_r = received reservation; and R = transmitted reservation. Then:

1. A station wishing to transmit must wait for a token with $P_r \leq P_m$.
2. While waiting, a station may reserve a future token at its priority level (P_m). If a data frame goes by, it sets the reservation field to its priority ($R \leftarrow P_m$) if the reservation field is less than its priority ($R_r < P_m$). If a token goes by, it sets the reservation field to its priority ($R \leftarrow P_m$) if $R_r < P_m$ and $P_m < P_r$. This has the effect of preempting any lower-priority reservations.
3. When a station seizes a token, it sets the token bit to 1, the reservation field to 0, and leaves the priority field unchanged.
4. Following transmission, a station issues a new token with the priority set to the maximum of P_r, R_r, and P_m, and a reservation set to the maximum of R_r and P_m.

   The effect of the above steps is to sort out competing claims and allow the waiting transmission of highest priority to seize the token as soon as possible. A moment's reflection reveals that, as is, the algorithm has a ratchet effect on priority, driving it to the highest used level and keeping it there. To avoid this, a station that raises the priority (issues a token that has a higher priority than the token that is received) has the responsibility of later lowering the priority to its previous level. For this purpose, a station that raises priority must remember both the old and the new priorities and downgrade the priority of the token at the appropriate time.

   To examine this process, we define two new variables: S_r = stack used to store old values of token priority and S_x = stack used to store new values assigned to the token. Each station maintains its own copy of these stacks. Assume that a station has seized a token and transmitted a frame at some priority (0 through 7). When that frame returns, the station must issue a new token. Before doing so, it examines the priority and reservation fields of the returned frame (Figure 6.7). If the reservation is not higher than the current priority, and if the station has no data to send at a level above the current priority, then the token is issued with the same priority as the returning frame. In other words, the station issues a new token with the same priority as the token it seized. The reservation bits are set to the maximum of the R_r and P_m. This assures that when the token priority is later downgraded, that it is not downgraded below the priority

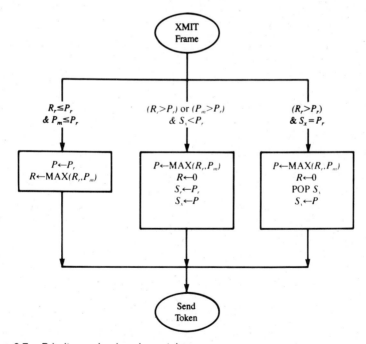

Figure 6.7.   Priority mechanism: issue token

level of queued data. If, when the station examines P_r and R_r, it finds that either a reservation has been made at a higher priority or the station itself has higher-priority data, then the priority of the token is upgraded and the reservation field in the token is set to zero. If this station was initially responsible for upgrading the old token ($P_r = S_x$), then it discards the old priority from its S_x stack and replaces it with the new priority; this avoids a two-step downgrade at a station. Otherwise ($S_x < P_r$), the station re- members the old priority ($S_r \leftarrow P_r$) and the new priority ($S_x \leftarrow P$) so that it can later perform the downgrading.

A station that has raised the priority level of a token is referred to as a stacking station. Having become a stacking station, the station will seize any token with a priority (P_r) equal to the top of its S_x stack to perform the downgrade (Figure 6.8). Ordinarily, the station simply down- grades the token to its old value ($P \leftarrow S_r$). However, if there is a reservation outstanding between the current priority and the stacked priority ($R_r < S_r$), then the station only lowers the priority to the reserved level. The station must stack this reserved priority for a later downgrading.

A station that has a frame to transmit at a nonzero priority must wait until it receives a token of equal or lower priority (Figure 6.9). If

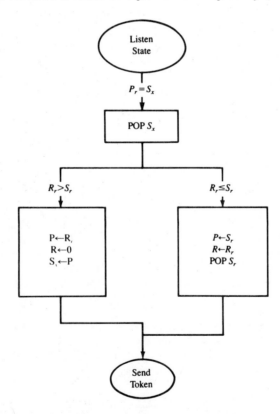

Figure 6.8.   Priority mechanism: alter token

such a token arrives, it simply transmits. While waiting, if it sees a frame with a reservation field value less than its desired priority, it sets the reservation field to its priority. If the waiting station sees a token with a priority above that of its message, it cannot transmit using that token. If such a token has a reservation field value less than its desired priority, it sets the reservation field to its priority. The exception to this last rule is if this station has a downgrade responsibility for this token. In that case, the sequence of events described in Figure 6.8 is followed.

We are now in a position to summarize the priority algorithm. A station having a higher priority than the current frame can reserve the next token for its priority level as the frame passes by. When the current transmitting station is finished, it issues a token at that higher priority. Stations of lower priority cannot seize the token, so it passes to the requesting station or an intermediate station of equal or higher priority with data to send.

The station that upgraded the priority level is responsible for downgrading it to its former level when all higher-priority stations are finished. When that station sees a token at the higher priority, it can assume that

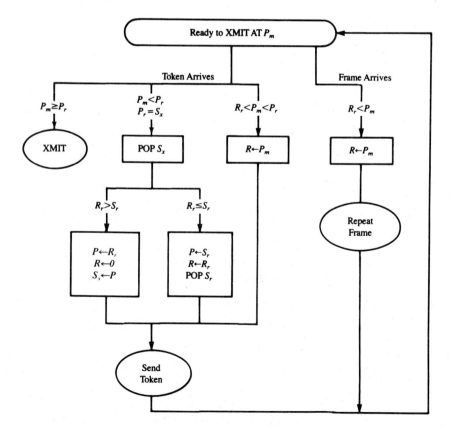

Figure 6.9. Priority mechanism: ready to transmit

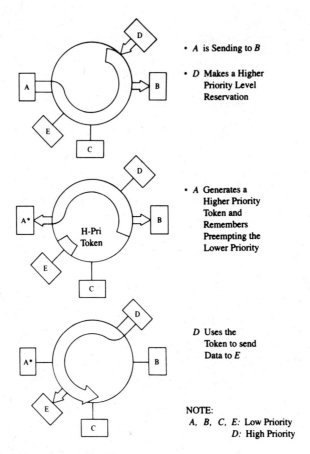

* A is Sending to B

* D Makes a Higher Priority Level Reservation

* A Generates a Higher Priority Token and Remembers Preempting the Lower Priority

D Uses the Token to send Data to E

NOTE:
A, B, C, E: Low Priority
D: High Priority

Figure 6.10. Token ring priority scheme

there is no more higher-priority traffic waiting, and it downgrades the token before passing it on. Figure 6.10 is an example.

Note that, in Figure 6.10, after *A* has issued a high-priority token, any station with high-priority data may seize the token. Suppose that, in addition to station *D*, station *C* now has high-priority data to send. *C* will seize the token, transmit its data frame, and reissue a high-priority token, which is then seized by *D*. By the time that a priority 3 token arrives at *A*, all intervening stations with high-priority data to send will have had the opportunity. It is now appropriate, therefore, for *A* to downgrade the token.

Maintenance

To overcome various error conditions, one station is designated as the active monitor (Figure 6.11). The active monitor periodically issues an Active-Monitor-Present control frame to assure other stations that there

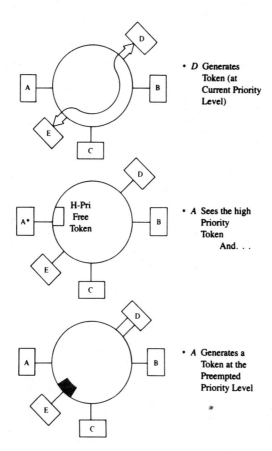

- *D* Generates Token (at Current Priority Level)

- *A* Sees the high Priority Token And. . .

- *A* Generates a Token at the Preempted Priority Level

Figure 6.10 (*continued*)

is an active monitor on the ring. To detect a lost-token condition, the active monitor uses a valid-frame timer that is greater than the time required to completely traverse the ring. The timer is reset after every valid token or frame. If the timer expires, the active monitor issues a token. To detect a persistently circulating frame, the monitor sets the monitor bit to one on any passing frame the first time it goes by. If it sees a frame with the monitor bit already set, it knows that the transmitting station failed to absorb the frame. The active monitor aborts the frame and transmits a token. The same strategy is used to detect a failure in the priority mechanism: no token should circulate the ring more than once at a constant nonzero priority level. Finally, if the active monitor detects evidence of another active monitor (via the Active-Monitor-Present frame), it immediately goes into standby monitor status.

In addition, all of the active stations on the ring cooperate to provide each station with a continuous update on the identity of its upstream neighbor. Each station periodically issues a standby-monitor-present

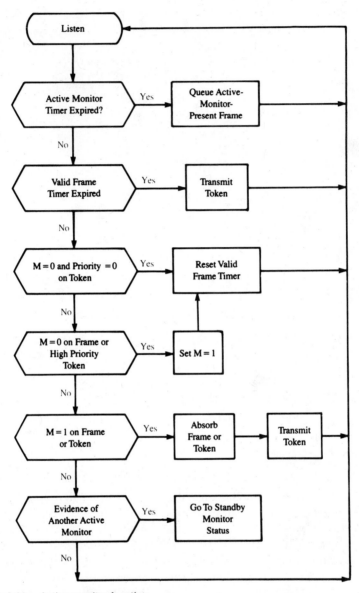

Figure 6.11. Active monitor function

(SMP) frame. Its downstream neighbor recognizes the frame as having originated from its immediate upstream neighbor because the *A* and *C* bits are zero. The station that recognizes such a frame sets the *A* and *C* bits to one and notes the source address; then after a pause, sends its own SMP frame. The absence of SMP frames can be used in fault isolation.

A number of MAC control frames are used to support the active and standby monitor present functions (Table 6.2). We have already described

Table 6.2.   KEY PARAMETER VALUES FOR MAC FRAMES

Frame Type	P_m	FC	DA	VI	SVI	SVV
Claim token	0	00 000011	All stations	X'0003'	X'02'–RUA	address
Duplicate address test	0	00 000000	MA	X'0007'		
Active monitor present	P_r^a	00 000101	All stations	X'0005'	X'02'–RUA	address
Standby monitor present	0	00 000110	All stations	X'0006'	X'02'–RUA	address
Beacon	0	00 000010	All stations	X'0002'	X'01'–RUA X'01'–Type	address[b]
Purge	0	00 000100	All stations	X'0004'	X'02'–RUA	address

RUA = received upstream neighbor's address
MA = This station's address

Notes:

[a]An AMP is transmitted at the ring service priority (P_r) that exists at the time a token is received after an AMP frame is queued. The default value for P_m for this frame is seven.

[b]X'0001' = Issued by a station during reconfiguration (for future study)
X'0002' = Continuous J symbols received
X'0003' = Timer TNT expired during claiming token; no Claim-Token frame received
X'0004' = Timer TNT expired during claiming token; Claim-Token (SA < MA) frame received

the active and standby monitor present frames. The claim-token frame is issued by a station that detects the loss of the active monitor. This frame is used to resolve contention among stations attempting to claim the status of active monitor. A claiming station sends a stream of claim-token frames and inspects the source address of received claim-token frames. (If the station hears something other than a claim-token frame, it reverts to repeater mode.) If the source address matches its own address, then is claim-token frame has made a complete circuit and the station becomes the active monitor. If the source address is less than its own address, the station ignores the incoming frame and continues to transmit claim-token frames. If the source address is greater than its own address, then the station reverts to a repeater mode. In this way, the contending station with the highest address becomes an active monitor.

The duplicate-address-test frame is transmitted as part of a station's initialization process. The frame is transmitted with a destination address equal to the station's address. If the frame returns with the address recognized bits set to one, then a duplicate address is detected; the station removes itself from the ring, indicating the error to station management.

The beacon frame is used to isolate a serious ring failure, such as a break in the ring. When a station is attempting the claim-token procedure, it will eventually time out if it does not come to a resolution (winning or losing). After timing out, the station issues a beacon to indicate the fault. Finally, the purge frame is used by the active monitor to clear the ring before issuing a new token.

6.3 MAC SERVICES

The services provided by the MAC layer allow the local LLC entity to exchange LLC data units with peer LLC entities.

The IEEE 802.5 service specification is an exact match to that defined in the LLC standard (Section 3.1).

6.4 PHYSICAL LAYER SPECIFICATION

Physical Layer Services

As always, the services provided by the physical layer are defined in terms of primitives and parameters. These are:

- PH-DATA.request (symbol)
- PH-DATA.indication (symbol)

The PH-DATA primitives support the transfer of data from a single MAC entity to all other MAC entities contained within the same local network defined by the medium. That is, data transmitted by one MAC entity using PH-DATA.request is received by all other MAC entities with a PH-DATA.indication. The symbol parameter can take on a value of binary one or zero, or two nondata symbols, J and K. The physical layer encodes and transmits each bit of data. Each active station attached to the medium receives the transmitted bits. As each bit is received, the physical layer generates a PH-DATA.indication.

It must be emphasized that this specification is an abstract description of services and does not imply any particular implementation. It does serve to illustrate that the MAC layer is substantially independent of the characteristics of the physical medium.

Medium-Independent Specification

The IEEE 802.5 standard includes a chapter entitled "Physical Layer," which provides the medium-independent aspects of the physical layer specification.

The standard specifies the use of data rates of 1 and 4 Mbps. Differential Manchester encoding (see Appendix B) is used. Figure 6.12 shows this encoding and includes encodings for the nondata symbols J and K. Unlike the data symbols, there is no transition in the middle of the bit time for J and K. For J, there is also no transition at the beginning of the bit time; for K there is a transition at the beginning of the bit time. The symbols J and K are normally transmitted in J–K pairs to avoid an accumulating dc component.

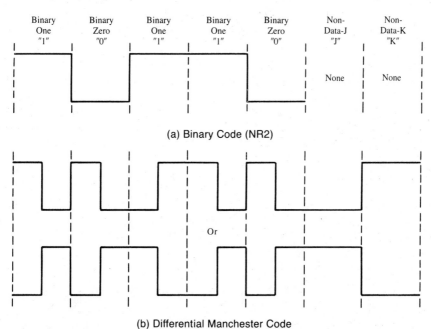

(a) Binary Code (NR2)

(b) Differential Manchester Code

Figure 6.12.   Example of symbol encoding

The standard also specifies the use of a latency buffer by the active monitor. Normally, the delay at each station is on the order of one bit time (e.g., 1 μs at 1 Mbps, 0.25, μs at 4 Mbps). At the active monitor, a latency buffer is inserted into the ring, so that incoming bits are buffered, and a delay equal to the buffer length is introduced. The buffer serves two distinct functions.

- *Assured minimum latency:* For the token to circulate continuously around the ring when no station is transmitting, the bit length (time, expressed in number of signal elements transmitted, for a signal element to complete one complete ring circuit) of the ring must be at least as long as the token, that is, 24 bits. This bit length is referred to as the ring latency. Because the delay in an actual ring is unknown ahead of time, the standard requires a latency buffer of at least 24 bits.
- *Phase jitter compensation:* A buffer can be used to compensate for jitter (see Appendix 6A). The standard specifies a maximum number of stations of 250, and assumes that this can produce a variation of up to 3 bits in the latency of the ring. This requires an elastic buffer with a length of 6 bits.

These two requirements are combined to produce a specification for a 30-bit latency buffer. The buffer is initialized to 27 bits. If the received signal at the active monitor station is slightly faster than the master oscillator, the buffer will expand, as required, to 28, 29, or 30 bits to avoid dropping bits. If the received signal is slow, the buffer will contract to 26, 25, or 24 bits to avoid adding bits to the repeated bit stream.

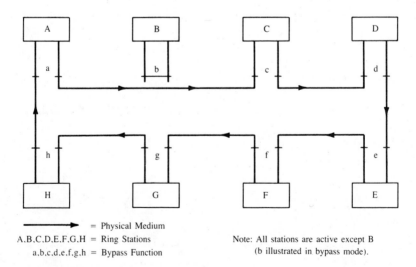

```
                              = Physical Medium
A,B,C,D,E,F,G,H = Ring Stations              Note: All stations are active except B
    a,b,c,d,e,f,g,h = Bypass Function                  (b illustrated in bypass mode).
```

Figure 6.13. Token ring configuration

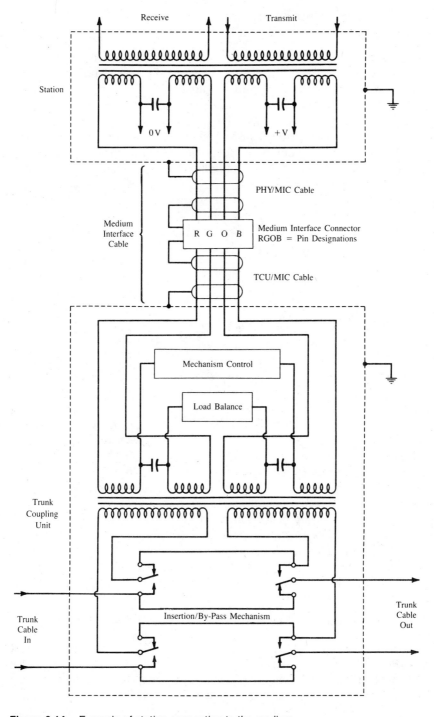

Figure 6.14. Example of station connection to the medium

Medium-Dependent Specification

The IEEE 802.5 standard specifies a connection from a station to a trunk coupling unit, as indicated in Figure 6.1. It is assumed that the repeating function is performed in the station, whereas the bypass function is performed in the trunk coupling unit (Figure 6-13). This provides considerable flexibility in the configuring of the network, including the use of a star-wiring arrangement (Chapter 1).

The standard specifies the transmission medium between the station and the trunk coupling unit and other aspects of the interface. The transmission medium consists of two 150-ohm shielded twisted pairs, one for transmission in each direction between station and a trunk coupling unit. Figure 6.14, from the standard, is an example of a connection. It shows the trunk coupling unit in bypass mode. The exact nature of the trunk coupling unit, however, is beyond the scope of the standard, as is the trunk medium [LOVE88]. These may be optimized for a specific environment.

APPENDIX 6A.   JITTER

On a twisted-pair or coaxial-cable ring LAN, digital signaling is generally used with biphase encoding, typically Differential Manchester. As data circulate around the ring, each receiver must recover the binary data from the received signal. To do this, the receiver must know the starting and ending times of each bit, so that it can sample the received signal properly. This requires that all the repeaters on the ring be synchronized, or clocked, together. Biphase codes are self-clocking; the signal includes a transition in the middle of each bit time. Thus, each repeater recovers clocking as well as data from the received signal. This clock recovery will deviate in a random fashion from the mid-bit transitions of the received signal for several reasons, including noise during transmission and imperfections in the receiver circuitry. The predominant reason, however, is delay distortion. Delay distortion is caused by the fact that the velocity of propagation of a signal through a guided medium varies with frequency. The effect is that some of the signal components of one pulse will spill over into other pulse positions; this is known as *intersymbol interference*. The resulting deviation of clock recovery is known as *timing jitter*.

As each repeater receives data, it recovers the clocking for two purposes: first to know when to sample the incoming signal to recover the data, and second, to use the clocking for transmitting the Differential Manchester signal to the next repeater. The repeater issues a clean signal with no distortion. However, since the clocking is recovered from the incoming signal, the timing error is not eliminated. Thus the digital pulse width will expand and contract in a random fashion as the signal travels around the ring, and the timing jitter accumulates. The cumulative effect of the jitter is to cause the bit latency, or *bit length,* of the ring to vary. However, unless the latency of the ring remains constant, bits will be dropped (not retransmitted) as the latency of the ring decreases or added as the latency increases.

Thus, timing jitter places a limitation on the number of repeaters in a ring. Although this limitation cannot be entirely overcome, several measures can be taken to improve matters [KELL83, HONG86]; these are illustrated in Figure 6.15. First, each repeater can include a phase-locked loop. This is a device that uses feedback to minimize the deviation from one bit time to the next. Although the use of phase-locked loops reduces the jitter, there is still an accumulation around the ring. A supplementary measure is to include a buffer in one of the repeaters, usually designated as the monitor repeater or station. Bits are written in using the recovered clock and are read out using a crystal master clock. The buffer is initialized to hold a certain number of bits and expands and contracts as needed. For example, the IEEE standard specifies a 6-bit buffer, which is initialized to hold three bits. That is, as bits come in, they are placed in the buffer for three bit times before being retransmitted. If the received signal at the monitor station is slightly faster than the master clock, the buffer will expand, as required, to 4, 5, or 6 bits to avoid dropping bits. If the received signal is slow, the buffer will contract to 2, 1, or 0 bits to avoid adding bits to the repeated bit stream. Thus, the cleaned-up signals that are retransmitted are purged of the timing jitter. This combination of phase-locked loops and a buffer significantly increases maximum feasible

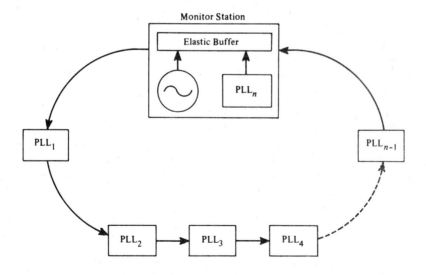

Figure 6.15.   Ring synchronization

ring size. The actual limit will depend on the characteristics of the transmission medium, which determine the amount of delay distortion, and therefore, the amount of accumulated jitter. For example, the IBM ring product specifies a maximum of 72 repeaters in a ring using unshielded twisted pair, and a maximum of 260 repeaters in a ring using shielded twisted pair.

7

Fiber Distributed
Data Interface

The accredited standards committee ASC X3T9.5 has produced a standard referred to as fiber distributed data interface (FDDI), which is in the process of becoming an ANSI standard [COOP86, ROSS86]. This standard specifies the medium access control (MAC) and the physical layers for a 100-Mbps optical fiber ring LAN. Use of the logical link control (LLC) standard (IEEE 802.2) is assumed. This chapter examines the FDDI standard.

7.1 SCOPE OF THE FDDI STANDARD

As with the IEEE 802.3, IEEE 802.4, and IEEE 802.5 standards, the FDDI standard encompasses both the MAC layer and the physical layer. Figure 7.1 depicts the architecture of the FDDI standard. Note that the standard assumes the use of the IEEE 802.2 standard, LLC. The standard is in four parts:

- Medium access control
- Physical protocol
- Physical medium dependent
- Layer management

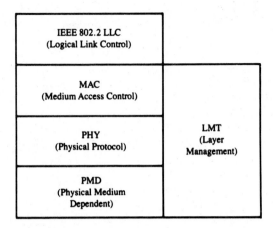

Figure 7.1.   FDDI architecture

The MAC layer is specified in terms of the MAC services and the MAC protocol. The MAC service specification defines in functional terms the service provided by FDDI to LLC or any other higher-level user. The interface includes facilities for transmitting and receiving protocol data units (PDUs), and provides per-operation status information for use by higher-layer error recovery procedures. It is assumed that the higher-level user will be LLC, but, because of the adherence of the FDDI and 802 standards to the principle of layering, this is not strictly necessary. In any case, this service specification hides the details of the MAC and physical layers from the MAC user. In particular, the use of a variety of transmission media should not be visible to the user except as it affects performance. The MAC protocol is the heart of the FDDI standard. The specification defines the frame structure and the interactions that take place between MAC entities.

The physical protocol (PHY) is the medium-independent portion of the physical layer. This includes a specification of the service interface with MAC. The interface specification defines facilities for passing a pair of serial bit streams between MAC and PHY. The PHY protocol specifies the encoding of digital data for transmission.

The physical medium dependent (PMD) sublayer of the physical layer defines and characterizes the fiber optic drivers and receivers, and other medium-dependent characteristics of the attachment of stations to the ring and of the cabling and connectors of the ring.

Layer management (LMT) provides the control necessary at the station level to manage the processes underway in the various FDDI layers such that a station may work cooperatively on a ring. LMT is part of a broader concept, referred to as station management (SMT), which may encompass processes at the LLC layer and above the LLC layer.

The FDDI standard is intended to support high-speed local network requirements, including what are referred to as backend and backbone applications. Appendix 7A elaborates on these requirements.

7.2 MAC PROTOCOL

Token Ring

As with IEEE 802.5, the FDDI MAC protocol is a token ring. The basic operation (not including priority and maintenance mechanisms) of the token ring is very similar for both 802.5 and FDDI. This subsection reviews the basic operation and points out some differences between the two protocols.

The FDDI token ring technique is based on the use of a small token frame that circulates around the ring when all stations are idle. A station wishing to transmit must wait until it detects a token passing by. It then seizes the token by aborting the token transmission as soon as the usable token is recognized. After the captured token is completely received, the station begins transmitting one or more frames.

There is now no token on the ring, so other stations wishing to transmit must wait. The frame on the ring will make a round trip and be purged by the transmitting station. The transmitting station inserts a new token on the ring when it has completed transmission of its frame. Note that if the bit length of the ring is greater than the length of a station's transmission, then a new token will appear before the leading edge of the current frame has returned to its transmitter for purging.

Figure 7.2 gives an example of ring operation. After station *A* has seized the token, it transmits frame F1, and immediately transmits a new token. F1 is addressed to station *C,* which copies it as it circulates past. The frame eventually returns to *A,* which absorbs it. Meanwhile, *B* seizes the token issued by *A* and transmits F2 followed by a token. This action could be repeated any number of times, so that at any one time, there may be multiple frames circulating the ring. Each station is responsible for absorbing its own frames based on the source address field.

Two differences between 802.5 and FDDI can be observed. First, an FDDI station does not attempt to seize a token by flipping a bit. Because of the high data rate of FDDI, it was considered impractical to impose this requirement. Second, in FDDI, a station releases a new token as soon as it completes frame transmission, even if it has not begun to receive its own transmission. Again, because of the high data rate, this technique is needed. Other differences between the two protocols will be mentioned as the description proceeds.

MAC Frames

Before discussing the details of the FDDI MAC protocol, we need to examine the frame structure. The standard expresses this structure in terms

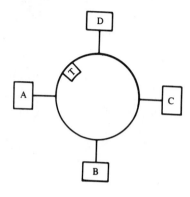

(a) *A* Awaiting Token

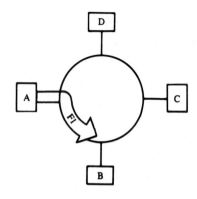

(b) *A* Seizes Token, Begins
Transmitting Frame F1

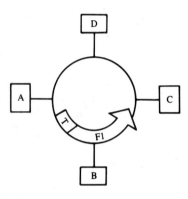

(c) *A* Appends Token to End of
Transmission

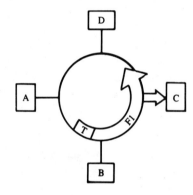

(d) *C* Copies Frame F1, Which Is
Addressed to It

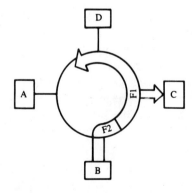

(e) *C* Continues to Copy F1; *B*
Seizes Token, Transmits F2

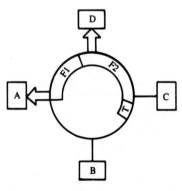

(f) *B* Emits Token; *D* Copies F2,
Which Is Addressed to It; *A* Absorbs F1

Figure 7.2. FDDI token operation

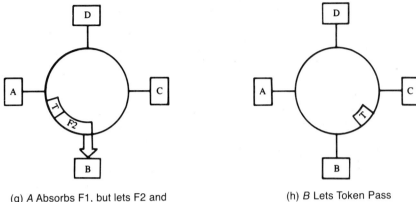

(g) *A* Absorbs F1, but lets F2 and
Token Pass; *B* Absorbs F2

(h) *B* Lets Token Pass

Figure 7.2. *Continued*

of symbols exchanged between MAC entities. Each symbol corresponds to four bits. This assignment was chosen because, at the physical layer, data are transmitted in four-bit chunks. However, MAC entities in fact must deal with individual bits, so the discussion that follows must sometimes refer to four-bit symbols and sometimes to bits.

Figure 7.3 depicts the formats of the frames generated by the FDDI protocol. The overall frame format consists of the following fields:

- *Preamble:* Synchronizes the frame with each station's clock. The originator of the frame uses a field of 16 idle symbols (64 bits); subsequent repeating stations may change the length of the field consistent with clocking requirements. The idle symbol is a nondata fill pattern. The actual form of a nondata symbol depends on the signal encoding on the medium.
- *Starting delimiter (SD):* Indicates the start of the frame. The SD consists of signaling patterns that are always distinguishable from data. It is coded as follows: JK, where J and K are nondata symbols.
- *Frame control (FC):* Has the bit format CLFFZZZ, where C indicates whether this is a synchronous or an asynchronous frame (explained later); L indicates the use of 16- or 48-bit addresses; FF indicates whether this is a LLC frame or a MAC control frame. In the latter case, the remaining bits indicate the type of MAC frame.
- *Destination address (DA):* Specifies the station(s) for which the frame is intended. It may be a unique physical address (one station), a multicast-group address (a group of stations), or a broadcast address (all stations on the local network). The ring may contain a mixture of 16-bit and 48-bit addresses.
- *Source address (SA):* Specifies the station that sent the frame.
- *Information:* Contains LLC data or information related to a control operation.
- *Frame check sequence (FCS):* A 32-bit cyclic redundancy check (see Appendix C), based on FC, DA, SA, and Information fields.

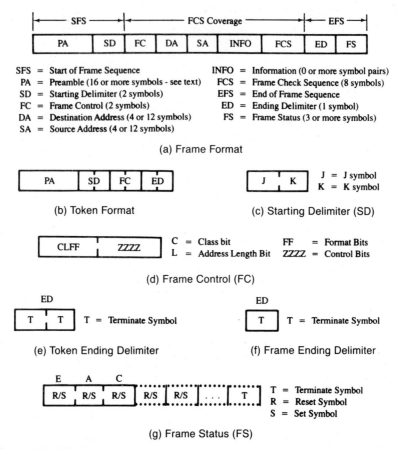

Figure 7.3.   FDDI frame format

- *Ending delimiter (ED):* Contains nondata symbols to indicate the end of the frame (except for the FS field). The delimiter is eight bits long for a token (two nondata T symbols), and four bits long (one T symbol) for all other frames. The variation is so that frames occupy an integral number of octets.
- *Frame status (FS):* Contains the error detected (E), address recognized (A), and frame copied (C) indicators. Each indicator is represented by a symbol, where R represents "off" or "false," and S represents "on" or "true." The FS field may contain additional trailing control indicators whose use is implementer defined. If there is an odd number of additional symbols, the FS field ends with a T symbol.

Address Fields.   The address field formats are shown in Figure 2.10. Although the exact structure of the 15-bit or 46-bit address is not defined in the standard, FDDI includes a recommended structure for further study. This structure is identical to that for IEEE 802.5 (see Figure 6.4), and the discussion in Section 6.2 is applicable.

The standard specifies that a mixture of 16-bit and 48-bit addresses may be employed on the ring. All stations shall have the capability to employ 16-bit addresses. A station with only 16-bit address capability shall be capable of functioning in a ring with stations concurrently operating with 48-bit addresses. To do so, the 16-bit station shall be capable of:

- Repeating frames with 48-bit addresses
- Recognizing the 48-bit broadcast address (all ones)
- Reacting correctly to Claim frames and Beacon frames (explained later) with 48-bit addresses

A station using 48-bit addresses shall have a minimum 16-bit address capability such that the station shall:

- Have a fully functional 16-bit individual address
- Recognize the 16-bit broadcast address (all ones)

Frame Control Field. The frame control field indicates which type of frame this is and also contains bits that specify details of operation. There are four types of frames, indicated by the FF bits. These are control, LLC, reserved for implementer, and reserved for future standardization. Table 7.1 lists the formats defined in the standard. Some of these are self-explanatory; others will be explained as the discussion proceeds.

Basic Operation

Having described the FDDI frame structure, we are now in a position to describe the MAC algorithm. To begin, we look at the basic operation, without the use of priority or ring maintenance functions.

A station that wishes to transmit waits until a token frame goes by, as indicated by a FC field with FF bits set to 00 and ZZZZ bits set to 0000. The station seizes the token by absorbing the remainder of the token from the ring before the entire FC field is repeated. After the captured token is completely received, the station may begin transmitting frames. The station may continue to transmit until it has no more data to transmit or until a token-holding timer (THT) expires.

Other stations listen to the ring and repeat passing frames. Each station introduces into the ring approximately a one-bit delay as the time to examine, copy, or change a bit as necessary. Each station can check passing bits for errors and can set the E indicator if an error is detected. If a station detects its own address, it sets the A indicator; it may also copy the frame, setting the C indicator. This allows the originating station to differentiate three conditions:

- Station nonexistent/nonactive
- Station exists but frame not copied
- Frame copied

Table 7.1.   FDDI FRAME TYPES

Type	FC Bits CLFF ZZZZ to ZZZZ	Description
Void	0X00 0000	Logically not a frame; ignored
Nonrestricted token	1000 0000	For synchronous and nonrestricted asynchronous transmission
Restricted token	1100 0000	For synchronous and restricted asynchronous transmission
MAC frames		
MAC	1L00 0001 to 1111	Used in MAC protocol
MAC Beacon	1L00 0010	Indicates serious ring failure
MAC Claim	1L00 0011	Used to determine which station creates a new token and initializes the ring
Station management frames		
Station management	0L00 0001 to 1111	Contains station management information
Next station addressing	0L00 1111	Used in station management
LLC frames		
Asynchronous	0L01 rPPP	Asynchronous transmission at priority PPP
Synchronous	1L01 rrrr	Synchronous transmission
Reserved frames		
Reserved for implementer	CL10 r000 to r111	Implementation-dependent
Reserved for future standardization	CL11 rrrr	To be used in future version of the standard

X = 0 or 1 bit
r = Reserved for future standardization
C = Class bit
L = Address length bit

The station that originates a frame is responsible for purging the frame from the ring. Each transmitted frame is absorbed as it returns to the originating station. The status indicators (E, A, C) in the ending delimiter are examined to determine the result of the transmission. However, if an error is reported, the MAC protocol does not attempt to retransmit the frame. This is the responsibility of LLC or some higher-layer protocol.

Capacity Allocation

The priority scheme used in 802.5 will not work in FDDI, as a station will often issue a token before its own transmitted frame returns. Hence, the use of a reservation field is not effective. Furthermore, the FDDI standard is intended to provide for greater control over the capacity of the network than 802.5 to meet the requirements for a high-speed local network (see Appendix 7A). Specifically, the FDDI capacity allocation scheme seeks to accommodate the following requirements:

- Support for a mixture of stream and bursty traffic.
- Support for multiframe dialogue.

To accommodate the first requirement, FDDI defines two types of traffic: synchronous and asynchronous. The scheme works as follows. A target token rotation time (TTRT) is defined; each station stores the same value for TTRT. Some or all stations may be provided a synchronous allocation (SA$_i$), which may vary among stations. The allocation must be set such that:

$$\Sigma SA_i + D\_Max + F\_Max + Token\_Time \leqslant TTRT$$

where

$$SA_i = \text{allocation for station } i$$

$$D\_Max = \text{propagation time for one complete circuit of the ring.}$$

$$F\_Max = \text{time required to transmit a maximum length frame (4500 octets).}$$

$$Token\_Time = \text{Time required to transmit a token.}$$

The assignment of values for SA$_i$ is by means of a SMT protocol involving the exchange of SMT PDUs. The protocol must assure that the above equation is satisfied. Initially, each station has a zero allocation and it must request a change in the allocation. Support for synchronous allocation is optional; a station that does not support synchronous allocation may only transmit asynchronous traffic.

All stations have the same value of TTRT and a separately assigned value of SA$_i$. In addition, several variables that are required for the operation of the capacity-allocation algorithm are maintained at each station:

- Token-rotation timer (TRT)
- Token-holding timer (THT)
- Late counter (LC)

Each station's TRT is initialized to TTRT; when it is enabled, it counts down until it expires at TRT = 0. It is then reset to TTRT and enabled again. LC is initialized at zero and is incremented when TRT expires. Thus LC records the number of times, if any, that TRT has expired since the token was last received at that station. The token is considered to arrive early if TRT has not expired since the station received the token, that is, if $LC = 0$.

When a station receives the token, its actions will depend on whether the token is early or late. If the token is early, the station saves the remaining time in TRT in THT; resets TRT, and enables TRT:

THT ← TRT

TRT ← TTRT

enable TRT

The station can then transmit according to the following rules:

1. It may transmit synchronous frames for a time SA_i.
2. After transmitting synchronous frames, or if there were no synchronous frames to transmit, THT is enabled. The station may transmit asynchronous frames only so long as $THT > 0$.

If a station receives a token and the token is late, then LC is set to zero, and TRT continues to run. The station can then transmit synchronous frames for a time SA_i. The station may not transmit any asynchronous frames.

This scheme is designed to assure that the time between successive sighting of a token is on the order of TTRT or less. Of this time, a given amount is always available for synchronous traffic and any excess capacity is available for asynchronous traffic. Because of random fluctuations

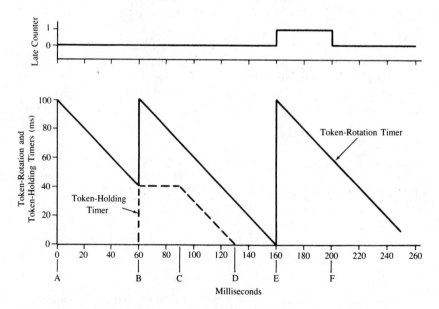

Figure 7.4. FDDI capacity allocation example [MCC088]

in traffic, the actual token circulation time may exceed TTRT [JOHN87, SEVC87], as demonstrated below.

The FDDI algorithm is similar to the 802.4 algorithm with only two classes of data, 6 and 4. Synchronous data corresponds to Class 6, and the value of SA_i in FDDI corresponds to the token holding time in 802.4. Finally, TTRT corresponds to TRT4. Since the sum of the SA_i (all the synchronous allocations) must be less than or equal to TTRT, the FDDI restrictions correspond to Case IIa in Figure 5.7.

Figure 7.4 illustrates the use of the station variables in FDDI by displaying the values of TRT, THT, and LC for a particular station. In this example, taken from [MCCO88], the TTRT is 100 milliseconds (ms). The stations's synchronous capacity allocation, SA_i, is 30 ms. The following events occur:

A. A token arrives early. The station has no frames to send. TRT is set to TTRT (100 ms) and begins to count down. The station allows the token to go by.

B. The token returns 60 ms later. Since TRT = 40 and LC = 0, the token is early. The station sets THT ← TRT and TRT ← TTRT, so that THT = 40 and TRT = 100. TRT is immediately enabled. The station has synchronous data to transmit and begins to do so.

C. After 30 ms, the station has consumed its synchronous allocation. It has asynchronous data to transmit, so it enables THT and begins transmitting.

D. THT expires, and the station must cease transmission of asynchronous frames. The station issues a token.

E. TRT expires. The station increments LC to 1 and resets TRT to 100.

F. The token arrives. Since LC is 1, the token is late, and no asynchronous data may be transmitted. At this point, the station also has no synchronous data to transmit. LC is reset to 0 and the token is allowed to go by.

Figure 7.5 provides a simplified example of a 4-station ring (compare Figure 5.8). We assume that the traffic consists of fixed-length frames,

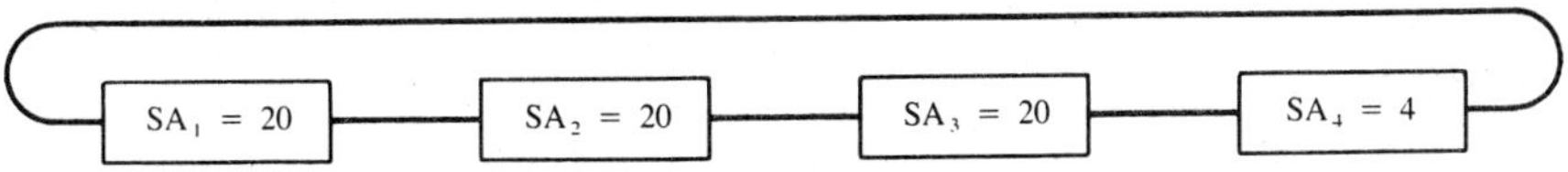

$SA_1 = 20$		$SA_2 = 20$		$SA_3 = 20$		$SA_4 = 4$	
TCT	XMIT	TCT	XMIT	TCT	XMIT	TCT	XMIT
4	20,76	100	20,0	120	20,0	140	20,0
160	20,0	84	20,16	100	20,0	100	20,0
100	20,0	100	20,0	84	20,16	100	20,0
100	20,0	100	20,0	100	20,0	84	20,16
100	20,0	100	20,0	100	20,0	100	20,0
84	20,16	100	20,0	100	20,0	100	20,0
100	20,0	84	20,16	100	20,0	100	20,0

Figure 7.5. Operation of FDDI capacity allocation scheme

and that TTRT = 100 frame times and SA_i = 20 frame times for all stations. We also assume that the total overhead during one complete token circulation is 4 frame times. The value in the left-hand column is the token circulation time actually experienced at that station for the previous rotation of the token. Thus, when the token arrives early, this value is equal to 100 − TRT. The right-hand value is the number of frames the station transmits; this is broken down into synchronous and asynchronous frames.

   The example begins after a period during which no data frames have been sent, so that the token has been circulating as rapidly as possible (4 frame times). Thus, when Station 1 receives the token, it measures a circulation time of 4 (its TRT = 96). It is therefore able to send not only its 20 synchronous frames but also 76 asynchronous frames; recall that THT is not enabled until after the station has sent its synchronous frames. Station 2 experiences a circulation time of 100 (20 frames + 76 frames + 4 overhead frames), but is nevertheless entitled to transmit its 20 synchronous frames. Note that if each station continues to transmit its maximum allowable synchronous frames, then the circulation time surges to 160, but soon stabilizes at 100. With a total synchronous utilization of 80 and an overhead of 4 frame times, there is an average capacity of 16 frame times available for asynchronous transmission. Note that if all stations always have a full backlog of asynchronous traffic, the opportunity to transmit asynchronous frames rotates among them.

   Asynchronous traffic can be further subdivided into eight levels of priority. Each station has a set of eight threshold values, $T\_Pr(1),\ldots,$ $T\_Pr(8)$, such that $T\_PR(i)$ = maximum time that a token can take to circulate and still permit priority i frames to be transmitted. The station can then transmit according to the following rule:

> After transmitting synchronous frames, or if there were no synchronous frames to transmit, THT is enabled and begins to run from its set value. The station may transmit asynchronous data of priority i only so long as $THT<T\_Pr(i)$. The maximum value of any of the $T\_Pr(i)$ must be no greater than TTRT.

This scheme is essentially the one used in the 802.4 token bus standard (see Figure 5.6).

   The above rule provides support for both stream and bursty traffic and, with the use of priorities, provides a great deal of flexibility. In addition, FDDI provides a mechanism that satisfies the requirement for dedicated multiframe traffic mentioned earlier and defined in Appendix 7A. When a station wishes to enter an extended dialogue it may gain control of all the unallocated (asynchronous) capacity on the ring by using a restricted token. The station captures a nonrestricted token, transmits the first frame of the dialog to the destination station, and then issues a restricted token. Only the station that received the last asynchronous frame

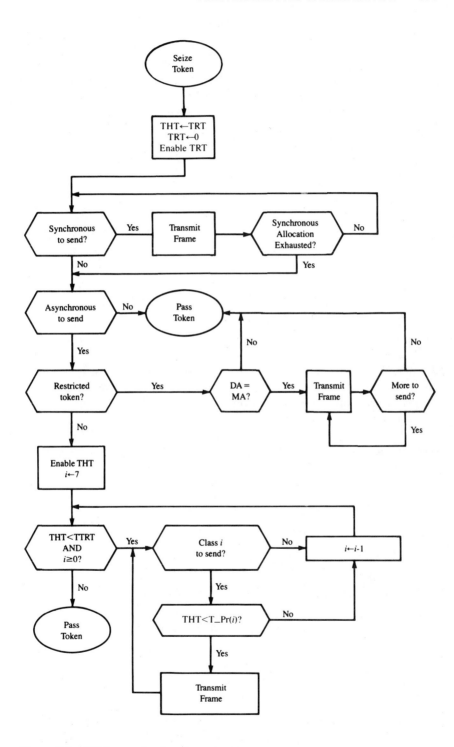

Figure 7.6.   FDDI capacity allocation scheme

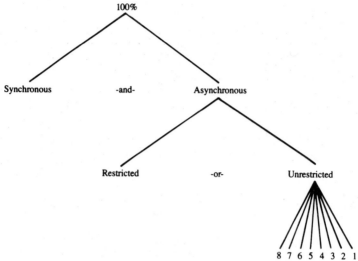

Figure 7.7. FDDI capacity allocation

may transmit asynchronous frames using the restricted token. The two stations may then exchange data frames and restricted tokens for an extended period, during which no other stations may transmit asynchronous frames. The standard assumes that restricted transmission is predetermined not to violate the TTRT limitation, and it does not mandate the use of THT during this mode. Synchronous frames may be transmitted by any station upon capture of either type of token.

Figure 7.6 depicts the complete capacity allocation scheme, and Figure 7.7 summarizes the relationship among the various types of traffic.

Ring Monitoring

The responsibility for monitoring the functioning of the token ring algorithm is distributed among all stations on the ring. Each station monitors the ring for invalid conditions requiring ring initialization. Invalid conditions include an extended period of inactivity or incorrect activity (e.g., persistent data frame). To detect the latter condition, each station keeps track of how long it has been since it last saw a valid token. If this time significantly exceeds TTRT, an error condition is assumed.

Three processes are involved in error detection and correction:

- Claim token process
- Initialization process
- Beacon process

Two MAC control frames are used: the Beacon frame and the Claim frame (Table 7.1).

Claim Token Process.   Any station detecting the need for initialization of the ring initiates the claim token process by issuing Claim frames. This is used to negotiate the value to be assigned to TTRT and to resolve contention among stations attempting to initialize the ring. Each claiming station sends a continuous stream of Claim frames. The information field of the Claim frame contains the station's bid for the value of TTRT. Each claiming station inspects incoming Claim frames and either defers (ceases to transmit its own Claim frames and repeats incoming frames) or not (continues to transmit its own Claim frames and absorbs incoming frames), according to the following arbitration hierarchy:

- The frame with the lowest TTRT has precedence.
- Given equal values of TTRT, the frame with the longest source address (48 versus 16 bits) has precedence.
- Given equal values of TTRT and equal address lengths, the frame with the highest address has precedence.

The process completes when one station receives its own Claim frame, which has made a complete circuit of the ring. At this point, the ring is filled with that station's Claim frames and all other stations have yielded. All stations store the value of TTRT contained in the latest received Claim frame. The result is that the smallest requested value for TTRT is stored by all stations and will be used to allocate capacity.

Initialization Process.   The station that has won the claim token process is responsible for initializing the ring. All the stations on the ring recognize the initialization process as a result of having seen one or more Claim frames. The initializing station issues a nonrestricted token. On the first circulation of the token, it may not be captured. Rather, each station uses the appearance of the token for transition from an initialization state to an operational state, and to reset its TRT.

Beacon Process.   The Beacon frame is used to isolate a serious ring failure such as a break in the ring. For example, when a station is attempting the claim token process, it will eventually time out if it does not come to a resolution (winning or losing).

Upon entering the beacon process, a station continuously transmits Beacon frames. A station always yields to Beacon frames received from an upstream station. Consequently, if the logical break persists, the Beacon frames of the station immediately downstream from the break will normally be propagated. If a station in the beacon process receives its own Beacon frames, it assumes that the logical ring has been restored, and it initiates the claim token process.

Table 7.2. **FDDI MAC SERVICE PRIMITIVES AND PARAMETERS**

MA-UNITDATA.request (FC-value (1), destination-address (1), M-SDU (1),
  requested-service-class (1), stream (1), FC-value (2), destination-address (2),
M-SDU (2), requested-service-class (2), stream (2), . . . , FC-value (n),
  destination-address (n), M-SDU (n), requested-service-class (n), stream (n),
  Token-class)

MA-UNITDATA-STATUS.indication (number-of-SDUs, transmission-status,
  provided-service-class)

MA-UNITDATA-indication (FC-value, destination-address, source-address,
  M-SDU, reception-status)

MA-TOKEN.request (requested-Token-class)

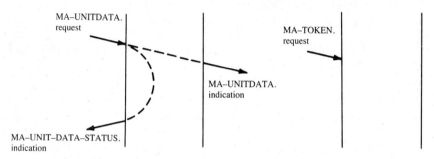

Figure 7.8.   FDDI MAC service timing

7.3 MAC SERVICES

The services provided by the MAC layer allow the local LLC entity to
exchange LLC data units with peer LLC entities. Table 7.2 lists the primitives and parameters that define the FDDI MAC service, and Figure 7.8
shows the interaction.

The FDDI service specification is a close but not exact match to
that expected in the LLC standard (see Section 3.1). It is probable that
the minor discrepancies will be resolved in a later version of the standard.
Because it is FDDI and not IEEE 802.2 that defines the functions of the
MAC layer, the service specification in the FDDI document should take
precedence.

In the MA-UNITDATA.request primitive, each set of parameters (FC-value, destination-address, M-SDU, requested-service-class,
stream) specifies one data unit for transmission and is referred to a *subrequest*. The FC-value parameter specifies the value of the frame control
field in the MAC frame (see Figure 7.3). If LLC is invoking MAC services, then the value should indicate that this is an LLC frame, and the
class and address length are specified. Requested-service-class may
either be synchronous or asynchronous; if asynchronous, the requested
token class and the priority may optionally be specified. The stream parameter is set to one in each subrequest except the last. Use of the stream
parameter requests that multiple data units be transmitted as a result of

the MA-UNITDATA.request. If TRT has expired or if a data unit is encountered that cannot be transmitted because of its associated requested-service-class and the current value of THT, then transmission is terminated. The standard leaves it as an implementation option for MAC to either transmit the remaining data units at the next access opportunity or require reissuance of MA-UNITDATA.request for the remaining data units. The token-class parameter specifies the class of token that MAC shall issue at the end of the request, if no other request is pending that can be honored. With requests for synchronous service, the token-class shall be the token-class that was captured; with requests for asynchronous service, it may be either restricted or nonrestricted.

The MA-UNITDATA-STATUS.indication primitive is passed from the MAC entity to the LLC user in response to an MA-UNITDATA.request. The number-of-SDUs parameter reports the number of data units transmitted on a given access opportunity as a result of this request. The transmission-status parameter indicates the success or the failure of the service provided for the previous associated MA-UNITDATA.request; this has local significance only. The provided-service-class parameter specifies the service class used for the data transfer.

When a MAC frame is received with an address match, the MAC entity will issue an MA-UNITDATA.indication. The FC-value parameter is the value of the received frame control field. The reception-status parameter consists of the following elements:

1. Frame-validity: The status is either FR-GOOD or FR-BAD. In the latter case, the reason for the error is reported as one of the following:

   - *invalid FCS:* Calculated FCS does not match received FCS
   - *length error:* Frame did not have valid data length
   - *internal error:* An internal error has occurred that prevents MAC from transferring to LLC a frame that has been acknowledged by the setting of the A and C indicators.

2. Frame status: The received E, A, and C indicator values.

The MA-TOKEN.request primitive is used by LLC to request the capture of the next token. Receipt of this primitive causes MAC to capture the next usable token. MAC retains the token until an MA-UNITDATA.request primitive is received from LLC or until TRT expires. In the former case, MAC acts on the request and then issues a token. In the latter case, MAC simply issues a token of the same token class as was captured.

The MA-TOKEN primitive may be used by LLC when data of a time-critical nature is to be transferred, but is not yet ready. The primitive minimizes the waiting time for the token.

7.4 PHYSICAL LAYER SPECIFICATION

Physical Layer Services

As always, the services provided by the physical layer are defined in terms of primitives and parameters. These are:

- PH-UNITDATA.request (PH-Request (symbol))
- PH-UNITDATA.indication (PH-Indication (symbol))
- PH-INVALID.indication (PH-Invalid)

The PH-UNITDATA primitives support the transfer of data from a single MAC entity to all other MAC entities contained within the same local network defined by the medium. That is, data transmitted by one MAC entity using PH-UNITDATA.request is received by all other MAC entities with a PH-UNITDATA.indication. As was mentioned, each symbol corresponds to four bit positions; allowable symbols include data symbols, representing four binary digits, and nondata symbols. The physical layer encodes and transmits each symbol. Each active station attached to the medium receives the transmitted symbols. As each symbol is received, the physical layer generates a PH-UNITDATA.indication.

It must be emphasized that this specification is an abstract description of services and does not imply any particular implementation. It does serve to illustrate that the MAC layer is substantially independent of the characteristics of the physical medium.

Physical Layer Protocol

The medium-independent portion of the physical layer specification is referred to as the physical layer protocol. In addition to defining the physical layer services, described previously, the physical layer protocol addresses data encoding and jitter.

Data Encoding. As is the case with the IEEE 802.4 optical fiber specification, the FDDI data encoding is based on the use of intensity modulation. In the case of the IEEE 802.4 specification, the incoming data is precoded in Manchester form before being submitted to the intensity modulation process, in order to provide transitions for synchronization. For FDDI, the use of Manchester precoding is not advisable. The disadvantage of this approach is that the efficiency is only 50 percent. That is, because there can be as many as two transitions per bit time, a signaling rate of 200 million signal elements per second (expressed as 200 Mbaud) is needed to achieve a data rate of 100 Mbps. At the high data rate of FDDI, this represents an unnecessary cost and technical burden.

To overcome the data rate burden imposed by Manchester intensity modulation, the FDDI standard specifies the use of a code referred to as

4B/5B. In this scheme, encoding is done four bits at a time; each four bits of data are encoded into a symbol with five cells such that each cell contains a single signal element (presence or absence of light). In effect, each set of four bits is encoded as five bits. The efficiency is thus raised to 80 percent; 100 Mbps is achieved with 125 Mbaud. The resulting savings is substantial: A 200-Mbaud transmitter/receiver can cost five to ten times that of a 125-Mbaud pair [JOSH86].

To understand how the 4B/5B code achieves synchronization, you need to know that there is actually a second stage of encoding [CONN87]; each element of the 4B/5B stream is treated as a binary value and encoded using a technique referred to as Nonreturn to Zero Inverted (NRZI) or Nonreturn to Zero-Mark (NRZ-M). In this code, a binary 1 is represented with a transition at the beginning of the bit interval and a binary 0 is represented with no transition at the beginning of the bit interval; there are no other transitions. The advantage of NRZI is that it employs differential encoding. In differential encoding, the signal is decoded by comparing the polarity of adjacent signal elements rather than the absolute value of a signal element. A benefit of this scheme is that it is generally more reliable to detect a transition in the presence of noise and distortion than to compare a value to a threshold. This aids the ultimate decoding of the signal after it has been converted back from optical to the electrical realm.

Now we are in a position to describe the 4B/5B code and to understand selections that were made. Table 7.3 shows the symbol encoding used in FDDI. As we are encoding 4 bits with a 5-bit pattern, there will be some patterns that are not needed. The codes selected to represent the 16 four-bit patterns are such that a transition is present at least twice for each 5-cell code on the medium. Given an NRZI format on the fiber, no more than three zeros in a row can be allowed, since, with NRZI, the absence of a line transition indicates a zero.

We can now summarize the FDDI encoding scheme.

1. A simple intensity modulation encoding is rejected because it does not provide synchronization; a string of 1s or 0s would have no transitions.
2. The 4B/5B code is chosen over Manchester because it is more efficient.
3. The 4B/5B code is further encoded using NRZI so that the resulting differential encoding will improve reception reliability.
4. The specific codes chosen for the encoding of the 16 four-bit data patterns guarantee no more than three zeros in a row; this provides for adequate synchronization.

Only 16 of the 32 possible code patterns are required to represent the input data. The remaining symbols are either declared invalid or as-

Table 7.3. 4B/5B CODE

Decimal	Code group	Symbol		Assignment
		Line state symbols		
00	00000	Q		Quiet
31	11111	I		Idle
04	00100	H		Halt
		Starting delimiter		
24	11000	J		1st of sequential SD pair
17	10001	K		2nd of sequential SD pair
		Data symbols		
			Hex	Binary
30	11110	0	0	0000
09	01001	1	1	0001
20	10100	2	2	0010
21	10101	3	3	0011
10	01010	4	4	0100
11	01011	5	5	0101
14	01110	6	6	0110
15	01111	7	7	0111
18	10010	8	8	1000
19	10011	9	9	1001
22	10110	A	A	1010
23	10111	B	B	1011
26	11010	C	C	1100
27	11011	D	D	1101
28	11100	E	E	1110
29	11101	F	F	1111
		Ending delimiter		
13	01101	T		Used to terminate the data stream
		Control indicators		
07	00111	R		Denoting logical ZERO (reset)
25	11001	S		Denoting logical ONE (set)
		Invalid code assignments		
01	00001	V or H		These code patterns shall not be
02	00010	V or H		transmitted because they violate
03	00011	V		consecutive code-bit zeros or
05	00101	V		duty cycle requirements. Codes
06	00110	V		01, 02, 08, and 16 shall, however,
08	01000	V or H		be interpreted as Halt when
12	01100	V		received.
16	10000	V or H		

signed special meaning as control symbols. For example, two of the patterns always occur in pairs and act as start delimiters for a frame.

Timing Jitter.   In Appendix 6A, we defined timing jitter as the deviation of clock recovery that can occur when the receiver attempts to recover clocking as well as data from the received signal. The clock recovery will deviate in a random fashion from the transitions of the received signal. If no countermeasures are taken, the jitter accumulates around the ring. We saw that the IEEE 802.5 standard specifies that only one clock will be used on the ring, and that the station that has the clock is responsible for eliminating jitter by means of an elastic buffer. If the ring as a whole runs ahead of or behind the master clock, the elastic buffer expands or contracts accordingly. Even with this technique, the accumulation of jitter places a limitation on the size of the ring.

This centralized clocking approach is inappropriate for a 100-Mbps fiber ring. At 100 Mbps, the bit time is only 10 ns, compared with a bit time of 250 ns at 4 Mbps. Thus the effects of distortion are more severe, and a centralized clocking scheme would put very tough and expensive demands on the phase-lock loop circuitry at each node. Therefore, the FDDI standard specifies the use of a distributed clocking scheme: each station uses its own autonomous clock source to transmit or repeat information onto the ring. Each station has its own elastic buffer of at least 10 bits. Data is clocked into the buffer at the clock rate recovered from the incoming stream, but is clocked out of the buffer at the station's autonomous clock rate. This distributed system is believed to be more robust and to minimize jitter. As a consequence of reclocking at each station, jitter does not limit the number of repeaters in the ring. However, the size of the elastic buffer limits frame size to a maximum of 4500 octets.

Physical Layer Medium Dependent

The medium-dependent portion of the physical layer specification defines the physical medium and specifies some reliability features [HAMS88] (Figure 7.9).

Physical Medium.   The FDDI standard specifies an optical fiber ring with a data rate of 100 Mbps, using the NRZI-4B/5B encoding scheme described previously. The wavelength specified for data transmission is 1300 nm. Virtually all fiber transmitters operate at 850, 1300, or 1550 nm. The cost and performance of the system increases as the wavelength increases. For local data communications, most systems today use an 850-nm light source. At distances of about 1 km and data rates of about 100 Mbps, however, this wavelength begins to be inadequate [MIER86]. On the other hand, the 1500-nm source requires the use of an expensive laser and is probably overkill for the FDDI application.

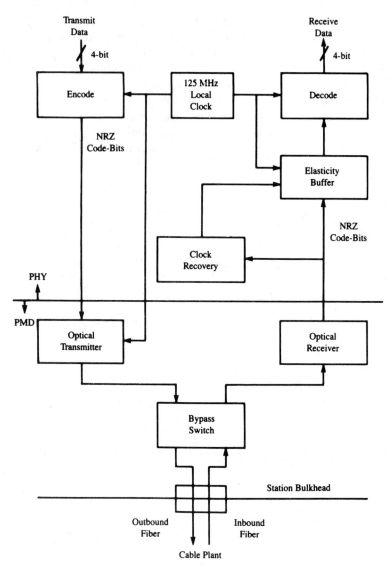

Figure 7.9.   FDDI physical layer block diagram [BURR86]

The specification indicates the use of multimode fiber transmission. Although today's long-distance networks rely primarily on single-mode fiber, that technology requires the use of lasers as light sources, rather than the cheaper and less powerful light emitting diodes (LEDs) which are adequate for the FDDI requirements. The dimensions of the multimode optical fiber cable are specified in terms of the diameter of the core of the fiber and the outer diameter of the cladding layer that surrounds the core. The combination specified in the standard is 62.5/125 μm. The standard lists as alternatives 50/125, 82/125, and 100/140 μm. In general, smaller diameters offer higher potential bandwidths but also higher connector loss. The 62.5/125 and 85/125 combinations seem the best overall compromise for the FDDI application.

Based on the characteristics defined previously, the maximum distance between adjacent repeaters is 2 km. The specifications were developed on the basis of up to 1000 physical connections and a total fiber path length of up to 200 km.

Reliability Specification.   Unlike the IEEE standards, the FDDI standard explicitly addresses the need for reliability by including specifications for reliability-enhancing techniques. Three techniques are included:

- *Station bypass:* A bad or powered-off station may be bypassed using an automatic optical bypass switch.
- *Wiring concentrator:* Wiring concentrators can be used in a star wiring strategy. This approach was discussed in Chapter 1.
- *Dual rings:* Two rings are employed to interconnect the stations in such a way that a failure of any station or link results in the reconfiguration of the network to maintain connectivity.

The concept of dual rings is illustrated in Figure 7.10 [ROSS87]. Stations participating in a dual ring are connected to their neighbors by two links that transmit in opposite direction. This creates two rings: a primary ring, and a secondary ring that circulates in the opposite direction. Under normal conditions, the secondary ring is idle. When a link failure occurs, the stations on either side of the link reconfigure as shown in Figure 7.10b. This isolates the link fault and restores a closed ring. In this figure, a dark dot represents a MAC attachment within the station. Thus, in the counter direction, signals are merely repeated, while the MAC protocol is only involved in the primary direction. Should a station itself fail, as shown in Figure 7.10c, then the stations on either side reconfigure to eliminate the failed station and both links to that station.

A network can be constructed with a mixture of single-ring and dual-ring capability. The FDDI standard defines two classes of stations:

- *Class A:* Connects to both primary and secondary rings. In the event of a failure, provisions are made within a Class A station to reconfigure the network using a combination of the operational links of the primary and secondary rings.
- *Class B:* Connects only to the primary ring. A failure can isolate a Class B station.

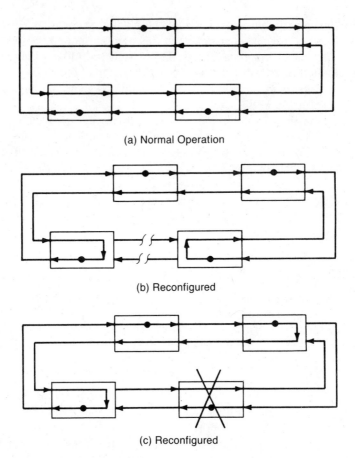

(a) Normal Operation

(b) Reconfigured

(c) Reconfigured

Figure 7.10. FDDI dual-ring operation

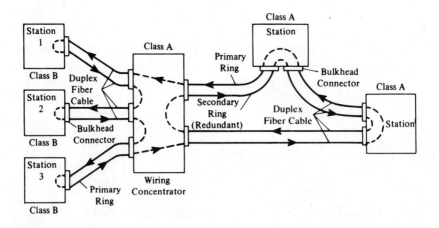

Figure 7.11. FDDI ring architecture

Figure 7.11 depicts the FDDI scheme. The user can equip stations that are of greater importance (including wiring concentrators) as Class A stations, insuring their higher availability. Stations of lesser importance can be configured as Class B stations, reducing their cost.

APPENDIX 7A.   REQUIREMENTS FOR HIGH-SPEED LOCAL NETWORKS

High-speed local networks are intended to meet a variety of requirements and to be used for applications where the higher cost of a high-speed LAN (compared to the IEEE 802 variety) is justified. Three general areas of application are addressed by FDDI [JOSH86]:

- Backend local networks
- High-speed office networks
- Backbone local networks

Backend Local Networks

Backend local networks are used in a computer-room environment to interconnect mainframe computers and mass storage devices [THOR79]. The key requirement here is for bulk data transfer among a limited number of devices in a small area. High reliability is also a requirement. Typical characteristics include:

- *High data rate:* To keep up with the high-volume demand, data rates of 50 to 100 Mbps are needed.
- *High-speed interface:* File transfer operations are typically performed through high-speed parallel I/O interfaces, rather than slower communications interfaces. Thus, the physical link between station and network must be high speed.
- *Distributed access:* For reasons of reliability and efficiency, a distributed MAC technique is used.
- *Limited distance:* Generally, a backend local network will be employed in a computer room or a small number of rooms.
- *Limited number of devices:* The number of expensive mainframes and mass storage devices found in the computer room is generally in the 10s of devices.

The FDDI network in a backend application is comprised of a preponderance of dual stations with relatively few single-ring stations.

The backend network introduces one new performance requirement that relates to the type of traffic to be handled. The backend network is more likely to see the file transfer application as opposed to interactive usage. For efficient operation, the MAC protocol should permit sustained use of the medium either by permitting transmissions of unbounded length or permitting a pair of devices to seize the channel for an indefinite period. In the latter case, MAC permits a multiframe dialogue between two devices, with no other data allowed on the medium for the duration of the dialogue. This permits a long sequence of data frames and acknowledgments to be interchanged. An example of the utility of this feature is its use to read from or write to high-performance disks. Without the ability to seize the bus temporarily, only one sector of the disk could be accessed per revolution—a totally unacceptable performance. The restricted token feature of the FDDI MAC protocol supports the multiframe dialogue requirement.

High-speed Office Networks

Traditionally, the office environment has included a variety of devices with low- to medium-speed data transfer requirements. The requirements of such an environment can be met in a cost-effective manner by the type of local network specified in the IEEE 802 standards. However, new applications in the office environment are being developed for which the limited speeds (1 to 10 Mpbs) of the typical local network are inadequate. Desktop image processors could soon increase network data flow by an unprecedented amount [BEVA86]. Examples of these applications include fax machines, document image processors, and graphics programs on personal computers. Resolutions as high as 400 $\times$ 400 per page are standard for these applications. Even with compression techniques, this will generate a tremendous load. Table 7.4 compares the load generated by image processing and some other office applications. In addition, optical disks are beginning to reach technical maturity and are being developed toward realistic desktop capacities exceeding 1 Gbyte. These new demands will require local networks with high speed that can support the larger numbers and greater geographic extent of office systems as compared to computer room systems. The FDDI network in this environment is likely to show a preponderance of single-ring stations to minimize the cost of connection.

Table 7.4. NETWORK LOAD COMPONENT COMPARISON

Traffic Type	Size in Bits
Compressed page image (400 $\times$ 400)	600,000
Compressed page image (200 $\times$ 200)	250,000
Word-processing page	20,000
Typical memo	3,500
Data processing transaction	500

Backbone Local Networks

The increasing use of distributed processing applications and personal computers has led to a need for a flexible strategy for local networking. Support of premises-wide data communications requires a networking and communications service that is capable of spanning the distances involved and that interconnects equipment in a single (perhaps large) building or a cluster of buildings. Although it is possible to develop a single local network to interconnect all the data processing equipment of a premises, this is probably not a practical alternative in most cases. There are several drawbacks:

- *Reliability:* With a single local network, a service interruption, even of short duration, could result in major disruption for users.
- *Capacity:* A single local network could be saturated as the number of devices attached to the network grows over time.
- *Cost:* A single network technology is not optimized for the diverse requirements for interconnection and communication. The presence of large numbers of low-cost microcomputers dictates that network support for these devices be provided at low cost. Local networks that support very low cost attachment will not be suitable for meeting the overall requirement.

A more attractive alternative is to employ lower-cost, lower-capacity local networks within buildings or departments and to link these networks with a higher-capacity (and therefore, higher-cost) local network. This latter network is referred to as a backbone local network.

Although many studies have shown that intradepartmental and intrabuilding communications greatly exceed interdepartmental and interbuilding communications, it is to be expected that the backbone local network in a large distributed processing environment will have to sustain high peak loads and, as the demand for communications grows over time, high sustained loads. Thus, a major requirement for the backbone is high capacity.

APPENDIX 7B.   A COMPARISON OF FDDI AND IEEE 802.5

The FDDI standard is based on the IEEE 802.5 standard. The X3T9.5 committee decided to adopt as much of 802.5 as possible, making changes only where necessary to exploit the high speeds of a fiber ring and to provide the service to be expected on a high-speed local network. This strategy has several advantages:

1. The token protocol is known to work effectively, particularly at high loads; thus there is no need and some risk in adopting a different approach.

Table 7.5. DIFFERENCES BETWEEN FDDI AND 802.5

FDDI	802.5
Optical fiber	Shielded twisted pair
100 Mbps	1 and 4 Mbps
NRZI-4B/5B code	Differential Manchester
Explicit reliability specification	No explicit reliability specification
Distributed clocking	Centralized clocking
Timed token rotation	Priority and reservation bits
New token after transmit	New token after receive
Seize token by absorption	Seizes token by flipping bit
FDDI frame structure	802.5 frame structure
4500-octet maximum frame size	No maximum frame size
16- and/or 48-bit addresses	16- or 48-bit addresses
Distributed recovery	Active monitor

2. The use of similar frame formats facilitates the internetworking of high- and low-speed rings.
3. Understanding of FDDI is facilitated for those already familiar with 802.5.
4. Implementation experience, particularly at the chip level, may be of benefit to vendors of FDDI systems and components.

Table 7.5 summarizes the key differences between 802.5 and FDDI.

8

MAC Bridges

An individual LAN is limited in terms of geographic scope, number of stations supported, and data-carrying capacity. To meet networking requirements, organizations are increasingly installing multiple LANs. With multiple LANs, there usually still remains the need to provide full interconnection. That is, it is usually required that a station on any one LAN be able to exchange data not only with other stations on the same LAN but also with stations on other LANs. When multiple networks are interconnected, the result is usually referred to as an *internet*. One means of providing this interconnection is the *MAC bridge*. As of this writing, there is no final standard for the MAC bridge. However, most of the technical work has been done. One specification has been developed by the 802.1 committee that is applicable to all types of LANs. At the same time, the 802.5 committee has developed a different specification specifically for 802.5 LANs. Both of these specifications are summarized in this chapter.

8.1 BRIDGE ARCHITECTURE AND OPERATION
Functions of a Bridge

The bridge is designed for use between local area networks (LANs) that use identical protocols for the physical and medium access layers (e.g., all conforming to IEEE 802.3 or all conforming to FDDI). In essence, a bridge operates at the MAC level and acts as a relay for frames between like networks. Because the networks all use the same protocols, the amount of processing required at the bridge is minimal.

Figure 8-1 illustrates the operation of a bridge between two LANs, A and B. The bridge performs the following functions:

- Read all frames transmitted on A, and accept those addressed to stations on B.
- Using the medium access control protocol for B, retransmit the frames onto B.
- Do the same for B-to-A traffic.

In addition to these basic functions, there are some interesting design considerations:

1. The bridge makes no modifications to the content or format of the frames it receives.
2. The bridge should contain enough buffer space to meet peak demands. Over a short period of time, frames may arrive faster than they can be transmitted.
3. The bridge must contain addressing and routing intelligence. At a minimum, the bridges must know which addresses are on each network in order to know which frames to forward. Further, there may be more than two networks in a sort of cascade configuration. The

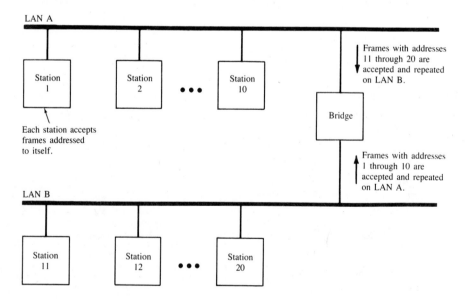

Figure 8.1. Bridge operation

bridge must be able to pass along frames intended for networks further on. The subject of routing is explored later in this section.

4. A bridge may connect more than two networks.

In summary, the bridge provides an extension to the LAN that requires no modification to the communications software in the stations attached to the LANs. It appears to all stations on the two (or more) LANs that there is a single LAN on which each station has a unique address. The station uses that unique address and need not explicitly discriminate between stations on the same LAN and stations on other LANs; the bridge takes care of that. Since the bridge operates as a MAC-level relay, the LLC level and above must be identical in the two end systems for successful end-to-end communications.

Since the bridge is used in a situation in which all of the LANs have the same characteristics, the reader may ask why not simply have one large LAN. Depending on circumstance, there are several reasons for the use of multiple LANs connected by bridges:

- *Reliability:* The danger in connecting all data processing devices in an organization to one network is that a fault on the network may disable communication for all devices. By using bridges, the network can be partitioned into self-contained units.
- *Performance:* In general, performance on a LAN declines with an increase in the number of devices or the length of the medium. A number of smaller LANs will often give improved performance if devices can be clustered so that *intra*-network traffic significantly exceeds *inter*-network traffic.
- *Security:* The establishment of multiple LANs may improve security of communications. It is desirable to keep different types of traffic (e.g., accounting, personnel, strategic planning) that have different security needs on physically separate media. At the same time, the different types of users with different level of security need to communicate through controlled and monitored mechanisms.
- *Geography:* Clearly, two separate LANs are needed to support devices clustered in two geographically distant locations. Even in the case of two buildings separated by a highway, it may be far easier to use a microwave bridge link than to attempt to string coaxial cable between the two buildings.

The description above has applied to the simplest sort of bridge. More sophisticated bridges can be used in more complex collections of LANs. These would include additional functions, such as:

- Each bridge can maintain status information on other bridges, together with the cost and number of bridge-to-bridge hops required to reach each network. This information may be updated by periodic exchanges of information among bridges. This allows the bridges to perform a dynamic routing function.

• A control mechanism can manage frame buffers in each bridge to overcome congestion. Under saturation conditions, the bridge can give precedence to en-route packets over new packets just entering the internet from an attached LAN, thus preserving the investment in line bandwidth and processing time already made in the en-route frame.

Bridge Protocol Architecture

The IEEE 802 committee has produced two specifications for bridges [IEEE88b, IEEE88c]. In both cases, the devices are referred to as MAC-level relays. In addition, all of the MAC standards suggest formats for a globally administered set of MAC station addresses across multiple homogeneous LANs. In this subsection, we examine the protocol architecture of these bridges.

Within the 802 architecture, the endpoint or station address is designated at the MAC level. At the LLC level, only an SAP address is specified. Thus, it is at the MAC level that a bridge can function. Figure 8-2a shows the simplest case, which consists of two LANs connected by a single bridge. The LANs employ the same MAC and LLC protocols. The bridge operates as previously described. A MAC frame whose destination is not on the immediate LAN is captured by the bridge, buffered briefly, and then transmitted on the other LAN. As far as the LLC layer is con-

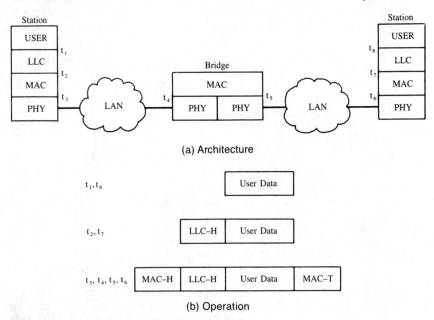

(a) Architecture

(b) Operation

Figure 8.2. Connection of two LANs by a bridge

cerned, there is a dialogue between peer LLC entities in the two endpoint stations. The bridge need not contain an LLC layer because it is merely serving to relay the MAC frames.

Figure 8-2b indicates the way in which data is encapsulated using a bridge. Data is provided by some user to LLC. The LLC entity appends a header and passes the resulting data unit to the MAC entity, which appends a header and a trailer to form a MAC frame. On the basis of the destination MAC address in the frame, it is captured by the bridge. The bridge does not strip off the MAC fields; its function is to relay the MAC frame intact to the destination LAN. Thus the frame is deposited on the destination LAN and captured by the destination station.

Routing

In the configuration of Figure 8-2, the bridge makes the decision to relay a frame on the basis of destination MAC address. In a more complex configuration, the bridge must also make a routing decision. Consider the configuration of Figure 8-3. Suppose that station 1 transmits a frame on LAN A intended for station 5. The frame will be read by both bridge 101 and bridge 102. For each bridge, the addressed station is not on a LAN

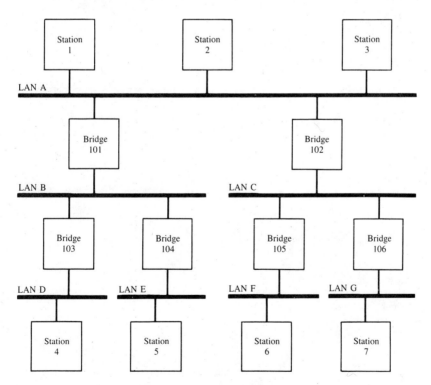

Figure 8.3. Internet configuration of bridges and LANs

to which the bridge is attached. Therefore, each bridge must make a decision of whether or not to retransmit the frame on its other LAN in order to move it closer to its intended destination. In this case, bridge 101 should repeat the frame on LAN B, whereas bridge 102 should refrain from retransmitting the frame. Once the frame has been transmitted on LAN B, it will be picked up by both bridges 103 and 104. Again, each must decide whether or not to forward the frame. In this case, bridge 104 should retransmit the frame on LAN E where it will be received by the destination, station 5.

Thus we see that, in the general case, the bridge must be equipped with a routing capability. When a bridge receives a frame, it must decide whether or not to forward it. If the bridge is attached to more than two networks, then it must decide whether or not to forward the frame and, if so, on which LAN the frame should be transmitted.

The routing decision may not always be a simple one. In Figure 8-4 bridge 107 is added to the previous configuration, directly linking LAN A and LAN E. Such an addition may be made to provide for higher overall internet availability. In this case, if Station 1 transmits a frame on LAN A intended for station 5 on LAN E, then either bridge 101 or bridge 107 could forward the frame. It would appear preferable for bridge 107 to

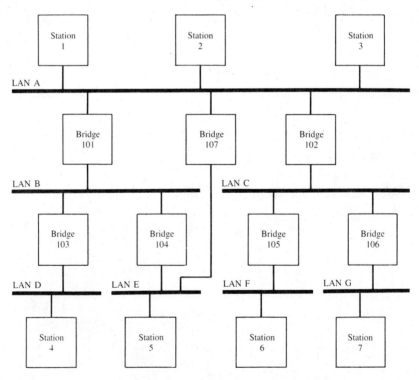

Figure 8.4. Internet configuration of bridges and LANs, with alternate routes

forward the frame, since it will involve only one "hop," whereas if the frame travels through bridge 101, it must suffer two hops. Another consideration is that there may be changes in the configuration. For example, bridge 107 may fail, in which case subsequent frames from station 1 to station 5 should go through bridge 101. So we can say that the routing capability must take into account the topology of the internet configuration and may need to be dynamically altered.

One final point: Figure 8-4 suggests that a bridge knows the identity of each station on each LAN. In a large configuration, such an arrangement is unwieldy. Furthermore, as stations are added to and dropped from LANs, all directories of station location must be updated. It would facilitate the development of a routing capability if all MAC-level addresses were in the form of a network part and a station part. For example, the IEEE 802.5 standard suggests that 16-bit MAC addresses consist of a 7-bit LAN number and an 8-bit station number, and that 48-bit addresses consist of a 14-bit LAN number and a 32-bit station number. In the remainder of this section, we assume that all MAC addresses include a LAN number and that routing is based on the use of that portion of the address only.

A variety of routing strategies have been proposed and implemented in recent years. The simplest, and most common strategy, is *fixed routing*. This strategy is suitable for small internets and for internets that are relatively stable. More recently, two groups within the IEEE 802 committee have developed specifications for routing strategies. The IEEE 802.1 group has issued a standard for routing based on the use of a *spanning tree* algorithm. The token ring committee, IEEE 802.5, has issued its own specification, referred to as *source routing*. We examine these three strategies in turn.

Fixed Routing

For fixed routing, a route is selected for each source-destination pair of LANs in the internet. If alternate routes are available between two LANs, then typically the route with the least number of hops is selected. The routes are fixed, or at least only change when there is a change in the topology of the internet.

Figure 8-5 suggests how fixed routing might be implemented. A central routing matrix is created to be stored perhaps at a network control center. The matrix shows, for each source-destination pair of LANs, the identity of the first bridge on the route. So for example, the route from LAN E to LAN F begins by going through bridge 107 to LAN A. Again consulting the matrix, the route from LAN A to LAN F goes through bridge 102 to LAN C. Finally, the route from LAN C to LAN F is directly through bridge 105. Thus the complete route from LAN E to LAN F is bridge 107, LAN A, bridge 102, LAN C, bridge 105.

Central Routing Matrix

Destination LAN

		A	B	C	D	E	F	G
	A	—	101	102	101	107	102	102
	B	101	—	101	103	104	101	101
Source LAN	C	102	102	—	102	102	105	106
	D	103	103	103	—	103	103	103
	E	107	104	107	104	—	107	107
	F	105	105	105	105	105	—	105
	G	106	106	106	106	106	106	—

Bridge 101 Table

from LAN A		from LAN B	
Dest	Next	Dest	Next
B	B	A	A
C	—	C	A
D	B	D	—
E	—	E	—
F	—	F	A
G	—	G	A

Bridge 102 Table

from LAN A		from LAN C	
Dest	Next	Dest	Next
B	—	A	A
C	C	B	A
D	—	D	A
E	—	E	A
F	C	F	—
G	C	G	—

Bridge 103 Table

from LAN B		from LAN D	
Dest	Next	Dest	Next
A	—	A	B
C	—	B	B
D	D	C	B
E	—	E	B
F	—	F	B
G	—	G	B

Bridge 104 Table

from LAN B		from LAN E	
Dest	Next	Dest	Next
A	—	A	—
C	—	B	B
D	—	C	—
E	E	D	B
F	—	F	—
G	—	G	—

Bridge 105 Table

from LAN C		from LAN F	
Dest	Next	Dest	Next
A	—	A	C
B	—	B	C
D	—	C	C
E	—	D	C
F	F	E	C
G	—	G	C

Bridge 106 Table

from LAN C		from LAN G	
Dest	Next	Dest	Next
A	—	A	C
B	—	B	C
D	—	C	C
E	—	D	C
F	—	E	C
G	G	F	C

Bridge 107 Table

from LAN A		from LAN E	
Dest	Next	Dest	Next
B	—	A	A
C	—	B	—
D	—	C	A
E	E	D	—
F	—	F	A
G	—	G	A

Figure 8.5. Fixed routing (using Figure 8.4)

From this overall matrix, routing tables can be developed and stored at each bridge. Each bridge needs one table for each LAN to which it attaches. The information for each table is derived from a single row of the matrix. For example, bridge 105 has two tables, one for frames arriving from LAN C and one for frames arriving from LAN F. The table shows, for each possible destination MAC address, the identity of the

LAN to which the bridge should forward the frame. The table labeled "from LAN C" is derived from the row labeled C in the routing matrix. Every entry in that row that contains bridge number 105 results in an entry in the corresponding table in bridge 105.

Once the directories have been established, routing is a simple matter. A bridge copies each incoming frame on each of its LANs. If the destination MAC address corresponds to an entry in its routing table, the frame is retransmitted on the appropriate LAN.

The fixed routing strategy is widely used in commercially available products. It has the advantage of simplicity and minimal processing requirements. However, in a complex internet, in which bridges may be dynamically added and in which failures must be allowed for, this strategy is too limited. We now turn to two more powerful alternatives.

8.2   THE SPANNING TREE APPROACH

The spanning tree approach is a mechanism in which bridges automatically develop a routing table and update that table in response to changing topology [BACK88, HART88, IEEE88b, PERL84]. The algorithm consists of three mechanisms:

- frame forwarding
- address learning
- loop resolution.

Frame Forwarding

In this scheme, a bridge maintains a *filtering database* for each port attached to a LAN. The database indicates the station addresses for which frames should be forwarded through that port. We can interpret this in the following fashion. For each port, a list of stations is maintained. A station is on the list if it is on the "same side" of the bridge as the port. For example, for bridge 102 of Figure 8-4, stations on LANs C, F, and G are on the same side of the bridge as the LAN A port, and stations on LANs A, B, D, and E are on the same side of the bridge as the LAN C port. When a frame is received on any port, the bridge must decide whether that frame is to be forwarded through the bridge and out through one of the bridge's other ports. Suppose that a bridge receives a MAC frame on port x. The following rules are applied (Figure 8-6):

1. Search the filtering database to determine if the MAC address is listed for any port except port x.
2. If the destination MAC address is not found, discard the frame.
3. If the destination address is in the filtering database for some port y, then determine whether port y is in a blocking or filtering state.

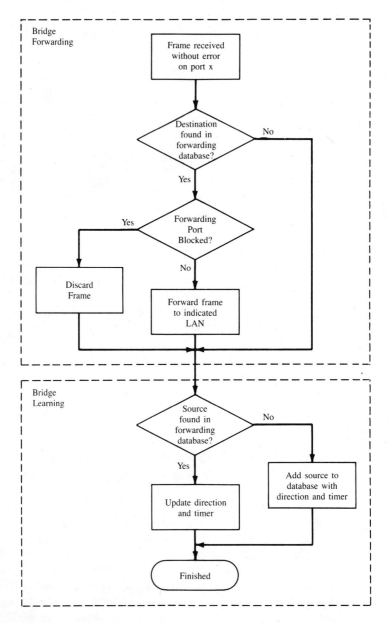

Figure 8.6. Bridge forwarding and learning

For reasons explained below, a port may sometimes be blocked, which prevents it from receiving or transmitting frames.

4. If port *y* is not blocked, transmit the frame through port *y* onto the LAN to which that port attaches.

Address Learning

The above scheme assumes that the bridge is already equipped with a filtering database that indicates the direction, from the bridge, of each destination station. This information can be preloaded into the bridge, as in static routing. However, an effective automatic mechanism for learning the direction of each station is desirable. A simple scheme for acquiring this information is based on the use of the source address field in each MAC frame (Figure 8-6).

The strategy is as follows. When a frame arrives in a particular port, it clearly has come from the direction of the incoming LAN. The source address field of the frame indicates the source station. Thus, a bridge can update its filtering database for that port on the basis of the source address field of each incoming frame. To allow for changes in topology, each element in the database is equipped with a timer. When a new element is added to the database, its timer is set. If the timer expires, then the element is eliminated from the database, since the corresponding direction information may no longer be valid. Each time a frame is received, its source address is checked against the database. If the element is already in the database, the entry is updated (the direction may have changed) and the timer is reset. If the element is not in the database, a new entry is created with its own timer.

The above discussion indicated that the individual entries in the database are station addresses. If a two-level address structure (LAN number, station number) is used, then only LAN addresses need to be entered in the database. Both schemes work the same. The only difference is that the use of station addresses requires a much larger database than the use of LAN addresses.

Spanning Tree Algorithm

The address learning mechanism described above is effective if the topology of the internet is a tree; that is, if there are no alternate routes in the network. The existence of alternate routes means that there is a closed loop. For example in Figure 8-4, the following is a closed loop: LAN A, bridge 101, LAN B, bridge 104, LAN E, bridge 107, LAN A.

To see the problem created by a closed loop, consider Figure 8-7. At time t0, station A transmits a frame addressed to station B. The frame is captured by both bridges. Each bridge updates its database to indicate that station A is in the direction of LAN X, and retransmits the frame on LAN Y. Say that bridge α retransmits at time t1 and bridge β a short time later, t2. Thus station B will receive two copies of the frame. Furthermore, each bridge will receive the other's transmission on LAN Y. Note that each transmission is a MAC frame with a source address of A and a

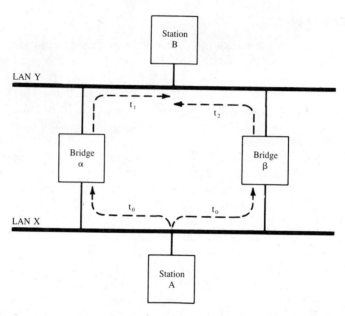

Figure 8.7. Loop of bridges

destination address of B. Thus each bridge will update its database to indicate that station A is in the direction of LAN Y. Neither bridge is now capable of forwarding a frame addressed to station A.

To overcome this problem, a simple result from graph theory is used: For any connected graph, consisting of nodes and edges connecting pairs of nodes, there is a spanning tree of edges that maintains the connectivity of the graph but contains no closed loops. In terms of internets, each LAN corresponds to a graph node, and each bridge corresponds to a graph edge. Thus, in Figure 8-4, the removal of one (and only one) of bridges 107, 101, or 104, results in a spanning tree. What is desired is to develop a simple algorithm by which the bridges of the internet can exchange sufficient information to automatically (without user intervention) derive a spanning tree. The algorithm must be dynamic. That is, when a topology change occurs, the bridges must be able to discover this fact and automatically derive a new spanning tree.

The algorithm is based on the use of the following:

1. Each bridge is assigned a unique identifier; in essence, the identifier consists of a MAC address for the bridge plus a priority level.
2. There is a special group MAC address that means "all bridges on this LAN." When a MAC frame is transmitted with the group address in the destination address field, all of the bridges on the LAN will capture that frame and interpret it as a frame addressed to itself.

3. Each port of a bridge is uniquely identified within the bridge, with a "port identifier."

With this information established, the bridges are able to exchange routing information in order to determine a spanning tree of the internet. We will explain the operation of the algorithm using Figures 8-8 and 8-9 as an example. The following concepts are needed in the creation of the spanning tree:

- *Root bridge:* The bridge with the lowest value of bridge identifier is chosen to be the root of the spanning tree.
- *Path cost:* Associated with each port on each bridge is a path cost, which is the cost of transmitting a frame onto a LAN through that port. A path between two stations will pass through zero or more bridges. At each bridge, the cost of transmission is added to give a total cost for a particular path. In the simplest case, all path costs would be assigned a value of 1; thus the cost of a path would simply be a count of the number of bridges along the path. Alternatively,

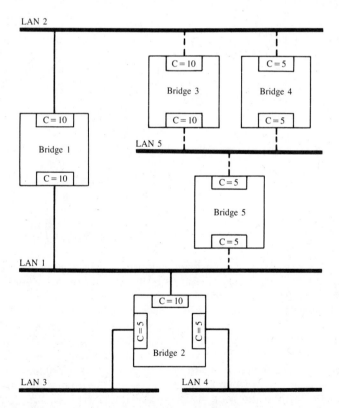

Figure 8.8. Example configuration for spanning tree algorithm

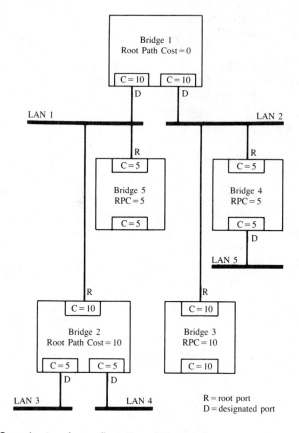

Figure 8.9. Spanning tree for configuration of Figure 8.8

costs could be assigned in inverse proportion to the data rate of the corresponding LAN, or any other criterion chosen by the network manager.

- *Root port:* Each bridge discovers the first hop on the minimum-cost path to the root bridge. The port used for that hop is labeled the root port.
- *Root path cost:* For each bridge, the cost of the path to the root bridge with minimum cost (the path the starts at the root port) is the root path cost for that bridge.
- *Designated bridge, designated port:* On each LAN, one bridge is chosen to be the designated bridge. This is the bridge on that LAN that provides the minimum cost path to the root bridge. This is the only bridge allowed to forward frames to and from the LAN for which it is the designated bridge. The port of the designated bridge that attaches the bridge to the LAN is the designated port. For all LANs to which the root bridge is attached, the root bridge is the designated bridge. All internet traffic to and from the LAN passes through the designated port.

In general terms, the spanning tree is constructed in the following fashion:

1. Determine the root bridge.
2. Determine the root port on all other bridges.
3. Determine the designated port on each LAN. This will be the port with the minimum root path cost. In the case of two or more bridges with the same root path cost, then the highest-priority bridge is chosen as the designated bridge. If the designated bridge has two or more ports attached to this LAN, then the port with the lowest value of port identifier is chosen.

By this process, when two LANs are directly connected by more than one bridge, all of the bridges but one are eliminated. This cuts any loops that involve two LANs. It can be demonstrated that this process also eliminates all loops involving more than two LANs and that connectivity is preserved. Thus, this process discovers a spanning tree for the given internet. In our example, the solid lines indicate the bridge ports that participate in the spanning tree.

The steps outlined above require that the bridges exchange information. The information is exchanged in the form of bridge protocol data units (BPDUs). A BPDU transmitted by one bridge is addressed to and received by all of the other bridges on the same LAN. Each BPDU contains the following information:

- The identifier of this bridge and the port on this bridge
- The identifier of the bridge that this bridge considers to be the root
- The root path cost for this bridge

To begin, all bridges consider themselves to be the root bridge. Each bridge will broadcast a BPDU on each of its LANs that asserts this fact. On any given LAN, only one claimant will have the lowest-valued identifier and will maintain its claim. Over time, as BPDUs propagate, the identity of the lowest-valued bridge identifier throughout the internet will be known to all bridges. The root bridge will regularly broadcast the fact that it is the root bridge on all of the LANs to which it is attached. This allows the bridges on those LANs to determine their root port and the fact that they are directly connected to the root bridge. Each of these bridges in turn broadcasts a BPDU on the other LANs to which it is attached (all LANs except the one on its root port), indicating that it is one hop away from the root bridge. This activity is propagated throughout the internet. Every time that a bridge receives a BPDU, it transmits BPDUs indicating the identity of the root bridge and the number of hops to reach the root bridge. On any LAN, the bridge claiming to be the one that is closest to the root becomes the designated bridge.

We can trace some of this activity with the configuration of Figure 8-8. At startup time, Bridges 1, 3, and 4 all transmit BPDUs on LAN 2 claiming to be the root bridge. When bridge 2 receives the transmission from bridge 1, it recognizes a superior claimant and defers. Bridge 3 has also received a claiming BPDU from bridge 5 via LAN 5. Bridge 3 recognizes that Bridge 1 has a superior claim to be the root bridge; it therefore assigns its LAN 2 port to be its root port, and sets the root path cost to 10. By similar actions, bridge 4 ends up with a root path cost of 5 via LAN 2; bridge 5 has a root path cost of 5 via LAN 1; and bridge 2 has a root path cost of 10 via LAN 1.

Now consider the assignment of designated bridges. On LAN 5, all three bridges transmit BPDUs attempting to assert a claim to be designated bridge. Bridge 3 defers because it receives BPDUs from the other bridges that have a lower root path cost. Bridges 4 and 5 have the same root path cost, but bridge 4 has the higher priority and therefore becomes the designated bridge.

The results of all this activity are shown in Figure 8-9. Only the designated bridge on each LAN is allowed to forward frames. All of the ports on all of the other bridges are placed in a blocking state. After the spanning tree is established, bridges continue to periodically exchange BPDUs to be able to react to any change in topology, cost assignments, or priority assignment. Any time that a bridge receives a BPDU on a port it makes two assessments:

1. If the BPDU arrives on a port that is considered the designated port, does the transmitting port have a better claim to be designated port?
2. Should this port be my root port?

The behavior of the bridges can be more precisely explained with reference to the state transition diagram of Figure 8-10. When a bridge is initialized, or when a bridge must participate in a change of configuration, all of its ports are placed in a listening state. For each port an associated timer is initialized to a value called *forward delay*. This timer is allowed to run down as long as no information is received to indicate that this port should be blocked from transmitting and receiving MAC frames. In the listening state, the spanning tree protocol information is received and transmitted, but station traffic is not forwarded to or from the bridge port, and MAC frames that arrive are not submitted to the learning process.

Once the forwarding timer expires, the bridge port transitions to the learning state, and the timer is reinitialized to the value of the forward delay parameter. Behavior in the learning state is exactly as in the listening state, with the exception that frames are submitted to the learning process. Once the forward delay timer expires a second time, the bridge port moves to the forwarding state. This means that this port is part of

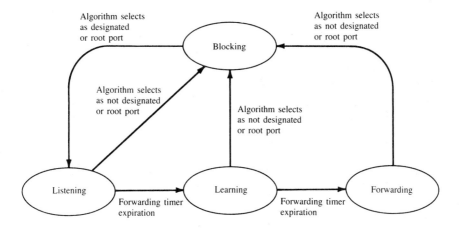

Figure 8.10.   Spanning tree state transition diagram for a bridge port

the spanning tree and will accept frames to be forwarded through the bridge and will transmit frames out of the bridge as appropriate.

If at any time, the bridge receives configuration information that indicates that this port should not be part of the spanning tree, the port is put in the blocking state. A future change in topology will move the port back to the listening state.

The motivation for this apparently complex process is to account for the propagation delays in communicating configuration information among the bridges. To move a state directly from a blocking state to a forwarding state risks having temporary data loops and the duplication and misordering of frames. Time is needed for new information to be received by all bridges and for other bridges to reply to inferior protocol information before starting to forward frames.

Bridge Protocol Data Units

The current version of the 802.1 standard defines two bridge protocol data units: the configuration BPDU and the topology change BPDU. Figure 8-11 illustrates the formats.

The **configuration BPDU** consists of the following fields:

- *Protocol version identifier (2 octets):* Identifies the spanning tree algorithm and protocol defined by 802.1. The value is all zeros.
- *BPDU type (1 octet):* The type of BPDU. For the configuration BPDU, the value is all zeros.

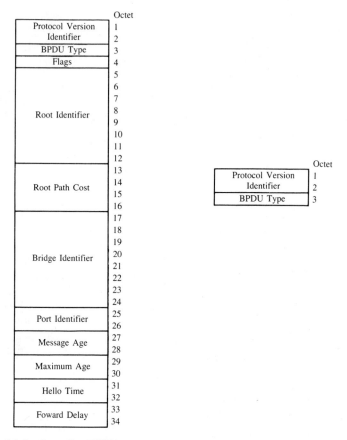

(a) Configuration BPDU   (b) Topology Change Notification BPDU

Figure 8.11.   Bridge protocol data units (BPDUs)

- *Flags (1 octet):* Consists of the Topology Change flag (bit 1 of octet 4) and the Topology Change Acknowledgment flag (bit 8 of octet 4). The use of these flags is explained below.
- *Root identifier (8 octets):* The unique bridge identifier of the bridge assumed to be the root by the bridge transmitting this BPDU. This parameter is conveyed to enable all bridges to agree on the root.
- *Root path cost (4 octets):* The cost of the path from the transmitting bridge to the bridge identified by the root identifier above. This parameter is conveyed to enable a bridge to decide which of the bridges attached to the LAN on which this BPDU has been received offers the lowest cost path to the root for that LAN.
- *Bridge identifier (8 octets):* The unique identifier of the bridge transmitting this BPDU. This parameter is conveyed to enable a bridge to decide, in the case of a LAN to which two or more bridges are attached and which offer equal cost paths to the root, which of the bridges should be selected as the designated bridge for that LAN.

- *Port identifier (2 octets):* The identifier of the port transmitting this BPDU. This identifier uniquely identifies a port on the transmitting bridge.
- *Message age (2 octets):* The age of the configuration message, which is the time since the generation of the configuration BPDU by the root which instigated the generation of this configuration BPDU. This parameter is conveyed to enable a bridge to discard information whose age exceeds the maximum age.
- *Maximum age (2 octets):* A timeout value to be used by all bridges in the internet. The value is set by the root. This parameter is conveyed to ensure that each bridge has a consistent value against which to test the age of stored configuration information.
- *Hello time (2 octets):* The time interval between the generation of configuration BPDUs by the root. This parameter is not directly used in the spanning tree algorithm but is conveyed to facilitate the monitoring of protocol performance by management functions.
- *Forward delay (2 octets):* A timeout value to be used by all bridges. The value is set by the root. This parameter is conveyed to ensure that each bridge uses a consistent value for the forward delay timer when transferring the state of a port to the forwarding state. This parameter is also used as the timeout value for ageing filtering database dynamic entries following changes in active topology.

The transmission of configuration BPDUs is triggered by the root (or a bridge that temporarily considers itself to be the root). The root will periodically (once every hello time) issue a configuration BPDU on all LANs to which it is attached. A bridge that receives a configuration BPDU on what it decides is its root port passes that information on to all the LANs for which it believes itself to be the designated bridge. Thus, in a stable configuration, the generation of a configuration BPDU by the root causes a cascade of configuration BPDUs throughout the spanning tree. This collection of BPDU transmissions is referred to as a *configuration message*.

A bridge may decide that it must change the topology of the spanning tree. For example, in Figure 8-9, if bridge 4 fails, it would cease to transmit configuration BPDUs as part of the periodic configuration messages. Bridge 3 would time out bridge 4 as the designated bridge on LAN 2 once the maximum age timer expires, and enter the listening state. Eventually, the port on LAN 2 of bridge 3 would enter the forwarding state. At this point, bridge 3 must notify the root of a change in topology. This is done by transmitting a *topology change notification BPDU* on the root port of the bridge. This BPDU consists merely of a protocol version identifier and a BPDU type field with a code for this type of BPDU.

The intent is to communicate the topology change notification to the root. In effect, this is done by relaying the change notification up the spanning tree to the root. To assure reliable delivery of the notification, the transmitting bridge will repeat the topology change notification BPDU until it receives an acknowledgment from the designated bridge for that LAN. The acknowledgment is carried in a configuration BPDU (Topology Change Acknowledgment flag). The designated bridge passes the notification to, or towards, the root using the same procedure.

When the root receives such a notification, or changes the topology itself (e.g., if a new root is declared), it will set the Topology Change flag in all configuration messages transmitted for some time. This time is such that all bridges will receive one or more configuration messages. While this flag is set, bridges use the value of forwarding delay to age out entries in the filtering database. When the flag is reset again, the bridges revert to using a filtering timer which, typically, is much longer. It is desirable to shorten the aging time during this period of reconfiguration because, after a topology change, stations may be in a new direction with respect to the bridge. Since a bridge must endure a wait of at least two forwarding times (see Figure 8-10) to transition from listening to forwarding, this will allow enough time for currently en-route frames to be delivered or eliminated by timeout.

8.3 SOURCE ROUTING

The source routing approach is a mechanism in which the sending station determines the route that the frame will follow and includes the routing information with the frame; bridges read the routing information to determine if they should forward the frame [DIXO88, HAMN88, PITT87b, BEDE86, PITT85, IEEE88c].

Basic Operation

The basic operation of the algorithm can be described with reference to the configuration of Figure 8-12. A frame from station X can reach station Z by either of the following routes:

- LAN 1, bridge B1, LAN 3, bridge B3, LAN 2
- LAN 1, bridge B2, LAN 4, bridge B4, LAN 2

Station X may choose one of these two routes and place the information, in the form of a sequence of LAN and bridge identifiers, in the frame to be transmitted. When a bridge receives a frame, it will forward that frame if the bridge is on the designated route; all other frames are discarded. In this case, if the first route above is specified, bridges B1 and B3 will forward the frame; if the second route is specified, bridges B2 and B4 will forward the frame.

Note that with this scheme bridges need not maintain routing tables. The bridge makes the decision whether or not to forward a frame solely on the basis of the routing information contained in the frame. All that is

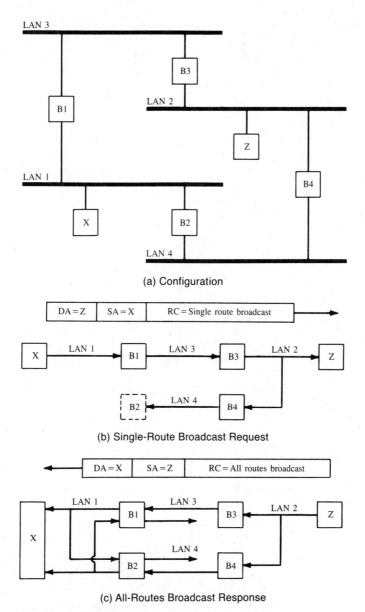

Figure 8.12.   Route discovery example [DIX088]

required is that the bridge know its own unique identifier and the identifier of each LAN to which it is attached. The responsibility for designing
the route falls to the source station.

For this scheme to work, there must be a mechanism by which a
station can determine a route to any destination station. Before dealing
with this issue, we need to discuss different types of routing directives.

Routing Directives and Addressing Modes

The source routing scheme developed by the IEEE 802.5 committee includes four different types of routing directives. Each frame that is transmitted includes an indicator of the type of routing desired. The four directive types are:

- *Null:* No routing is desired. In this case, the frame can only be delivered to stations on the same LAN as the source station.
- *Specific route (nonbroadcast):* The frame includes a route, consisting of a sequence of LAN numbers and bridge numbers that defines a unique route from the source station to the destination station. Only bridges on that route forward the frame, and only a single copy of the frame is delivered to the destination station.
- *All-paths (broadcast):* The frame will reach each LAN of the internet by all possible routes. Thus each bridge will forward each frame once to each of its ports in a direction away from the source node and multiple copies of the frame may appear on a LAN. The destination station will receive one copy of the frame for each possible route through the network.
- *Spanning-tree (broadcast):* Regardless of the destination address of the frame, the frame will appear once, and only once, on each LAN in the internet. For this effect to be achieved, the frame is forwarded by all bridges that are on a spanning tree (with the source node as the root) of the internet. The destination station receives a single copy of the frame.

Let us first examine the potential application of each of these four types of routing, and then examine the mechanisms that may be employed to achieve them. First, consider null routing. In this case the bridges that share the LAN with the source station are told not to forward the frame. This will be done if the intended destination is on the same LAN as the source station. Specific routing is used when the two stations are not on the same LAN and the source station knows a route that can be used to reach the destination station. Only the bridges on that route will forward the frame.

The remaining two types of routing can be used by the source to discover a route to the destination. For example, the source station can use all-paths broadcasting to send a request frame to the intended destination. The destination returns a response frame, using specific routing, on each of the routes followed by the incoming request frame. The source station can pick one of these routes and send future frames on that route. Alternatively, the source station could use spanning-tree broadcasting to send a single request frame to the destination station. The destination station could send its response frame via all-paths broadcasting. The incoming frames would reveal all of the possible routes to the destination station, and the source station could pick one of these for future transmissions. Finally, spanning-tree broadcasting could be used for group addressing as discussed below.

Now consider the mechanisms for implementing these various routing directives. Each frame must include an indicator of which of the four types of routing is required. For null routing, the frame is ignored by the bridge. For specific routing, the frame includes an ordered list of LAN numbers and bridge numbers. When a bridge receives a specifically routed frame, it forwards the frame if, and only if, the routing information contains the sequence LAN i, Bridge x, LAN j, where:

LAN i = LAN from which the frame arrived
Bridge x = this bridge
LAN j = another LAN to which this bridge is attached.

For all-paths broadcasting, the source station marks the frame for this type of routing, but includes no routing information. Each bridge that forwards the frame will add its bridge number and the outgoing LAN number to the frame's routing information field. Thus, when the frame reaches its destination, it will include a sequenced list of all LANs and bridges visited. To prevent the endless repetition and looping of frames, a bridge obeys the following rule. When an all-paths broadcast frame is received, the bridge examines the routing information field. If the field contains the number of a LAN to which the bridge is attached, the bridge will refrain from forwarding the frame on that LAN. Put another way, the bridge will only forward the frame to a LAN that the frame has not already visited.

Finally, for spanning-tree broadcasting, a spanning tree of the internet must be developed. This can either be done automatically, as in the 802.1 specification, or manually. In either case, as with the 802.1 strategy, one bridge on each LAN is the designated bridge for that LAN and is the only one that forwards single-route frames.

It is worth noting the relationship between addressing mode and routing directive. Recall from Chapter 2, that there are three types of MAC addresses:

- *Individual:* the address specifies a unique destination station.
- *Group:* the address specifies a group of destination addresses; this is also referred to as *multicast*.
- *All-stations:* the addresses specifies all stations that are capable of receiving this frame; this is also referred to as *broadcast*. We will refrain from using this latter term since it is also used in the source routing terminology.

In the case of a single, isolated LAN, group and all-stations addresses refer to stations on the same LAN as the source station. In an internet, it may be desirable to transmit a frame to multiple stations on

Table 8.1. EFFECTS OF VARIOUS COMBINATIONS OF ADDRESSING AND SOURCE ROUTING

Addressing Mode	Routing Specification			
	No Routing	Nonbroadcast	All Routes	Single-Route
Individual	Received by station if it is on the same LAN	Received by station if it is on one of the LANs on the route	Received by station if it is on any LAN	Received by station if it is on any LAN
Group	Received by all group members on the same LAN	Received by all group members on all LANs visited on this route	Received by all group members on all LANs	Received by all group members on all LANs
All-Stations	Received by all stations on the same LAN	Received by all stations on all LANs visited on this route	Received by all stations on all LANs	Received by all stations on all LANs

multiple LANs. Indeed, because a set of LANs interconnected by bridges should appear to the user as a single LAN, the ability to do group and all-stations addressing across the entire internet is mandatory.

Table 8-1 summarizes the relationship between routing specification and addressing mode. If no routing is specified, then all addresses refer only to the immediate LAN. If specific routing is specified, then addresses may refer to any station on any LAN visited on the specific route. From an addressing point of view, this combination is not generally useful for group and all-stations addressing. If either the all-paths or spanning-tree specification is included in a frame, then all stations on the internet can be addressed. Thus, the total internet acts a single network from the point of view of MAC addresses. Because less traffic is generated by the spanning-tree specification, this is to be preferred for group and all-stations addressing. Note also that the spanning-tree directive in source routing is equivalent to the 802.1 spanning tree approach. Thus, the latter supports both group and all-stations addressing.

Route Discovery and Selection

With source routing, bridges are relieved of the burden of storing and using routing information. Thus the burden falls on the stations that wish to transmit frames. Clearly, some mechanism is needed by which the source stations can know the route to each destination for which frames are to be sent. Three strategies suggest themselves.

1. Manually load the information into each station. This is simple and effective but has several drawbacks. First, any time that the configuration is changed, the routing information at all stations must be updated. Secondly, this approach does not provide for automatic adjustment in the face of the failure of a bridge or LAN.
2. One station on a LAN can query other stations on the same LAN for routing information about distant stations. This approach may reduce the overall amount of routing messages that must be transmitted, compared to option 3 below. However, at least one station on each LAN must have the needed routing information, so this is not a complete solution.
3. When a station needs to learn the route to a destination station, it engages in a dynamic route discovery procedure.

Option 3 is the most flexible and the one that is specified by IEEE 802.5. As was mentioned earlier, two approaches are possible. The source station can transmit an all-paths request frame to the destination. Thus, all possible routes to the destination are discovered. The destination station can send back a specific-route response on each of the discovered routes. This allows the source to choose which route to follow in subsequently transmitting the frame. However, this approach generates quite a bit of both forward and backward traffic, and requires the destination station to receive and transmit a number of frames. An alternative approach is for the source station to transmit a spanning-tree request frame. Only one copy of this frame will reach the destination. The destination responds with an all-paths response frame, which generates all possible routes back to the source. Again, the source can choose among these alternative routes. This latter approach is the one specified in the 802.5 document.

An additional refinement is added to the 802.5 mechanism. When a spanning-tree or all-paths request frame is transmitted, a field is included that indicates the maximum frame size that can be supported on this route. As each bridge forwards the frame, it sets this field to the least value of the received field, the value of the maximum frame size supported by the bridge, and the value of the maximum frame size supported by the LAN on which the frame is to be transmitted.

Figure 8-12 illustrates the latter approach. Assume that the spanning tree that has been chosen for this internet consists of bridges B1, B3, and B4. In this example, station X wishes to discover a route to station Z. Station X issues a spanning-tree request frame. Bridge B2 is not on the spanning tree and so does not forward the frame. The other bridges do forward the frame and it reaches station Z. Note that bridge B4 forwards the frame to LAN 4, although this is not necessary; it is simply an effect of the spanning-tree mechanism. When Z receives this frame, it responds with an all-paths frame. Two messages reach X: one on the path LAN 2, B3, LAN 3, B1, LAN 1, and the other on the path LAN 2, B4, LAN 4, B2, LAN 1. Note that frames that arrived by the latter route are received by bridge B1 and forwarded onto LAN 3. However, when bridge B3 receives this frame, it sees in the routing information field that the frame has already visited LAN 2; therefore it does not forward the frame. A similar fate occurs for the frame that follows the first route and is forwarded by bridge B2.

Once a collection of routes has been discovered, the source station needs to select one of the routes. The 802.5 specification does not dictate a selection criterion, but suggests the following possible criteria. Choose the route corresponding to the response message with the following characteristics:

- The first response frame received. This is a measure of minimum delay.
- The first response with less than n bridge designators.
- The response with the minimum number of hops (fewest bridge designators), received within a time window.
- The first response with a frame size larger than a specified value. This corresponds to the minimum-delay route that can handle the anticipated size of frames to be transmitted.
- The response with the largest allowed frame size, received within a time window.

- The first response with less than n bridge designators, and with a frame size larger than a specified value.
- The response with the fewest hops which also satisfies frame size criteria, received within a time window.
- The response with the largest frame size and the number of hops less than n, within a time window.

Another point to consider is how often to update a route. Routes should certainly be changed in response to network failures and perhaps should be changed in response to network congestion. If connection-oriented logical link control is used (see Chapter 3), then one possibility is to rediscover the route with each new connection. Another alternative, which works with either connection-oriented or connectionless service, is to associate a timer with each selected route, and rediscover the route when its time expires.

Frame Format

With source routing, changes must be made to the MAC frame format. Figure 8-13 shows the frame format specified by the IEEE 802.5 source routing document. Recall that the first bit of the destination address indicates whether the address is an individual address or a group address.

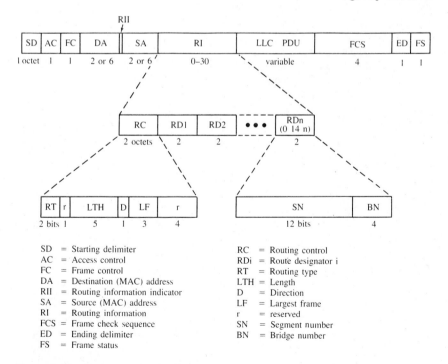

SD	= Starting delimiter	RC	= Routing control
AC	= Access control	RDi	= Route designator i
FC	= Frame control	RT	= Routing type
DA	= Destination (MAC) address	LTH	= Length
RII	= Routing information indicator	D	= Direction
SA	= Source (MAC) address	LF	= Largest frame
RI	= Routing information	r	= reserved
FCS	= Frame check sequence	SN	= Segment number
ED	= Ending delimiter	BN	= Bridge number
FS	= Frame status		

Figure 8.13. Source routing formats

Table 8.2. **CODING FOR LARGEST-FRAME FIELD**

Code	Value (octets)	Application
000	516	ISO subnetwork, including LLC header
001	1470	802.3 LANs
010	2052	80X24 character screen with control
011	4472	FDDI; 802.5 with 9 ms token-holding timer
100	8144	802.4
101	11454	802.5 with 23 ms token-holding timer
110	17800	802.5 with 36 ms token-holding timer
111	initial value	

Clearly, a source address must always be an individual address, and the corresponding bit is unused. To accommodate source routing, this bit becomes the routing information indicator (RII). The RII bit is set to zero to indicate null routing and to one to indicate that routing information is present in the frame. In the latter case, a new field is added to the MAC frame, the routing information field which consists of a routing control field followed by from 0 to 14 route designation fields. The routing control field consists of the following subfields:

- *Routing type (2 bits):* indicates the type of routing directive with the following interpretation:
    0X = specific route
    10 = all-paths route
    11 = spanning-tree route
- *Length (5 bits):* indicates the length of the routing information control field, in octets. The value is an even number between 2 and 30.
- *Direction (1 bit):* indicates to a bridge whether the frame is traveling from the originating station to the target or vice versa. Its use allows the list of route designation fields to appear in the same order for frames traveling in both directions along the route.
- *Largest frame (3 bits):* specifies the largest size of the MAC information field that may be transmitted on this route. This field is encoded to indicate certain common sizes, as indicated in Table 8-2. When a bridge receives a frame, it updates this field if the specified size exceeds what the bridge can handle or its adjoining LANs allow. In this way, the route discovery process also discovers the maximum frame size that can be handled on a particular route.

The remainder of the routing information field consists of a sequence of route designators, each designator corresponding to one hop. The route designator consists of a 12-bit segment number (LAN number) and a 4-bit bridge number.

A

The OSI Reference Model

Throughout this book, reference is made to both the concepts and the specifics of the open systems interconnection (OSI) reference model. For the reader unfamiliar with the OSI model, this appendix provides a brief overview. Greater detail can be found in another book in this series [STAL87b].

A.1 MOTIVATION

When work is done that involves more than one computer, additional elements must be added to the system: the hardware and the software to support the communication between or among the systems. Communications hardware is reasonably standard and generally presents few problems. However, when communication is desired among heterogeneous (different vendors, different models of same vendor) machines, the software development effort can be a nightmare. Different vendors use different data formats and data exchange conventions. Even within one vendor's product line, different model computers may communicate in unique ways.

As the use of computer communications and computer networking proliferates, a one-at-a-time special-purpose approach to communications software development is too costly to be acceptable. The only alternative is for computer vendors to adopt and implement a common set of conventions. For this to happen, a set of international or at least national standards must be promulgated by appropriate organizations. Such standards have two effects:

- Vendors feel encouraged to implement the standards because the wide usage of the standards would make their products less marketable without them.
- Customers are in a position to require that the standards be implemented by any vendor wishing to propose equipment to them.

It should become clear from the ensuing discussion that no single standard will suffice. The task of communication in a truly cooperative way between applications on different computers is too complex to be handled as a unit. The problem must be broken down into manageable parts. Hence, before one can develop standards, there should be a structure or *architecture* that defines the communications tasks.

This line of reasoning led the International Organization for Standardization (ISO) in 1977 to establish a subcommittee to develop such an architecture. The result was the *Open Systems Interconnection* (OSI) reference model, which is a framework for defining standards for linking heterogeneous computers. The OSI model provides the basis for connecting *open* systems for distributed applications processing. The term

Table A.1. PURPOSE OF THE OSI MODEL (ISO 7498)

The purpose of this International Standard Reference Model of Open Systems Interconnection is to provide a common basis for the coordination of standards development for the purpose of systems interconnection, while allowing existing standards to be placed into perspective within the overall Reference Model.

The term Open Systems Interconnection (OSI) qualifies standards for the exchange of information among systems that are "open" to one another for this purpose by virtue of their mutual use of the applicable standards.

The fact that a system is open does not imply any particular systems implementation, technology, or means of interconnection, but refers to the mutual recognition and support of the applicable standards.

It is also the purpose of this International Standard to identify areas for developing or improving standards, and to provide a common reference for maintaining consistency of all related standards. It is not the intent of this International Standard either to serve as an implementation specification, or to be a basis for appraising the conformance of actual implementations, or to provide a sufficient level of detail to define precisely the services and protocols of the interconnection architecture. Rather, this International Standard provides a conceptual and functional framework which allows international teams of experts to work productively and independently on the development of standards for each layer of the Reference Model of OSI.

open denotes the ability of any two systems conforming to the reference model and the associated standards to connect.

Table A.1 extracted from the basic OSI document [ISO84d] summarizes the purpose of the model.

A.2 CONCEPTS

A widely accepted structuring technique, and the one chosen by ISO, is *layering*. The communications functions are partitioned into a vertical set of layers. Each layer performs a related subset of the functions required to communicate with another system. It relies on the next lower layer to perform more primitive functions and to conceal the details of those functions. It provides services to the next higher layer. Ideally, the layers should be defined so that changes in one layer do not require changes in the other layers. Thus, we have broken down one problem into a number of more manageable subproblems.

The task of the ISO subcommittee was to define a set of layers and the services performed by each layer. The partitioning should group functions logically, should have enough layers to make each layer manageably small, but should not have so many layers that the processing overhead imposed by the collection of layers is burdensome. The principles by which ISO went about its task are summarized in Table A.2. The resulting OSI reference model has seven layers, which are listed with a brief definition in Table A.3. Table A.4 provides ISO's justification for the selection of these layers.

Table A.3 defines, in general terms, the functions that must be performed in a system for it to communicate. Of course, it takes two to communicate, so the same set of layered functions must exist in two systems. Communication is achieved by having the corresponding (*peer*) layers in two systems communicate. The peer layers communicate by means of a set of rules or conventions known as a *protocol*. The key elements of a protocol are:

- *Syntax:* Includes such things as data format and signal levels.
- *Semantics:* Includes control information for coordination and error handling.
- *Timing:* Includes speed matching and sequencing.

Figure A.1 illustrates the OSI model. Each system contains the seven layers. Communication is between applications in the systems, labeled AP X and AP Y in Figure A.1. If AP X wishes to send a message to AP Y, it invokes the application layer (layer 7). Layer 7 establishes a peer relationship with layer 7 of the target machine, using a layer 7 protocol. This protocol requires services from layer 6, so the two layer 6

Table A.2. PRINCIPLES USED IN DETERMINING THE OSI LAYERS (ISO 7498)

1. Do not create so many layers as to make the system engineering task of describing and integrating the layers more difficult than necessary.

2. Create a boundary at a point where the description of services can be small and the number of interactions across the boundary are minimized.

3. Create separate layers to handle functions that are manifestly different in the process performed or the technology involved.

4. Collect similar functions into the same layer.

5. Select boundaries at a point that past experience has demonstrated to be successful.

6. Create a layer of easily localized functions so that the layer could be totally redesigned and its protocols changed in a major way to take advantage of new advances in architectural, hardware, or software technology without changing the services expected from and provided to the adjacent layers.

7. Create a boundary where it may be useful at some point in time to have the corresponding interface standardized.

8. Create a layer where there is a need for a different level of abstraction in the handling of data (e.g., morphology, syntax, semantics).

9. Allow changes of functions or protocols to be made within a layer without affecting other layers.

10. Create for each layer boundaries with its upper and lower layer only.

Similar principles have been applied to sublayering:

11. Create further subgrouping and organization or functions to form sublayers within a layer in cases where distinct communication services need it.

12. Create, where needed, two or more sublayers with a common, and therefore, minimal functionality to allow interface operation with adjacent layers.

13. Allow bypassing of sublayers.

---

entities use a protocol of their own, and so on down to the physical layer, which actually passes the bits through a transmission medium.

Note that there is no direct communication between peer layers except at the physical layer. Even at that layer, the OSI model does not stipulate that two systems be directly connected. For example, a packet-switched or circuit-switched network may be used to provide the communications link. This point should become clearer later, when we discuss the network layer.

The attractiveness of the OSI approach is that it promises to solve the heterogeneous computer communications problem. Two systems, no matter how different, can communicate effectively if they have the following in common.

- They implement the same set of communications functions.
- These functions are organized into the same set of layers. Peer layers must provide the same functions, but note that it is not necessary that they provide them in the same way.
- Peer layers must share a common protocol.

Table A.3.   **THE OSI LAYERS**

Layer	Definition
1. Physical	Concerned with transmission of unstructured bit stream over physical link; involves such parameters as signal voltage swing and bit duration; deals with the mechanical, electrical, and procedural characteristics to establish, maintain, and deactivate the physical link.
2. Data link	Provides for the reliable transfer of data across the physical link; sends blocks of data (frames) with the necessary synchronization, error control, and flow control.
3. Network	Provides upper layers with independence from the data transmission and switching technologies used to connect systems; responsible for establishing, maintaining, and terminating connections.
4. Transport	Provides reliable, transparent transfer of data between end points; provides end-to-end error recovery and flow control.
5. Session	Provides the control structure for communication between applications; establishes, manages, and terminates connections (sessions) between cooperating applications.
6. Presentation	Performs generally useful transformations on data to provide a standardized application interface and to provide common communications services; examples: encryption, text compression, reformatting.
7. Application	Provides services to the users of the OSI environment; examples: transaction server, file transfer protocol, network management.

To ensure the above, standards are needed. Standards must define the functions and services to be provided by a layer (but not how it is to be done—that may differ from system to system). Standards must also define the protocols between peer layers (each protocol must be identical for the two peer layers). The OSI model, by defining a seven-layer architecture, provides a framework for defining these standards.

Some useful OSI terminology is illustrated in Figure A.2. For simplicity, any layer is referred to as the (N) *layer,* and names of constructs associated with that layer are also preceded by (N). Within a system, there are one or more active entities in each layer. An (N) *entity* implements functions of the (N) layer and also the protocol for communicating with (N) entities in other systems. An example of an entity is a process in a multiprocessing system. Or it could simply be a subroutine. There might be multiple identical (N) entities, if this is convenient or efficient for a given system. There might also be differing (N) entities, corresponding to different protocol standards at that level. Each (N) entity implements a protocol for communicating with (N) entities in other systems.

Table A.4.   JUSTIFICATION OF THE OSI LAYERS (ISO 7498)

a. It is essential that the architecture permit usage of a realistic variety of physical media for interconnection with different control procedures (e.g., V.24, V.25, X.21, etc.). Application of principles 3, 5, and 8 [Table A.2] leads to identification of a *Physical Layer* as the lowest layer in the architecture.

b. Some physical communication media (e.g., telephone line) require specific techniques to be used to transmit data between systems despite a relatively high error rate (i.e., an error rate not acceptable for the great majority of applications). These specific techniques are used in data-link control procedures that have been studied and standardized for a number of years. It must also be recognized that new physical communication media (e.g., fiber optics) will require different data-link control procedures. Application of principles 3, 5, and 8 leads to identification of a *Data Link Layer* on top of the Physical Layer in the architecture.

c. In the open systems architecture, some systems will act as the final destination of data. Some systems may act only as intermediate nodes (forwarding data to other systems). Application of principles 3, 5, and 7 leads to identification of a *Network Layer* on top of the Data Link Layer. Network oriented protocols, such as routing, for example, will be grouped in this layer. Thus, the Network Layer will provide a connection path (network-connection) between a pair of transport-entities, including the case where intermediate nodes are involved.

d. Control of data transportation from source end-system to destination end-system (which is not performed in intermediate nodes) is the last function to be performed to provide the totality of the transport-service. Thus, the upper layer in the transport-service part of the architecture is the *Transport Layer,* on top of the Network Layer. This Transport Layer relieves higher layer entities from any concern with the transportation of data between them.

e. There is a need to organize and synchronize dialogue, and to manage the exchange of data. Application of principles 3 and 4 leads to the identification of a *Session Layer* on top of the Transport Layer.

f. The remaining set of general interest functions are those related to representation and manipulation of structured data for the benefit of application programs. Application of principles 3 and 4 leads to identification of a *Presentation Layer* on top of the Session Layer.

g. Finally, there are applications consisting of application processes that perform information processing. An aspect of these applications processes and the protocols by which they communicate comprise the *Application Layer* as the highest layer of the architecture.

Each entity communicates with entities in the layers above and below it across an interface. The interface is realized as one or more *service access points* (SAPs).

To clarify these terms as well as some functions common to all layers, refer to Fig. A.3. The functions we wish to discuss are:

• Encapsulation
• Segmentation

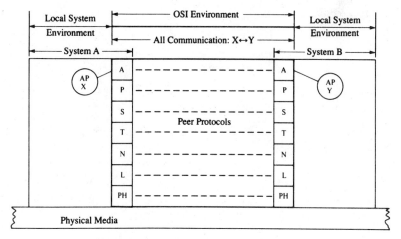

Figure A.1.   The OSI environment

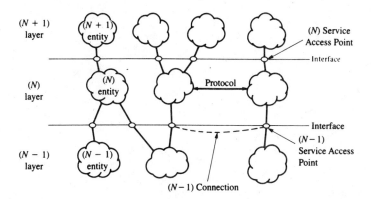

Figure A.2.   The layer concept

- Connection establishment
- Flow control
- Error control
- Multiplexing

The most common way in which protocols are realized is by a process of *encapsulation*. When AP X has a message to send to AP Y, it transfers those data to a (7) entity in the application layer. A *header* is appended to the data that contains the required information for the peer layer 7 protocol; this is referred to as an encapsulation of the data. The original data, plus the header, is now passed as a unit to layer 6. The (6) entity treats the whole unit as data, and appends its own header (a second encapsulation). This process continues down through layer 2, which gen-

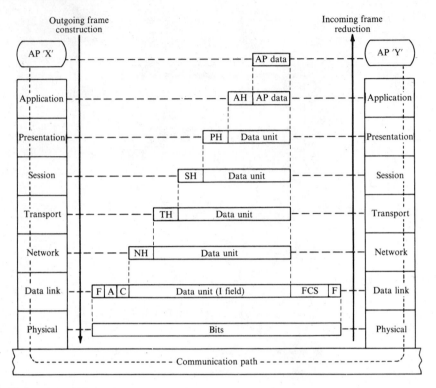

Figure A.3. OSI operation

erally adds both a header and a trailer, with the trailer containing a frame check sequence (FCS) for error detection. This layer 2 unit, called a *frame,* is then transmitted by the physical layer onto the transmission medium. When the frame is received by the target system, the reverse process occurs. As the data ascend, each layer strips off the outermost header, acts on the protocol information contained therein, and passes the remainder up to the next layer.

At each stage of the process, a layer may *segment* the data unit it receives from the next higher layer into several parts to accommodate its own requirements. These data units must then be reassembled by the corresponding peer layer before being passed up.

When two peer entities wish to exchange data, this may be done with or without a prior *connection.* Example of both approaches are provided in the discussion of LLC. A connection can exist at any layer of the hierarchy. In the abstract, a connection is established between two (N) entities by identifying a connection endpoint, $(N - 1)$ CEP, within an $(N - 1)$ SAP for each (N) entity. A connection facilitates flow control and error control. *Flow control* is a function performed by an (N) entity to limit the amount or rate of data it receives from another (N) entity. This function is needed to ensure that the receiving (N) entity does not experience overflow. *Error control* refers to mechanisms to detect and correct errors that occur in the transmission of data units between peer entities.

Multiplexing can occur in two directions. *Upward* multiplexing means that multiple (N) connections are multiplexed on, or share, a single ($N - 1$) connection. This may be needed to make more efficient use of the ($N - 1$) service or to provide several (N) connections in an environment where only a single ($N - 1$) connection exists. *Downward* multiplexing, or *splitting*, means that a single (N) connection is built on top of multiple ($N - 1$) connections, the traffic on the (N) connection being divided among the various ($N - 1$) connections. This technique may be used to improve reliability, performance, or efficiency.

A.3   LAYERS

Physical Layer

The *physical layer* covers the physical interface between devices and the rules by which bits are passed from one to another. The physical layer has four important characteristics:

- Mechanical
- Electrical
- Functional
- Procedural

Examples of standards at this layer are RS-232-C, RS-449/422/423, and portions of X.21.

Data Link Layer

Although the physical layer provides only a raw bit-stream service, the *data link layer* attempts to make the physical link reliable and provides the means to activate, maintain, and deactivate the link. The principal service provided by the data link layer to the higher layers is that of error detection and control. Thus, with a fully functional data link layer protocol, the next higher layer may assume virtually error-free transmission over the link. However, if communication is between two systems that are not directly connected, the connection will comprise a number of data links in tandem, each functioning independently. Thus the higher layers are not relieved of an error control responsibility.

Examples of standards at this layer are HDLC, LAP-B, LAP-D, and LLC.

Network Layer

The basic service of the *network layer* is to provide for the transparent transfer of data between transport entities. It relieves the transport layer of the need to know anything about the underlying data transmission and switching technologies used to connect systems. The network service is responsible for establishing, maintaining, and terminating connections across the intervening communications facility.

It is at this layer that the concept of a protocol becomes a little fuzzy. This is best illustrated with reference to Fig. A.4, which shows two stations that are communicating, not via direct link, but via a packet-switched network. The stations have direct links to the network nodes. The layer 1 and 2 protocols are station-node protocols (local). Layers 4 through 7 are clearly protocols between (N) entities in the two stations. Layer 3 is a little bit of both.

The principal dialogue is between the station and its node; the station sends addressed packets to the node for delivery across the network. It requests a virtual circuit connection, uses the connection to transmit data, and terminates the connection. All of this is done by means of a station-node protocol. However, because packets are exchanged and virtual circuits are set up between two stations, there are aspects of a station-station protocol as well.

There is a spectrum of possibilities for intervening communications facilities to be managed by the network layer. At one extreme, the simplest, there is a direct link between stations. In this case, there may be little or no need for a network layer, as the data link layer can perform the necessary functions of managing the link. Between extremes, the most common use of layer 3 is to handle the details of using a communication network. In this case, the network entity in the station must provide the network with sufficient information to switch and route data to

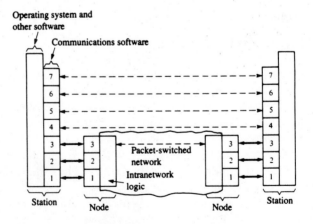

Figure A.4. Communication across a network

another station. At the other extreme, two stations might wish to communicate but are not even connected to the same network. Rather, they are connected to networks that, directly or indirectly, are connected to each other. One approach to providing for data transfer in such a case is to use an Internet Protocol (IP) that sits on top of a network protocol and is used by a transport protocol. IP is responsible for internetwork routing and delivery, and relies on a layer 3 at each network for intranetwork services. IP is sometimes referred to as *layer 3.5*.

The best known example of layer 3 is the X.25 layer 3 standard. The X.25 standard refers to itself as an interface between a station and a node (using our terminology). In the context of the OSI model, it is actually a station-node protocol.

Transport Layer

The purpose of layer 4 is to provide a reliable mechanism for the exchange of data between processes in different systems. The *transport layer* ensures that data units are delivered error-free, in sequence, with no losses or duplications. The transport layer may also be concerned with optimizing the use of network services and providing a requested quality of service to session entities. For example, the session entity might specify acceptable error rates, maximum delay, priority, and security. In effect, the transport layer serves as the user's liaison with the communications facility.

The size and the complexity of a transport protocol depends on the type of service it can get from layer 3. For a reliable layer 3 with a virtual circuit capability, a minimal layer 4 is required. If layer 3 is unreliable, the layer 4 protocol should include extensive error detection and recovery. Accordingly, ISO has defined five classes of transport protocol, each oriented toward a different underlying service.

Session Layer

The *session layer* provides the mechanism for controlling the dialogue between presentation entities. At a minimum, the session layer provides a means for two presentation entities to establish and use a connection, called a *session*. In addition it may provide some of the following services:

- *Dialogue type:* This can be two-way simultaneous, two-way alternate, or one-way.
- *Recovery:* The session layer can provide a checkpointing mechanism so that if a failure of some sort occurs between checkpoints, the session entity can retransmit all data since the last checkpoint.

Presentation Layer

The presentation layer offers application programs and terminal handler programs a set of data transformation services. Services that this layer would typically provide include:

- *Data translation:* Code and character set translation.
- *Formatting:* Modification of data layout.
- *Syntax selection:* Initial selection and subsequent modification of the transformations used.

Examples of presentation protocols are text compression, encryption, and virtual terminal protocol. A virtual terminal protocol converts between specific terminal characteristics and a generic or virtual model used by application programs.

Application Layer

The *application layer* provides a means for application processes to access the OSI environment. This layer contains management functions and generally useful mechanisms to support distributed applications. Examples of protocols at this level are virtual file protocol and job transfer and manipulation protocol.

A.4 PERSPECTIVES ON THE OSI MODEL

Figure A.5 provides two useful perspectives on the OSI architecture. The annotation along the right side suggests viewing the seven layers in three parts. The lower three layers contain the logic for a host to interact with a network. The host is physically attached to the network, uses a data link protocol to reliably communicate with the network, and uses a net-

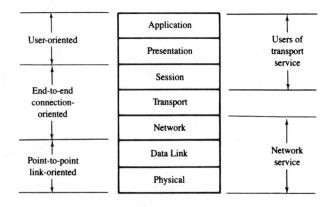

Figure A.5. Perspectives on the OSI architecture

work protocol to request data exchange with another device on the network and to request network services (e.g., priority). The X.25 standard for packet-switched networks actually encompasses all three layers. Continuing from this perspective, the transport layer provides a reliable end-to-end connection regardless of the intervening network facility. Finally, the upper three layers, taken together, are involved in the exchange of data between end users and making use of a transport connection for reliable data transfer.

Another perspective is suggested by the annotation on the left. Again, consider host systems attached to a common network. The lower two layers deal with the link between the host system and the network. The next three layers are all involved in transferring data from one host to another. The network layer makes use of the communication network facilities to transfer data from one host to another; the transport layer ensures that the transfer is reliable; and the session layer manages the flow of data over the logical connection. Finally, the upper two layers are oriented to the user's concerns, including considerations of the application to be performed and any formatting issues.

B

Encoding of Digital Data
for Transmission

The primary application of local networks is the transmission of digital data. As was discussed in Chapter 1, there are two general techniques for this:

- *Baseband:* The digital data is transmitted as a digital signal, consisting of sequence of constant-voltage pulses.
- *Broadband:* The digital data is transmitted as an analog signal, which is a continuously varying electromagnetic wave.

In both of these cases, some form of encoding is required. That is, the digital data (binary 1s and 0s) must be represented by signal elements that are suitable for transmission over the given medium and that can be recognized by the receiver and decoded to reproduce the transmitted data. Typically, the form of the encoding is chosen to optimize the transmission, in terms cost, performance, and/or reliability. This appendix provides a brief survey of some of the more common encoding techniques. More detail can be found in [STAL88].

B.1   DIGITAL DATA, DIGITAL SIGNALS

NRZ Codes

The most common, and easiest, way to transmit digital signals is to use two different voltage levels for the two binary digits. For example, the absence of voltage (which is also the absence of current) can be used to represent binary 0, whereas a constant positive voltage is used to represent binary 1. More commonly, a negative voltage is used to represent one binary value, and a positive voltage is used to represent the other (Figure B.1a). This code is known as Nonreturn-to-Zero-Level (NRZ-L).

A variation on NRZ is NRZI (nonreturn to zero, invert on ones). As with NRZ-L, NRZI maintains a constant voltage pulse for the duration of a bit time. The data itself is encoded as the presence or absence of a signal transition at the beginning of the bit time. A transition (low-to-high or high-to-low) at the beginning of a bit time denotes a binary 1 for that bit time; no transition indicates a binary 0 (Figure B.1b).

NRZI is an example of *differential encoding*. In differential encoding, the signal is decoded by comparing the polarity of adjacent signal

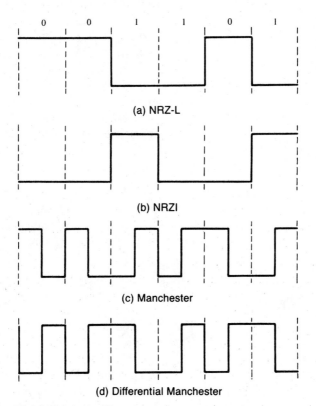

(a) NRZ-L

(b) NRZI

(c) Manchester

(d) Differential Manchester

Figure B.1.   Digital signal encoding

elements rather than the absolute value of a signal element. One benefit of this scheme is that it may be more reliable to detect a transition in the presence of noise than to compare a value to a threshold. Another benefit is that, with a complex transmission layout, it is easy to lose the sense of the polarity of the signal. For example, on a multidrop twisted-pair line, if the leads from an attached device to the twisted pair are accidentally inverted, all 1s and 0s will be inverted unless differential encoding is used.

Biphase Codes

There are several disadvantages to NRZ transmission. Since it is difficult to determine where one bit ends and another begins, there needs to be some means of keeping the transmitter and receiver *clocked* or synchronized. Also, there is a direct-current (dc) component during each bit time that will accumulate if 1s or 0s predominate. Thus alternating-current (ac) coupling, which uses a transformer and provides excellent electrical isolation between data communicating devices and their environment, is not possible. Furthermore, the dc component can cause plating or other deterioration at attachment contacts.

There is a set of alternative coding techniques, grouped under the term *biphase,* which overcomes these disadvantages. Two of these biphase techniques, Manchester and Differential Manchester, are commonly used for digital signaling in local networks. All of the biphase schemes require at least one transition per bit time and may have as many as two transitions. Thus, the maximum modulation rate is twice that for NRZ; this means that the bandwidth or transmission capacity consumed is correspondingly greater. To compensate for this, the biphase schemes have several advantages:

- *Synchronization:* Because there is a predictable transition during each bit time, the receiver can synchronize on that transition. For this reason, the biphase codes are known as self-clocking codes.
- *No dc component:* Because of the transition in each bit time, biphase codes have no dc component, yielding the benefits described earlier.
- *Error detection:* The absence of an expected transition can be used to detect errors. Noise on the line would have to invert the signal both before and after the expected transition to cause an undetected error.

In the *Manchester code* (Figure B.1c), there is a transition at the middle of each bit period. The mid-bit transition serves as a clock and also as data: a high-to-low transition represents a zero, and a low-to-high transition represents a one. In *Differential Manchester* (Figure B.1d), the mid-bit transition is used only to provide clocking. The encoding of a 0 (1) is represented by the presence (absence) of a transition at the beginning of the bit period. Differential Manchester exhibits the further advantage of differential encoding in addition to those listed above.

B.2   DIGITAL DATA, ANALOG SIGNALS

The basis for analog signaling is a continuous constant-frequency signal known as the *carrier signal*. Digital data are encoded by modulating one of the three characteristics of the carrier: amplitude, frequency, or phase, or some combination of these. Figure B.2 illustrates the three basic forms of modulation of analog signals for digital data:

- Amplitude-shift keying (ASK)
- Frequency-shift keying (FSK)
- Phase-shift keying (PSK)

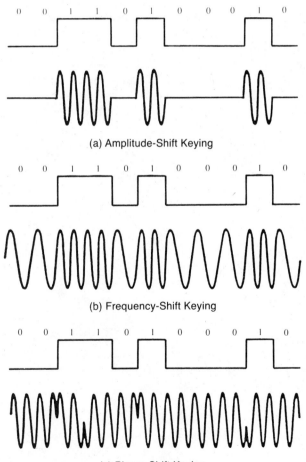

(a) Amplitude-Shift Keying

(b) Frequency-Shift Keying

(c) Phase-Shift Keying

Figure B.2.   Modulation of analog signals for digital data

In all these cases, the resulting signal contains a range of frequencies on both sides of the carrier frequency. That range is referred to as the *bandwidth* of the signal.

In ASK, the two binary values are represented by two different amplitudes of the carrier frequency. In some cases, one of the amplitudes is zero; that is, one binary digit is represented by the presence, at constant amplitude, of the carrier, the other by the absence of the carrier. ASK is susceptible to sudden gain changes and is a rather inefficient modulation technique. On voice-grade lines, it is typically used only up to 1200 bps.

In FSK, the two binary values are represented by two different frequencies near the carrier frequency. This scheme is less susceptible to error than ASK. On voice-grade lines, it is typically used up to 1200 bps. It is also commonly used for high frequency (3 to 30 MHz) radio transmission. It can also be used at even higher frequencies on local networks that use coaxial cable.

In PSK, the phase of the carrier signal is shifted to represent data. Figure B.2c is an example of a two-phase system. In this system, a zero is represented by sending a signal burst of the same phase as the previous signal burst sent. A one is represented by sending a signal burst of opposite phase to the previous one. PSK can use more than two phase shifts. A four-phase system would encode two bits with each signal burst. The PSK technique is more noise resistant and efficient than FSK; on a voice-grade line, rates up to 9600 bps are achieved.

Finally, the techniques discussed previously may be combined. A common combination is PSK and ASK, where some or all of the phase shifts may occur at one of two amplitudes.

C

Error Detection

C.1 THE ERROR DETECTION PROCESS

Any data transmission is subject to errors. Causes of errors include [STAL88]:

- *Attenuation:* The strength of a signal decreases with distance over any transmission medium. With sufficient attenuation, it becomes difficult for the receiver to recover the data from the received signal.
- *Attenuation distortion:* Attenuation is an increasing function of frequency. Thus, frequency components of a signal are differentially affected, which introduces distortion into the signal.
- *Delay distortion:* The velocity of propagation of a signal through a guided medium varies with frequency; the velocity tends to be highest near the center frequency of the signal and fall off toward the two edges of the signal's bandwidth. This causes the intersymbol interference described in Chapter 1.
- *Noise:* Noise is any unwanted signal that combines with, and hence, distorts the signal intended for reception. Varieties include thermal noise, intermodulation noise, crosstalk, and impulse noise.
- *Collisions:* In a bus or tree topology, if two stations transmit at the same time, their signals overlap and neither signal can be successfully received.

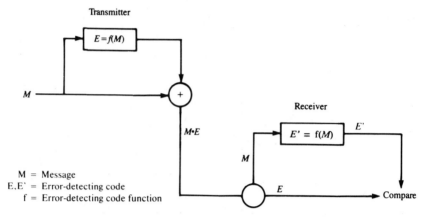

Figure C.1. Error detection

Because of these impairments, a MAC entity may receive a frame from a peer MAC entity in which some bits have changed value. Accordingly, the MAC protocol entity must perform error detection to avoid delivering incorrect data to the user.

The error detection procedure is illustrated in Figure C.1. On transmission, a calculation is performed on the bits of the frame to be transmitted; the result is inserted as an additional field in the frame. On reception, the same calculation is performed on the received bits and the calculated result is compared to the value stored in the incoming frame. If there is a discrepancy, the receiver assumes that an error has occurred and discards the frame.

The error-detecting code used by the three IEEE 802 MAC protocols and the FDDI MAC protocol is a 32-bit cyclic redundancy check (CRC), the details of which are described in the remainder of this appendix.

C.2 THE CYCLIC REDUNDANCY CHECK

Let us begin by describing the general operation of the CRC. Given a k-bit frame or message, the transmitter generates an n-bit sequence, known as a *frame check sequence* (FCS) so that the resulting frame, consisting of $k + n$ bits, is exactly divisible by some predetermined number. The receiver then divides the incoming frame by the same number and, if there is no remainder, assumes that there was no error.

To clarify the above, we present the procedure in several ways:

- Modulo 2 arithmetic.
- Polynomials.
- Shift registers and exclusive-or gates.

First, we work with binary numbers and modulo 2 arithmetic. Modulo 2 arithmetic uses binary addition with no carries, which is just the exclusive-or operation.

Examples

$$
\begin{array}{r}
1111 \\
+\,1010 \\
\hline
0101
\end{array}
\qquad
\begin{array}{r}
11001 \\
\times \quad\ 11 \\
\hline
11001 \\
11001 \\
\hline
101011
\end{array}
$$

Now define:

$T = (k + n)$-bit frame to be transmitted,
    with $n < k$

$M = k$-bit message, the first k bits of T

$F = n$-bit FCS, the last n bits of T

$P = $ pattern of $n + 1$ bits;
    this is the predetermined divisor mentioned above

We would like T/P to have no remainder. It should be clear that

$$T = 2^n M + F$$

That is, by multiplying M by 2^n, we have in effect shifted it to the left by n bits and padded out the result with 0's. Adding F gives us the concatenation of M and F, which is T. Now we want T to be exactly divisible by P. Suppose that we divided $2^n M$ by P:

$$\frac{2^n M}{P} = Q + \frac{R}{P} \qquad\qquad \text{(C-1)}$$

There is a quotient and a remainder. Because division is binary, the remainder is always one bit less than the divisor. We will use this remainder as our FCS. Then

$$T = 2^n M + R$$

Question: Does this R satisfy our condition? To see that it does, consider

$$\frac{T}{P} = \frac{2^n M + R}{P}$$

substituting equation (C-1), we have

$$\frac{T}{P} = Q + \frac{R}{P} + \frac{R}{P}$$

However, any binary number added to itself modulo 2 yields zero. Thus,

$$\frac{T}{P} = Q + \frac{R + R}{P} = Q$$

There is no remainder, and therefore T is exactly divisible by P. Thus, the FCS is easily generated: Simply divide 2^nM by P and use the remainder as the FCS. On reception, the receiver will divide T by P and will get no remainder if there have been no errors.

A simple example of the procedure is now presented:

1. Given

$$\begin{aligned}
\text{Message } M &= 1010001101 \text{ (10 bits)} \\
\text{Pattern } P &= 110101 \text{ (6 bits)} \\
\text{FCS } R &= \text{to be calculated (5 bits)}
\end{aligned}$$

2. The message is multiplied by 2^5, yielding 101000110100000
3. This product is divided by P:

```
                  1101010110 ← Q
P → 110101 ) 101000110100000 ← 2ⁿM
             110101
             111011
             110101
              111010
              110101
               111110
               110101
                101100
                110101
                110010
                110101
                  1110 ← R
```

4. The remainder ($R = 01110$) is added to 2^nM to give $T = 101000110101110$, which is transmitted.

5. If there are no errors, the receiver receives T intact. The received frame is divided by P:

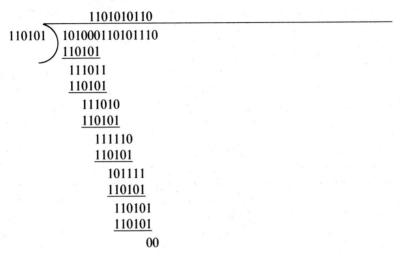

As there is no remainder, it is assumed that there have been no errors.

The pattern P is chosen to be one bit longer than the desired FCS, and the exact bit pattern chosen depends on the type of errors expected. At minimum, both the high- and low-order bits of P must be 1.

The occurrence of an error is easily expressed. An error results in the reversal of a bit. Mathematically, this is equivalent to taking the exclusive-or of the bit and $1: 0 + 1 = 1; 1 + 1 = 0$. Thus the errors in an $(n + k)$-bit frame can be represented by an $(n + k)$-bit field with 1's in each error position. The resulting frame T_r can be expressed as

$$T_r = T + E$$

where

T = transmitted frame

E = error pattern with 1s in positions where errors occur

T_r = received frame

The receiver will fail to detect an error if and only if T_r is divisible by P; that is, if and only if E is divisible by P. Intuitively, this seems an unlikely occurrence.

A second way of viewing the CRC process is to express all values as polynomials in a dummy variable X with binary coefficients. The coefficients correspond to the bits in the binary number. For example, for

$M = 110011$, we have $M(X) = X^5 + X^4 + X + 1$, and for $P = 11001$, we have $P(X) = X^4 + X^3 + 1$. Arithmetic operations are again modulo 2. The CRC process can now be described as:

1. $\dfrac{X^n M(X)}{P(X)} = Q(X) + \dfrac{R(X)}{P(X)}$

2. $T(X) = X^n M(X) + R(X)$

An error $E(X)$ will only be undetectable if it is divisible by $P(X)$. It can be shown [PETE61] that all of the following are not divisible by $P(X)$ and hence are detectable:

1. All single-bit errors.
2. All double-bit errors, as long as $P(X)$ has a factor with at least three terms.
3. Any odd number of errors, as long as $P(X)$ *contains a factor* $(X + 1)$.
4. Any burst error for which the length of the burst is less than the length of the FCS.
5. Most larger burst errors.

The first assertion is clear. A single-bit error can be represented by $E(X) = X^i$ for some i. We have said that for $P(X)$ both the first and last terms must be nonzero. Thus $P(X)$ has at least two terms and cannot divide the one-term $E(X)$. Similarly, a two-bit error can be represented by $E(X) = X^i + X^j = X^i(1 + X^{j-i})$ for some i and j with $i > j$. Thus $P(X)$ must divide either X^i or $(1 + X^{j-i})$. We have shown that it does not divide X^i, and it can be shown [PETE61] that it does not divide $(1 + X^{j-i})$ except for very large values of $j - i$, beyond the practical frame length. To see the third assertion, assume that $E(X)$ has an odd number of terms and is divisible by $(X + 1)$. Then we can express $E(X)$ as $(E(X) = (X + 1)F(X)$. Then $E(1) = (1 + 1)F(1) = 0$ since $1 + 1 = 0$. But $E(1)$ will be 0 if and only if $E(X)$ contains an even number of terms. For the fourth assertion, we define a burst of length j as a string of bits beginning and ending with 1 and containing intervening 1's and 0's. This can be represented as $E(X) = X^i(X^{j-1} + \ldots + 1)$ where i expresses how far the burst is shifted from the right-hand end. We know that $P(X)$ does not divide X^i. For $j < n$, where n is the length of the FCS, $P(X)$ will not divide the second factor, since $P(X)$ is of higher order.

Finally, it can be shown that if all error patterns are considered equally probable, then for a burst of length $r + 1$, the probability that $E(X)$ is divisible by $P(X)$ is $1/2^{r-1}$, and for a longer burst, the probability is $1/2^r$ [PETE61].

Four versions of *P(X)* are widely used:

$$CRC\text{-}12 = X^{12} + X^{11} + X^3 + X^2 + X + 1$$
$$CRC\text{-}16 = X^{16} + X^{15} + X^2 + 1$$
$$CRC\text{-}CCITT = X^{16} + X^{12} + X^5 + 1$$
$$CRC\text{-}32 = X^{32} + X^{26} + X^{23} + X^{22} + X^{16} + X^{12} + X^{11}$$
$$+ X^{10} + X^8 + X^7 + X^5 + X^4 + X^2 + X + 1$$

The CRC-12 system is used for transmission of streams of 6-bit characters and generates a 12-bit FCS. Both CRC-16 and CRC-CCITT are popular for blocks of 8-bit characters, in the United States and Europe respectively, and both result in a 16-bit FCS. The CRC-32 is specified as an option in a number of data link control standards, and is the one used in IEEE 802 and FDDI.

As a final representation, Figure C.2 shows that the CRC process can be implemented easily as a dividing circuit consisting of exclusive-or gates and a shift register. The circuit is implemented as follows:

1. The register contains *n* bits, equal to the length of the FCS.
2. There are up to *n* exclusive-or gates.
3. The presence or absence of a gate corresponds to the presence or absence of a term in the divisor polynomial, *P(X)*.

In this example, we use:

Message $M = 1010001101$; $M(X) = X^9 + X^7 + X^3 + X^2 + 1$
Divisor $P = 110101$; $P(X) = X^5 + X^4 + X^2 + 1,$

which were used earlier in the discussion.

The process begins with the shift register cleared (all zeros). The message, or dividend, is then entered, one bit at a time, starting with the most significant (leftmost) bit. As no feedback occurs until a one dividend bit arrives at the most significant end of the register, the first four operations are simple shifts. Whenever a one bit arrives at the left end, a one is subtracted (exclusive-or) from the second and fifth bits on the next shift. This is identical to the binary long division process illustrated earlier. The process continues through all the bits of the message, plus four zero bits. These latter bits account for shifting *M* to the left four positions to accommodate the FCS. After the last bit is processed, the shift register contains the remainder (FCS), which can then be transmitted.

At the receiver, the same logic is used. As each bit of *M* arrives, it is inserted into the shift register at A. If there have been no errors, the

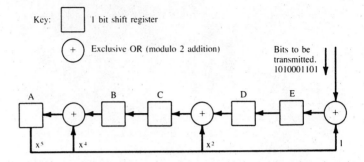

Key: ☐ 1 bit shift register

⊕ Exclusive OR (modulo 2 addition)

Bits to be transmitted.
1010001101

Contents of shift registers:

	A	B	C	D	E	Input bit	
Initial contents:	0	0	0	0	0		
Step 1	0	0	0	0	1	1	
Step 2	0	0	0	1	0	0	
Step 3	0	0	1	0	1	1	
Step 4	0	1	0	1	0	0	
Step 5	1	0	1	0	0	0	Message to be sent
Step 6	1	1	1	0	1	0	
Step 7	0	1	1	1	0	1	
Step 8	1	1	1	0	1	1	
Step 9	0	1	1	1	1	0	
Step 10	1	1	1	1	1	1	
Step 11	0	1	0	1	1	0	
Step 12	1	0	1	1	0	0	
Step 13	1	1	0	0	1	0	Five 0's added
Step 14	0	0	1	1	1	0	
Step 15	0	1	1	1	0	0	

Remainder (which is sent
as the five check bits)

Figure C.2. Circuit with shift registers for dividing by the polynomial
$(X^5 + X^4 + X^2 + 1)$

shift register should contain the bit pattern for *R* at the conclusion of *M*. The transmitted bits of *R* now begin to arrive, and the effect is to zero out the register so that, at the conclusion of reception, the register contains all 0s.

The shift register implementation makes clear the power of the CRC algorithm. Due to the feedback arrangement, the state of the shift register depends, in a complex way, on the past history of bits presented. Thus it will take an extremely rare combination of errors to fool the system. Further, it is evident that the CRC algorithm is easy to implement in hardware.

C.3 APPLICATION TO IEEE 802 AND FDDI

As was mentioned, the IEEE 802 and FDDI MAC protocols all use the CRC-32 divisor:

$$P(X) = X^{32} + X^{26} + X^{23} + X^{22} + X^{16} + X^{12} + X^{11}$$
$$+ X^{10} + X^{8} + X^{7} + X^{5} + X^{4} + X^{2} + X + 1.$$

Several refinements are added to the process described previously. Specifically, the 32-bits FCS is defined to be the ones complement of:

$$R(X) = [X^{32}M(X) + X^{k}L(X)]/P(X)$$

where

$$L(X) = X^{31} + X^{30} + X^{29} + ... + X^{2} + X + 1$$

and

$$k = \text{number of bits in } M$$

The addition of $X^{k}L(X)$ to $X^{32}M(X)$ is equivalent to inverting the first 32 bits of $M(X)$. It can be accomplished in a shift register implementation such as Figure C.2, by presetting the register to all ones initially, instead of all zeros. This term is present to detect erroneous addition or deletion of zero bits at the leading end of $M(X)$. The procedure described in Section C.2 will produce the same result for two messages that differ only in the number of leading zeros.

The complementing of $R(X)$ by the transmitter at the completion of the division insures that the transmitted sequence has a property that permits the receiver to detect addition or deletion of trailing zeros that may appear as a result of errors. Again, the procedure described in Section C.2 will produce the same result at the receiver for two transmissions that differ only in the number or trailing zeros.

At the receiver, the reverse operations must be done to perform error detection. Using a shift register implementation, the initial content of the receiver's register is set to all ones. If there have been no transmission errors, the final remainder after division of the incoming bits, including the FCS, by $P(X)$ will be the unique 32 bit sequence:

1100 0111 0000 0100 1101 1101 0111 1011

Thus, instead of comparing the result to the received FCS, the receiver computes a value and compares it to this unique bit pattern.

References

ABRA86 Abraham, M. Running Ethernet modems over broadband cable. *Data Communications*, May 1986.

ABRA70 Abramson, N. The ALOHA system—Another alternative for computer communications. *Proceedings, Fall Joint Computer Conference*, 1970.

ALLA86 Allan, R. MAP carrier-band specs bound for change. *Electronic Design*, February 20, 1986.

ANSI86a American National Standards Institute. *FDDI Token Ring Media Access Control (MAC)*. Draft Proposed American National Standard, ASC X3T9.5, Revision 10, February 28, 1986.

ANSI87b American National Standards Institute. *FDDI Station Management (SMT)*. Draft Proposed American National Standard, ASC X3T9.5, Revision 2.1, April 16, 1987.

ANSI86b American National Standards Institute. *FDDI Physical Layer Protocol (PHY)*. Draft Proposed American National Standard, ASC X3T9.5, Revision 14, October 20, 1986.

ANSI87a American National Standards Institute. *FDDI Physical Layer Medium Dependent (PMD)*. Draft Proposed American National Standard, ASC X3T9.5, Revision 7, February 20, 1987.

BACK88 Backes, F. "Transparent Bridges for Interconnection of IEEE 802 LANs." *IEEE Network*, January 1988.

BEDE86 Bederman, S. "Source Routing," *Data Communications*, February 1986.

BELL82 Bell Telephone Laboratories. *Transmission Systems for Communications*, 1982.

BEVA86 Bevan, M. Image processing may cause future problems with network loading. *Data Communications,* March 1986.

BIER88 Biersack, E. "Performance Improvements of the IEEE 802.2 LLC Type 2 Protocol." *Proceedings, 13th Conference on Local Computer Networks,* October 1988.

BUCK86 Buckley, F. An overview of the IEEE computer society standards process. *Proceedings, Computer Standards Conference,* May 1986.

BURR86 Burr, W. The FDDI optical data link. *IEEE Communications Magazine,* May 1986.

BUX83 Bux, W., F. Closs, K. Kuemmerle, H. Keller, and H. Mueller. Architecture and design of a reliable token-ring network. *IEEE Journal on Selected Areas in Communications,* November 1983.

CERN84 Cerni, D. *Standards in Process: Foundations and Profiles of ISDN and OSI Studies.* National Telecommunications and Information Administration, Report 84-710, December 1984.

CHAP82 Chapin, A. Connectionless data transmission. *Computer Communications Review,* April 1982.

CHRI79 Christensen, G. Links between computer-room networks. *Telecommunications,* February 1979.

CLAN82 Clancy, G., et al. The IEEE 802 committee states its case concerning its local network standards efforts. *Data Communications,* April 1982.

COHE85 Cohen, E., and W. Wilkens. The IEEE role in telecommunications standards. *IEEE Communications Magazine,* January 1985.

CONN87 Connor, G., P. Scott, and S. Vesuna. Serial data races at parallel rates for the best of both worlds. *Electronic Design,* January 22, 1987.

COOP86 Cooper, S. ANSI network holds promise for fiber's future. *Data Communications,* December 1986.

CROW86 Crowder R. MAP, PROWAY, and IEEE 802: A marriage of standards for automation. *Proceedings, IEEE INFOCOM '86,* April 1986.

DERF86 Derfler, F., and W. Stallings. The IBM token-ring LAN. *PC Magazine,* March 11, 1986.

DIX80 Digital Equipment Corporation, Intel Corporation, and Xerox Corporation. *The Ethernet: A Local Area Network: Data Link Layer and Physical Layer Specifications.* Version 1.0, September 30, 1980.

DIX82 Digital Equipment Corporation, Intel Corporation, and Xerox Corporation. *The Ethernet: A Local Area Network: Data Link Layer and Physical Layer Specifications.* Version 2.0, November 1982.

DIX083 Dixon, R., N. Strole, and J. Markov. A token-ring network for local data communications. *IBM Systems Journal,* Nos. 1/2, 1983.

DIX087 Dixon, R. Lore of the token ring. *IEEE Network,* January 1987.

DIX088 Dixon, R., and D. Pitt, "Addressing, Bridging, and Source Routing." *IEEE Network,* January 1988.

DOUG86 Douglas, R. IEEE token bus standard status. *Proceedings, Phoenix Conference on Computers and Communications,* March 1986.

FARM69 Farmer, W., and E. Newhall. An experimental distributed switching system to handle bursty computer traffic. *Proceedings, ACM Symposium on Problems in the Optimization of Data Communications,* 1969.

FIEL86 Field, J. Logical link control. *Proceedings, IEEE INFOCOM '86,* April 1986.

FLAT84 Flatman, A. Low-cost local network for small systems grows from IEEE 802.3 standard. *Electronic Design,* July 26, 1984.

FORR86 Forrest, S. Optical detectors: Three contenders. *IEEE Spectrum,* May 1986.

FREE81 Freeman, R. *Telecommunication Transmission Handbook.* New York: Wiley, 1981.

FREE85 Freeman, R. *Reference Manual for Telecommunications Engineering.* New York: Wiley, 1985.

GAND85 Gandhi, S. *Implementing StarLAN with the Intel 82588 Controller.* Intel Application Note AP-236. Reprinted in Microcommunications Handbook, Intel, 1986.

HAMN88 Hamner, M., and G. Samsen, "Source Routing Bridge Implementation." *IEEE Network,* January 1988.

HAMS88 Hamstra, J. "FDDI Design Tradeoffs." *Proceedings, 13th Conference on Local Computer Networks,* October 1988.

HART88 Hart, J. "Extending the IEEE 802.1 MAC Bridge Standard to Remote Bridges." *IEEE Network,* January 1988.

HONG86 Hong, J. Timing jitter. *Data Communications,* February 1986.

HOPK79 Hopkins, G. Multimode communications on the MITRENET. *Proceedings, Local Area Communications Network Symposium,* 1979.

HOPK80 Hopkins, G., and P. Wagner. *Multiple Access Digital Communications System.* U.S. Patent 4,210,780, July 1, 1980.

IEEE85a The Institute of Electrical and Electronics Engineers. *Logical Link Control.* American National Standard ANSI/IEEE Std 802.2, 1985.

IEEE85b The Institute of Electrical and Electronics Engineers. *Carrier Sense Multiple Access with Collision Detection (CSMA/CD) Access Method and Physical Layer Specifications.* American National Standard ANSI/IEEE Std 802.3, 1985.

IEEE85c The Institute of Electrical and Electronics Engineers. *Token-Passing Bus Access Method and Physical Layer Specifications.* American National Standard ANSI/IEEE Std 802.4, 1985.

IEEE85d The Institute of Electrical and Electronics Engineers. *Token Ring Access Method and Physical Layer Specifications.* American National Standard ANSI/IEEE Std 802.5, 1985.

IEEE86 IEEE Computer Society. *IEEE Standard 802.1: Overview, Interworking, and Systems Management,* August 1986.

IEEE88a The Institute of Electrical and Electronics Engineers. *IEEE Standard 802.1: Overview and Architecture.* July 1988.

IEEE88b The Institute of Electrical and Electronics Engineers. *IEEE Standard 802.1: MAC Bridges.* September 1988.

IEEE88c The Institute of Electrical and Electronics Engineers. *IEEE 802.5, Appendix D: Multi-ring Networks (Source Routing).* November 1988.

ISA85 Instrument Society of America. *PROWAY-LAN Industrial Data Highway.* Standard ISA-S72.01-1985, 1985.

ISO84a International Organization for Standardization. *High-Level Data Link Control Procedures—Frame Structure,* ISO 3309, 1984.

ISO84b International Organization for Standardization. *High-Level Data Link Control Procedures—Consolidation of Elements of Procedure,* ISO 4335, 1984.

ISO84c International Organization for Standardization. *High-Level Data Link*

Control Procedures—Consolidation of Classes of Procedure, ISO 7809, 1984.

ISO84d International Organization for Standardization. *Open Systems Intercon-nection—Basic Reference Model,* ISO 7498, 1984.

ISO87a International Organization for Standardization. *Logical Link Control,* IS 8802/2, 1987.

ISO87b International Organization for Standardization. *Carrier Sense Multiple Access with Collision Detection (CSMA/CD) Access Method and Physical Layer Specifications,* IS 8802/3, 1987.

ISO87c International Organization for Standardization. *Token-Passing Bus Access Method and Physical Layer Specifications,* IS 8802/4, 1987.

ISO87d International Organization for Standardization. *Token Ring Access Method and Physical Layer Specifications,* IS 8802/5, 1987.

JAYA87 Jayasumana, A. "Performance Analysis of Token Bus-Priority Scheme," *Proceeding, INFOCOM '87,* 1987.

JOHN87 Johnson, M. "Proof that Timing Requirements of the FDDI Token Ring Protocol Are Satisfied." *IEEE Transactions on Communications,* June 1987.

JONE85 Jones, K. Cheapernet makes local area networking more affordable. *Mini-Micro Systems,* January 1985.

JORD85 Jordan, E., ed. *Reference Data for Engineers: Radio, Electronics, Computer, and Communications.* Indianapolis, IN: Howard W. Sams & Co., 1985.

JOSH86 Joshi, S. High-performance networks: A focus on the fiber distributed data interface (FDDI) standard. *IEEE Micro,* June 1986.

KAMI86 Kaminski, M. Protocols for communicating in the factory. *IEEE Spectrum,* April 1986.

KELL83 Keller, H., H. Meyer, and H. Mueller. Transmission design criteria for a synchronous token ring. *IEEE Journal on Selected Areas in Communications,* November 1983.

KELL84 Kelley, R., J. Jones, V. Bhatt, and P. Pate. "Transceiver Design and Implementation Experience in an Ethernet-Compatible Fiber Optic Local Area Network." *Proceedings, INFOCOM 84,* 1984.

KLEI86 Klein, M., and T. Balph. Carrierband is low-cost, single-channel solution for MAP. *Computer Design,* February 1, 1986.

KUMM87 Kummerle, K., J. Limb, and F. Tobagi. *Advances in Local Area Networks.* New York: IEEE Press, 1987.

LOHS85 Lohse, E. The role of the ISO in telecommunications and information systems standardization. *IEEE Communications Magazine,* January 1985.

LOVE88 Love, R. "Specifying the Physical Layer in a LAN Standard: A Comparison of CSMA/CD and Token Ring." *Proceedings, 13th Conference on Local Computer Networks,* October 1988.

MCCO88 McCool, J. "FDDI: Getting to know the Inside of the Ring." *Data Communications,* March 1988.

METC76 Metcalfe, R., and D. Boggs. Ethernet: Distributed packet switching for local computer networks. *Communications of the ACM,* July 1976.

METC77 Metcalfe, R., D. Boggs, C. Thacker, and B. Lampson. *Multipoint Data Communication System with Collision Detection.* U.S. Patent 4,063,220, 1977.

METC83 Metcalfe, R. Controller/transceiver board drives Ethernet into PC domain. *Mini-Micro Systems*, January 1983.

MIER83 Mier, E. "Ethernet Controversy Flares as IEEE Readies a Standard." *Data Communications*, June 1983.

MIER86 Mier, E. Light sources and wavelengths. *Data Communications*, February 1986.

MILL82 Miller, C., and D. Thompson. Making a case for token passing in local networks. *Data Communications*, March 1982.

NSPA 79 National Standards Policy Advisory Committee. *National Policy on Standards for the United States*. 1979. Reprinted in [CERN84].

OETT79 Oetting, J. A comparison of modulation techniques for digital radio. *IEEE Transactions on Communications*, December 1979.

PARL85 Parlatore, P. Hooking into AT&T networks. *Systems & Software*, September 1985.

PERL84 Perlman, R. "An Algorithm for Distributed Computation of a Spanning Tree." *Proceedings, Ninth Data Communications Symposium*, 1984.

PETE61 Peterson, W., and D. Brown. Cyclic codes for error detection. *Proceedings of the IRE*, January 1961.

PHIN83 Phinney T., and G. Jelatis. Error handling in the IEEE 802 token-passing bus LAN. *IEEE Journal on Selected Areas in Communications*, November 1983.

PITT85 Pitt, D., K. Sy, and R. Donnan. "Source Routing for Bridged Local Area Networks." *Proceedings, Globecom '85*, December 1985. Reprinted in [KUMM87].

PITT87a Pitt, D. Standards for the token ring. *IEEE Network*, January 1987.

PITT87b Pitt, D., and Winkler, J. "Table-Free Bridging." *IEEE Journal on Selected Areas in Communications*, December 1987.

RATN83 Ratner, D. "How Broadband Modems Operate on Token-Passing Nets." *Data Communications*, June 1983.

RAWS78 Rawson, E., and R. Metcalfe. "Fibernet: Multimode Optical Fibers for Local Computer Networks." *IEEE Transactions on Communications*, July 1978.

RELC87 Relcom, Inc. *Carrier-Band Network Handbook, Second Edition*. Forest Grove, OR, 1987.

ROBE75 Roberts, L. ALOHA packet system with and without slots and capture. *Computer Communications Review*, April 1975.

ROBI86 Robinson, G. Accredited standards committee for the information processing systems, X3. *Proceedings, Computer Standards Conference*, May 1986.

ROSE82 Rosenthal, R., ed. *The Selection of Local Area Computer Networks*. National Bureau of Standards Special Publication 500-96, November 1982.

ROSS86 Ross, F. FDDI—A tutorial. *IEEE Communications Magazine*, May 1986.

ROSS87 Ross, F. Rings are 'round for good! *IEEE Network*, January 1987.

RUBY88 Ruby, D. "How Do Today's Broadband LANs Compare to Ethernet?" *Data Communications*, July 1988.

SALT79 Saltzer, J., and K. Pogran. A star-shaped ring network with high maintainability. *Proceedings, Local Area Communications Network Symposium*, 1979.

SALT83 Saltzer, J., K. Pogran, and D. Clark. Why a ring? *Computer Networks,* March 1983.

SALW83 Salwen, H. In praise of ring architecture for local area networks. *Computer Design,* March 1983.

SCHO88 Scholl, F., and M. Coden. "Passive Optical Star Systems for Fiber Optic Local Area Networks." *IEEE Journal on Selected Areas in Communications,* July 1988.

SEVC87 Sevcik, K., and M. Johnson. "Cycle Time Properties of the FDDI Token Ring Protocol." *IEEE Transactions on Software Engineering,* March 1987.

SHER86a Sherr, S. IEEE and information systems. *Proceedings, Computer Standards Conference,* May 1986.

SHER86b Sherr, S. ANSI and information systems. *Proceedings, Computer Standards Conference,* May 1986.

SHOC82 Shoch, J., Y. Dalal, D. Redell, and R. Crane. Evolution of the Ethernet local computer network. *Computer,* August 1982.

STAH82 Stahlman, M. Inside Wang's local net architecture. *Data Communications,* January 1982.

STAL88 Stallings, W. *Data and Computer Communications, Second Ed.* New York: Macmillan, 1988.

STAL90a Stallings, W. *Handbook of Computer-Communications Standards: Volume I: The Open Systems Interconnection (OSI) Model and OSI-Related Standards, Second Edition.* Indianapolis, IN: Howard W. Sams & Co., 1990.

STAL90b Stallings, W. *Handbook of Computer-Communications Standards: Volume III: The TCP/IP Protocol Suite, Second Edition.* Indianapolis, IN: Howard W. Sams & Co., 1990.

STAL90c Stallings, W. *Local Networks: An Introduction, Third Edition.* New York: Macmillan, 1990.

STIE81 Stieglitz, M. Local network access tradeoffs. *Computer Design,* October 1981.

STIX88 Stix, G. "Telephone Wiring: A Conduit for Networking Standards." *IEEE Spectrum,* June 1988.

STRO83 Strole, N. A local communication network based on interconnected token-access rings: A tutorial. *IBM Journal of Research and Development,* September 1983.

STRO86 Strole, N. How IBM addresses LAN requirements with the token ring. *Data Communications,* February 1986.

STRO87 Strole, N. The IBM token-ring network—A functional overview. *IEEE Network,* January 1987.

THOR79 Thornton, J. Back-end network approaches. *Computer,* February 1979.

WERN86 Wernli, M. The choices in designing a fiber-optic network. *Data Communications,* June 1986.

WILK87 Wilkens, W. "Standards for Communications." *IEEE Communications Magazine,* July 1987.

YEN83 Yen, C., and R. Crawford. Distribution and equalization of signal on coaxial cables used in 10-Mbits baseband local area networks. *IEEE Transactions on Communications,* October 1983.

Index